D0758269

A.L.T.

VILLARD V NEW YORK

A.L.T.

ANDRÉ LEON TALLEY

A MEMOIR

Published in the United States by Villard Books, an imprint of The Random House Ballantine Publishing Group, a division of Random House, Inc., New York, and simultaneously in Canada by Random House of Canada Limited, Toronto.

Library of Congress Cataloging-in-Publication Data

Talley, André Leon.
A.L.T.: a memoir / André Leon Talley.
p. cm.
ISBN 0-375-50828-7
1. Talley, André Leon. 2. Vreeland, Diana. 3. Davis, Bennie Frances, d. 1989. 4. Fashion editors—United States—Biography. 5. African American fashion editors—Biography. I. Title.

TT505 .T29 A3 2003
746.9'2'092—dc21 2002033056
[B]

Villard Books website address: www.villard.com

Printed in the United States of America on acid-free paper

24689753
First Edition

Book design by Casey Hampton

FOR MY GRANDMOTHER,

BENNIE FRANCES,

AND FOR ALL GRANDMOTHERS

INTRODUCTION

In 1989, I was forty years old. Friends were already calling me Monsieur Vogue. I loved working at the magazine, and then, as its creative director, I was on the way to a happy yet totally unpredictable life. But that year turned out to be very difficult, because in 1989 I lost the two women who were most important in my life: the grandmother who raised me, Bennie Frances Davis, and my surrogate mother, the Empress of Style, Diana Vreeland. Both had been ill for some while, and each had fought a brave fight to the end. Their deaths broke my heart.

My grandmother had worked hard all her life. So had Diana Vreeland. After my grandmother had raised her own four children (having lost two in childbirth), worked as a maid, and been widowed, she raised me. Five days a week, she cleaned men's dormitory rooms at Duke University. Our house was heavy with love and full of a lot of odds and ends, leftover furniture from the dorm rooms that male students would give to her after completion of semesters or upon graduation.

Both my grandmother and Diana Vreeland kept immaculate houses—except that Vreeland, who might have three or four maids running around in a frenzy in her small, luxurious apartment in New York, never did the scrubbing, the polishing, or the cooking. Laundry was something she ordered done. My grandmother was responsible not only for doing laundry, cooking meals twice a day, and working five days a week, she was also an active member of her church, eldest sister to seven siblings, and favorite aunt to many nieces and nephews.

Two years prior to her passing, my grandmother was diagnosed with leukemia. She did her best to hide her illness from her loved ones, and I didn't learn of her condition until one Sunday when I had to rush from New York to North Carolina, where I found her in a wheelchair in the emergency room at Duke University Hospital. She sat there in her robe, surrounded by her favorite nieces, Bena, Doris, and Georgia. It was only then that I learned that for months she had been going to see a Dr. Cox at an outpatient clinic, where she had taken oral chemotherapy. I spent that long night on a hospital bed adjacent to hers in the emergency ward, watching her sleep and praying for a miracle.

It is no small task to learn to sit back and take it easy after a lifetime of backbreaking labor. With great dignity, both my grandmother and Diana Vreeland refused to let illness limit them. To the extent that she could, my grandmother put up a tough fight, never giving in. She would go about the business of baking, cooking, light dusting, and going to church. Mrs. Vreeland, as I always called my surrogate fashion mother, shut her elegant lacquer red doors and took to her bed, where I would sit by her side and read aloud, as she sat on top of the luxurious covers, impeccably turned out, with her toes and nails in her favorite vibrant red varnish.

Mama, as I called my grandmother, never wore red varnish. The only time she wore lip rouge was on Sundays for church. Two days before she died, she was still hobbling over with her walker to the red velvet Georgian daybed that I had installed in the bay window of her bedroom suite, to gently pull the covers up to my chin as I napped on the chaise in my silent vigil. When she turned ninety, I threw her a lavish surprise birthday party. She wore a navy blue Calvin Klein suit and let me pin a huge corsage to her lapel as she stood in front of her tiered cake, surrounded by all of our family.

For years, Christmas posed the problem of how to spend the most important holiday with the two women I loved most, when one lived in New York, the other in Durham, North Carolina, and neither had any intention of spending the holiday in the other place. Sometime in the mid-1980s, I found the way. I would go up to Mrs. Vreeland—Christmas Eve, just the two of us, quietly at home, having dinner, exchanging gifts, talking about everything under the sun. At 7:00 A.M., I would be on the first flight out of La Guardia to Durham, where I would arrive in time for my grandmother's huge Southern welcome of a Christmas homecoming. Grits, hot biscuits, sausage and country ham, Grandma's molasses (a jar of which I still keep unopened in my kitchen cupboards), were always ready to be served, with my grandmother saying grace.

In September 1988, for the first time in her life other than childbirth, my grandmother entered the hospital. She did not like the idea of spending even one night there. After having spent a lifetime of believing in going home to her reward, she had always hoped to die peacefully in her own bed. I wanted that for her; unfortunately, she died at Duke Hospital, on March 3, 1989, at around 4:28 P.M. The only family member present was my cousin, her niece Georgia Nunn Purefoy.

At home, she would move around the new house on Swarthmore Road with her walker. Some Sundays, we still went to our family church on Mt. Sinai Road, in Orange County, and she never entered with her walker until the very last time, in January of 1989. On that last Sunday, in a navy Chanel suit, she leaned on my arm for support and entered the church as graceful and proud as she had always been.

At home in her bedroom four days before she died, she began talking incessantly about her own mother, my beloved great-grandmother China. She told me how she remembered that shortly before her mother died, she had suffered from the same kinds of headaches she herself was having then. Stoic, noble, and dignified, she would tell me story after story about her own mother. I knew she was very ill, but I didn't realize it would be the end that week.

At *Vogue*, I had recently become creative director, following Anna Wintour from *HG* only seven months before my grandmother passed on. Two nights before my grandmother died, I asked her if she would mind if I made a brief trip back to New York City, for work. Then I would return for the weekend.

"Not at all, Ray," she said, calling me by her favorite nickname. "Just as long as you come home on the weekend."

"I'll be back by Saturday," I told her.

"Have a good trip, and send my regards to your friend Mrs. Vreeland."

Except for the constant dull headache and the touch of the soles of her feet, which were very cool, how was anyone to know the time of her death was near?

She still wanted to sit up, comb her hair, get dressed, and the only unusual request was her asking me, for the first time ever, to massage her arms. In her beautifully decorated room, she desired things like a dip of her favorite Railroad Mills Snuff or some fatback meat. Both were unthinkable in her condition, but before I left for New York, I slipped her a tiny morsel of each, when no other relations were around to tell me not to. When I left Durham, she was still at home. My mother, Alma Ruth Talley, told me on the telephone, that the morning before she died, my grandmother had put on her very favorite red corduroy skirt and vest, and a blouse. This sounded like a good sign.

The next day, however, when I made my daily telephone check, things had taken a turn for the worse. With no other recourse (thinking back on it now, I should have rushed to the airport and taken the first plane back to Durham), I called my cousin Georgia and asked her what she would do in a case like this. She told me it would be best to have her taken to the hospital. I instructed my mother to call an ambulance and get her to the hospital as fast as she could.

At the time, *Vogue* was going to print its first issue with Madonna on the cover. They needed me to do a sound bite for a television interview to promote the issue. It would take no longer than two or three minutes, but I had to film it in New York, in the layout department. That sad day, I was leaning against a Formica countertop, doing "Vogue-speak" on Madonna. As soon as the taping had finished, I ran to my office and called Mama's hospital room. The phone rang and rang. No answer. I felt it, *My God,* I kept praying for a miracle, that she or Cousin Georgia would pick up on the other end. I dialed the number over and over. Later I learned that at that very moment, they had been performing that final drastic act, with those horrible things attached to her chest, trying to jump-start her heart. She was gone.

The shock came over me in waves as I sat alone in my office. When I finally got through, Dr. Cox informed me of her death in the gentlest possible tone. I told no one at *Vogue.* I just picked up my things and walked out the door, down Madison Avenue, to my apartment on West Twenty-third, and crawled under the covers until Saturday morning, when I took the first plane home. I could not forgive myself for not having been there with her in her last moments. It was, I felt and still feel strongly, what she would have wished. I kept replaying in my mind the conversation we'd had before I left; if only she had said, "No, Ray, I'd want you to stay here with me," I would have stayed. My one consolation was that the night before she died I spoke to her, and the last thing I said to her was "I love you."

Her reply, the very last words I ever heard her speak, was "I love you, too."

That was in March 1989. I went home to organize the funeral. I had the good fortune to have my cousin Georgia, who had been one of my grandmother's favorite nieces and who had been there most of that last afternoon, tell me that she had seen her in a peaceful state. I was glad that, if I could not have been with her, she had at least been visited by someone who loved her and whom she loved; she had not been alone on the journey.

The funeral was very difficult for me. It is almost impossible to say good-bye to someone you love so much, even if you know from your religious upbringing that she's going to a better place; it is difficult to reckon with loss. The worst thing about her funeral was that the undertakers inadvertently lowered her coffin into the vault with her feet facing north and her head positioned south. The old folks always say that a person should be buried almost the opposite way, with the head facing the sun as it rises in the east, so that on the day of Resurrection the spirit can rise up and walk. Against the protests of many of my female cousins, I had my grandmother disinterred a week after her funeral and her coffin turned around, with head and feet planted properly for her awakening on that Great Getting Up Morning. For her grave marker, I designed a somber obelisk of dark Georgia granite and had it cut to my own height, so that it could always be as if my figure were watching over her final resting place.

I knew Bennie Frances Davis had loved me and thought of me until the very end—I was, after all, her only grandchild. I felt very, very fortunate to have had her, but the loss was great. Being an only child is a hard thing. The older you get, the more you feel the loneliness of it. One is lucky if, at my age, one's parents are still alive on this planet.

I returned to work as soon as I could. Mrs. Vreeland, who had lost most of her sight and was bedridden by then, did her best to give me comfort. I spent many evenings and most of my weekends reading to her. I know that, when they hear this story, people sometimes like to think of me reading to Mrs. Vreeland from behind a screen, well out of sight and using a megaphone. This is rubbish. We were the closest of friends, and I made all the noise I wanted to right there in front of her. I had been raised in a black Southern family, and if there was one thing I could do, it was tell a story. I wore myself out reading to Mrs. Vreeland. I had always loved her, but that year, she truly became the core of my life.

The last conversation I had with her was, as it had been with my grandmother, over the telephone, that same August. She had helped me profoundly through the difficult process of coming to terms with my grandmother's death, and I called one day to tell her that I had, on my own, made a further step toward recovering my inner strength: I had joined Harlem's Abyssinian Baptist Church. Abyssinian Baptist was much larger and more urbane than the church in which my grandmother had raised me, but it reminded me of it nonetheless. The singing was much the same, and the uplifting spirit of the place took me back to memories of my childhood. Dr. Calvin O. Butts III, the famous reverend of the church, clearly espoused the values my grandmother had worked so hard to instill in me, and listening to his sermons encouraged me to reflect upon my life and brought me some serenity.

"That's marvelous, André, simply marvelous," she said, her voice strong. I could imagine her lying there in her blue boudoir, wrapped in a neat robe, and propped up on pillows atop her perfectly made bed. Her beautiful feet would have been resting on a pillow of their own, and sporting a perfect pedicure of crimson. When she said good-bye after a short, uneventful conversation, she said the thing she always said to me at the end of a conversation: "Just keep the news coming."

The doctors tried to revive her, too, but like my grandmother, she left peacefully when her time had come.

It was on Monday afternoon that her grandson, Alexander Vreeland, called me at home to tell me that my surrogate mother in the world of *Vogue* had passed. I had just come from around the corner, where I'd had my first salon manicure at a Korean shop, when Alexander reached me and told me he wanted to be the first to let me know. I was deeply touched that in his grief he could remember how much his grandmother and I had meant to each other. I was also moved by Alexander's invitation to attend his grandmother's private services in a side chapel of Saint Thomas Church on Fifth Avenue; no one came but me, the immediate family, and the two black nurses who had taken care of Mrs. Vreeland in her last days. This was the same church in which, so many years ago, and wearing a medieval wimple that covered her right up to her throat, she had married T. Reed Vreeland. In her excitement about the wedding, she had forgotten to send out the invitations, so few of their friends and guests had showed up.

When the services ended, I had the opportunity to talk to the two nurses. Both reported that she had spoken incessantly about her mother, about how she was going to see her beautiful mother dancing, how she herself wanted to go dancing in a beautiful dress.

I think that when I am ready to pass on, I will see both of my mothers: the grandmother who raised me and the spiritual mother who helped make my dreams come true. I can imagine that my grandmother will have come from the beauty parlor with a halo of perfect bluish snow-white curls, and Diana Vreeland will be waiting in her red Georgian dwarf armchair—her favorite chair from her hill-red seraglio—with a decanter of vodka and two small glasses on the table beside her. In her hands she'll hold a book for the two of us to read together, and when she first sees me, she'll smile, and say, "Right-o André, let's get crackin'!"

Bennie Frances Davis and Diana Vreeland were two brave, strong women preparing for the last journey, seeing some of the same sights along the way. They had courage and strength that I have yet to see in any man—the courage to battle pain, disease, loss of sight, loss of loved ones, and loss of independence with the simple resolve to maintain their personal dignity. I believe that for both of them, this strength came from a sure sense of rootedness in the past, from vast stores of self-confidence, and from what I can only believe is God's mercy.

I still continued to go to church after Mrs. Vreeland died, but I found that I needed comfort of a different kind as well. I needed a change of scenery to help me sort things out. I went back to Paris, where I had lived for a while as Paris bureau chief of *Women's Wear Daily*, and retraced my steps through the French landscape I so dearly loved. Anna Wintour, my editor at *Vogue*, also granted me as much time as I needed to do research for a tribute to Mrs. Vreeland; so from Paris I traveled to England, to meet Mrs. Vreeland's one surviving niece. She turned out to be a lovely woman, much more robust and typically British in appearance than Mrs. Vreeland had been. The one thing she wanted to know of me was if her aunt Diana had been a believer?

I told her that Mrs. Vreeland had believed in God in her own way. Once or twice I remember her lifting her hands in a prayerlike position, at table or when propped up on her bed in a *levée de la reine* position. She would say, "Thank you, God, for this extraordinary life and all your bountiful blessings!" These were serious moments, when the tone of her conversation turned to lyrical rapture. I remember her once at table, raising her hands above her head in a dramatic, almost Martha Graham gesture of exaltation and praise. She may not have spoken of God often, but the goodness of God was in her at all times. I never spent a disheartening moment in her presence; even sitting with her silently was a joy.

My grandmother and Mrs. Vreeland were the most important figures in my life, and their guidance continues to inform my every decision. Although they are physically gone, I feel them with me at every moment, my two good angels, each looking over one of my shoulders. I speak to them both, often, in the silent language of memory-speak.

At the end of the rainbow that has led me to a successful career in the world of fashion and at *Vogue*, I find that the things that are most important to me are not the gossamer and gilt of the world I live in now, but my deep Southern roots. The catty anecdotes in which books about fashion abound may be titillating, but they are not what ultimately matters. What matters is a sense of place, a sense of self.

The precious memories of my two great anchors still linger with me, every day in every step of the journey. The love and protection of these two women still guide me as I move through this life. If I hope only one thing, it is that these chantings of memory—the gifts of the sounds, scents, and visions of a childhood and young manhood full of love—will sing to other kindred souls and spirits. The unconditional love that passed into eternity in 1989 has kept me ploughing on, through the roughest waters, with silent whispers of gratitude.

Durham is an industrial town, home to tobacco fortunes and Duke University. It is my hometown, the place where my grandmother reared me and taught me about loving God and living well. Our street was a typical American street. Our house, the first on the left as one entered Cornell Street from Morehead Avenue, had the oldest, grandest sycamore on the block. I don't know how old that tree was, but it dwarfed all others for what seemed to me to be miles around. In spring and summer, it gave abundant shade, and in autumn, it dropped so many leaves that I had to rake them up almost every day. This was hard work but gave me an excuse to start a leaf bonfire, whose scent and heat were a thrill to me on a crisp autumn day. It was also a perfect place to light up the imagination and dream of faraway, exotic places.

My parents, William Carroll Talley and Alma Ruth Davis, were both raised in North Carolina: my mother in a house down the street on Morehead Avenue, my father in Roxboro, another tobacco hamlet, half an hour away. Sometime in 1947 they met at a party. They were married in a minister's house, in Washington, D.C., where they had moved, believing they could make a better life.

This is all I know of their courtship and early life together, since my father died in 1993. Three years ago, when I was staying at Karl Lagerfeld's house in Biarritz, I called my mother to ask her more about her romance and her wedding. When did they decide to marry? How long had they dated? Did she have any precious memories she wanted to share with me about my birth and early life? She obviously did not want to talk about or remember any of these things. She ended our phone conversation by telling me I didn't need to know any of the details of her marriage to my father.

I was born on October 16, 1948. My parents brought me straight to Durham that Christmas. My mother's mother, "Mama," her mother, China, and her younger (and favorite) daughter, Dorothy Bee, all lived in the same house. My parents decided to leave me in this house full of women. So they kept me, Great-grandmother China, Mama, and Aunt Dorothy Bee. I lived at 1007 Cornell until I left to go to Brown University in 1970. It was the only home I've ever known, except for sporadic summer visits to my parents during my teens. I went to Lyon Park Elementary School, a two-minute walk to the end of Cornell Street, to Whitted Junior High School, across town in the swanky black bourgeois section of Durham, and Hillside High School. Each school stands to this day, though Lyon Park has been abandoned for decades.

Though my grandmother's house was modest and the walls were newspaper-thin in the cold of winter, I was blessed to be in a home so full of love, so full of nurturing. Our house had no luxuries, except for cleanliness, fresh air in summer, hot fires in winter, and the spirit of God.

When I was small, my grandmother used to tell me a story about when I was a baby—a story that I am fond of. According to her, I was an infant always doing things in the reverse. For instance, I had my own ideas about how to learn to crawl. Instead of crawling like other babies, I sat down on my bottom with my legs straight out in front of me and scooted my legs to propel myself forward.

Although I rarely attended grade school in Washington, I remember my parents had a huge apartment with a spacious dining room and two big bedrooms with huge windows on Gerard Street, Northwest. The living room and entrance hall were airy, full of light; that's all I remember. Other than those things, I recall little, except coffee splashes against the kitchen wall during one of my parents' violent disputes. The translucent lines of brown liquid running down the pale lemon yellow walls from a coffeepot dashed from the hands of either my mother or father is a vivid memory. The point is that a coffeepot was thrown; I never asked by whom. I was never told why. They remained married for ten years before they divorced.

Our family life at my grandmother's house was, like anyone's, full of births, deaths, happy events and sad; the difference between our family and some was that scandals and difficulties were whispered about for years but never spoken out loud. The word *cancer,* for example, never came out of any of my aunts' mouths. The grown-ups would say, "She has a *C,* you know." Children, of course, hear and understand all. When I was nine, the news came to me that my mother had decided to divorce my dad. I found out one fall day while seated in my father's brand-new car, parked under that sycamore tree, with the window rolled up. My father and his favorite brother stood a few feet away from the car; through the raised window floated the words "Talley has a *D* now," as if I couldn't figure out that *D* stood for a divorce.

It also stood for depression, desperation, and despair, which combined to change the entire course of my mother's life, after her divorce. She became a different person, dark, brooding, withdrawn, distant. For a while she imagined a bright future with a man of means who was courting her. But that hope extinguished the morning she opened her mailbox and found an envelope with an invitation to his church wedding—to a younger woman.

That boyfriend, Waddy (whom I had always disliked when my mother took me by taxi to his dusty, gloomy apartment), had betrayed her for a registered nurse. My mother's life went into a full tailspin. Her hair turned white, and from that moment forward she slid into her own world of bitterness and removed herself from mine. Although I do care for and respect my mother and would do anything for her, when I called to ask her about her own wedding bells, she did not want to share her own memories of happier times. I have provided and will always provide for her as she continues her life, but she figures little in my story.

My father, meanwhile, took up his active role as hepcat sugar daddy to what seemed to me an inexhaustible supply of younger, firm-bodied women. Nevertheless, he continued to uphold his moral duty, as a father, and as a Masonic Lodge member. He was a God-fearing man, never delinquent with his support envelopes—weekly or biweekly letters stuffed with cash, since in those days, our family didn't write checks or have credit cards. Everything was done in cash. Every bill paid in cash. He left my upbringing in my capable grandmother's hands. Yet his frequent visits, on holidays and otherwise, were moments of great happiness for me. Sometimes I wished my father had been more involved in my upbringing—especially when my grandmother (or Grandmother China, when she was still living) would tear a branch from a fruit tree and make a switch with which to apply punishment to my pajama-covered backside. I disliked this system wholeheartedly. But what man or woman today can't look back and say those switch whippings helped to mold one into a responsible adult?

I do not mean to suggest that my childhood involved physical abuse from my grandmothers—far from it! One reason those punishments stand out in my mind is how infrequently they were administered; I took notice when they came. And I know it pained Mama and her mother, China, to inflict punishment. They did not enjoy disciplining me, but they felt it was the right thing to do. It was a system passed down from one generation to another. I believe I have grown up to be the sort of man they wanted me to be—committed to church and charity, trying to be a good citizen—so who is to say their old-fashioned, down-home approach is wrong?

I realize now how very blessed I was to lead a sheltered life as a young boy—to live in a world that revolved around church, religion, Sunday school, and house duties, in a house of nurturing, mature women who had lived hard lives and survived with dignity. I may have lacked the everyday presence of a male role model, but I found those in church, in my pastors.

It is an entirely different thing to write a column for *Vogue* called

StyleFax (which was my editor, Anna Wintour's idea) than to live solely in the service of peace and brotherhood. However, I do feel I have tried, in my own way, to live in a way that Dr. King would approve of, exactly as I have tried to live according to my grandmother's and Mrs. Vreeland's precepts.

Every day I strive to be a better, kinder, more tolerant, patient, and forgiving human being. I try to use my position in life to bring beauty and joy into other people's lives. Certainly, I have weathered and survived the chiffon trenches of fashion for nearly three decades, but during that time I have not lost my sense of values or of place. Balzac's brilliant sentence sums up my daily mantra: There is far more happiness in another's happiness than in your own."

A.L.T.

CHAPTER ONE

I shall begin by writing about luxury. I can't be sure exactly what image you'll drum up, but I suspect that it will either be swathed in silk and brocade or dressed in a custom-made English suit. You have every right to suppose this is what I'd mean. After all, high fashion *is* luxury—the luxury of the most beautiful fabrics, tailored to perfection; the luxury of the clothes' presentation at runway shows, beautifully orchestrated luncheons, or designers' showrooms; the luxury of having a lifestyle that permits one either the leisure to wear such clothes or the leisure to have opinions about them. If I tell you, "I am going to write about luxury," perhaps you will think, *André wants to write down what he learned from Diana Vreeland, that self-appointed queen of splendor.* Or *André intends to memorialize the heyday of hedonism with the fashion elite.* Or *André is about to wax rapturous about the perfect lines of a be-*

spoke shoe. And you wouldn't be entirely wrong. Sooner or later, I am going to talk about all of these things.

But they are not what I mean by luxury.

The truth is that I live on a relatively grand scale, because that's the way fashion is: By its very nature, it is larger than life. It's fickle, it's flamboyant, and it's fabulous. But at the same time, it does not provide the boundaries a person needs in order to live a sane, happy life in service not only to oneself but also to others. Fashion is no substitute for family, and I do not believe I could ever have learned to appreciate haute couture had I not learned to appreciate simpler things first.

Long before I became Mrs. Vreeland's assistant at the Costume Institute of New York's Metropolitan Museum of Art, long, long before I became the Paris fashion editor at *WWD,* or Paris bureau chief at *W,* or creative director (and now, once again, an editor) at *Vogue,* I was an African-American man raised by his hardworking grandmother in North Carolina. My grandmother never tried to force me to subscribe to a particular code of behavior, but growing up in her house, I learned how to live just by watching her work, pray, and go about the business of making a home for me. Her life was not easy, but because it was based on clear, sound principles of good behavior, it lacked the tortured complexity that I now so often see around me. Her code of ethics, always unspoken, was nonetheless perfectly straightforward: Church and family, the focal points, were inextricably bound together. She worked hard at her job and kept a clean, welcoming home, so that those in her care (her own mother and I) could be well provided for, and so that we could all serve God. What this meant at a practical level was that every surface in our home glowed—not only through the application of soap, paste wax, or ammonia, but also through the underlying working of love. What it also meant was that my childhood was, by anyone's standards, a rich one. Faith, Hope, Charity: Add Luxury to the list, because it was that important, taken that seriously in our home.

My earliest experiences of luxury, then, were not experiences of surfeit and sumptuousness, but of the beauty of ordinary tasks done well and in a good frame of mind; of simple things suited to their purpose and well cared for. I will get to evenings with Mrs. Vreeland eventually, and to New York in the '70s, and to silk faille bespoke shoes, but for me, the only place to begin talking about luxury is with my grandmother's crisp white sheets.

When I was a child, my great-grandmother China (and my grandmother, when China became too frail), boiled our laundry in a big black iron cauldron in the yard. She would set up everything under our peach trees, for shade. She would build a good fire from wood she had chopped herself. Sheets and table linens always had to be allowed to simmer, and anything white (such as towels, nightgowns, or my Sunday shirts) would be left to boil the longest. The temperature in that cauldron was so high, my great-grandmother or grandmother had to use a rod as thick as a forearm, cut from the limb of a tree, to stir the laundry around the enormous pot. Once clean, the wash was transferred to huge zinc rinsing tubs that rested either on a wooden table or on the tree stump that was normally reserved for the death whack on the neck of a soon-to-be-eaten chicken. The sheets and other whites got a weekly dose of bluing agent, to prevent them from turning yellow, and my grandmother or great-grandmother would wring them out thoroughly by hand before hanging them to dry. I can still see my grandmother, her apron full of clothespins, walking the length of our silvery clothesline (which stretched all the way from the porch to a tree far at the back of the property) with a rag in hand, wiping the natural dust and pollen off the line before she would entrust her laundry to it.

The wall of white sheets flapped in the wind like huge sails rigged by wooden clothespins. They stretched the entire length of our deep backyard. And I loved to run past and between the drying sheets, feeling their roughness on my outstretched hands and inhaling the fresh smell of cotton dried in the open air.

The convenience of a modern tumble dryer doesn't really compensate for the loss of that wonderful smell. That warm, delicious odor came inside on the folded sheets, which my grandmother stacked shoulder-high on the table. And then she ironed them.

Remember that my grandmother was not a woman of leisure, no bored housewife searching for ways to occupy her time. Until she retired at sixty-five, she worked five mornings a week at her job, and before she left to begin this hard work, she did a lot of hard work at home. On bitter cold, frost-encrusted mornings when I was a child, she would go outside with an ax to chop wood for the stove and our fires. (I sometimes volunteered for this task, but she always said she could chop better and more quickly than I could.) Her night head scarf would still be in place, protecting her curls, and she would be wearing nothing warmer than a pink quilted bed jacket over her flannel nightgown. After she chopped the wood, she started all the fires, put up a steaming breakfast of scrambled eggs, bacon, grits, and coffee, got me ready for school, and still managed to be at work by 7:30 A.M. (On Sundays she rose even earlier to make her special Sunday breakfast, which included cured country ham, sausages, and homemade biscuits.) After all this work, and after performing manual labor all day, she came home not to rest on the sofa, but to do more work. Every Thursday evening, without fail, she ironed every sheet and pillowcase for three beds—hers, mine, and Great-grandma China's, until China passed on in January 1960. She did this with an old electric iron. I remember her standing at the ironing board for what seemed hours at a time, sprinkling the sheets with water before she pressed them, to make them more pliable.

As late as 1983, I would sometimes iron my sheets as a form of therapeutic reconnection to my home; but to anyone with a modern sensibility, the idea of ironing sheets is unthinkable. Who has time, when permanent-press (or permanently none-too-smooth) linens can be thrown in the washer and dryer, then tossed on the bed? To my grandmother, however, pressed sheets were a necessity of a well-run, tasteful home. If we could have that luxury—which cost only her willingness for one more labor-intensive task and the time it took to perform it—then she would see to it that we did. Her sheets were always plain white, but they were of high quality, thick Egyptian cotton; and they were always, always immaculate.

Sheets like that are a true delight. Our house was often chilly in the winter, but there was no pleasure more delicious than climbing into a bed piled six-deep with homemade quilts and snuggling down into those crispy, crispy, clean, clean, clean white sheets. Sleep was never so fine as between those sheets, cooked, ironed, and arranged by loving hands.

Our house was full of such simple luxuries. Until I left home, I never used a towel that hadn't been ironed—and had no idea how much I would miss them when I was out in the world. My boxer shorts, always white, or pale blue for Sunday, were pressed smooth, and my Sunday shirts starched to a shine. The handkerchiefs my grandmother would tuck into her purse before leaving for church were folded neat as letters. And the curtains in her house were, quite plainly, a joy to look out at the world through. In the kitchen she often had printed curtains, but the rest of the curtains were white organdy, with deep ruffles and tiebacks; the kind of curtains you only see now in movies about days gone by. At regular intervals, she would ask that the curtains be taken down (one of many household tasks for which my height particularly suited me) and would launder them so well that they dazzled the eye. Like everything else in the house, they were meticulously ironed and arranged. Even the lace doilies on the backs of chairs were starched.

Of course, these luxuries are only luxuries if you see them that way. We always had clothes to wear and food on the table, but we lived on limited means. Our roof leaked buckets of water when the snow melted, and if the pipes froze, my grandmother heated water on the wood-burning stove so I could take a "bird bath" before school. Of course, the toilet didn't flush during hard freezing spells, so at those times we took turns dumping buckets of water down the commode as a hygienic measure. The wind had a way of screaming through our paper-thin walls, but my grandmother never lit a fire in her own bedroom at night. (She always said this was for health reasons—and indeed, I hardly ever remember her taking ill until she grew old.) The love we had for one another was the only luxury we had in that house, but because of that love, and because of my grandmother's faith, our simple life was suffused with dignity and grace.

My grandmother taught me very early to seek out the clean lines of true elegance. Luxury in the greatest sense, in the grand sense, could be something as simple as watching two or three cardinals cavorting outside my bedroom window, or receiving from my uncle's big, callused hands a basket of tomatoes, freshly picked and still smelling of the salt and sunshine of the vine. It might be a glossy, store-bought bow on a birthday present wrapped in glossier paper from the five-and-dime. There was tremendous beauty in the white picket fence that divided my grandmother's rose garden from her occasional experiments at vegetable gardening, especially when that fence stood out, in the fall of the year, against the blanket of scarlet and yellow sycamore leaves that drifted down to cover our yard. And though my grandmother had no formal training as a gardener, had never read a gardening book, and had no big bags of Miracle-Gro to assist her, her peach trees, rosebushes, and begonias were lush, and the terra-cotta pots of red geraniums she kept on our porch in summer were among the finest in the neighborhood. She had a natural green thumb. Anything she touched blossomed.

It was likely the very plainness of my grandmother's home that trained me to be an aesthete—not in the sense of someone who seeks out, like the protagonist of Joris Karl Huysmans's *Against the Grain,* ever more rarefied aesthetic pleasures, but in the truer sense, of one whose life is governed by his experience of and relationship to beauty. Certainly by the time I was six or seven years old, I was a luxury addict. I loved waking up on Sunday mornings, savoring my breakfast, and then carefully stepping into my best clothes. I loved watching my grandmother perform the ministrations she did only on that day—the application of such wonders as powder and lipstick. And although I had rarely eaten in anyone else's kitchen, I knew it was a stroke of good fortune always to be presented with the delicious food she cooked me. (I will return to talk about it more fully later, as my grandmother's cooking was of such epic proportions that it deserves its own chapter.) And when beautiful things came into the house, they always made a profound impression on me.

I will never forget the yellow paisley pajamas my grandmother bought for my twelfth birthday. Until that time, my pajamas had been, like my underwear, white or pale blue cotton. But that year, for whatever reason, my grandmother went downtown to a Main Street store called Belk's and picked out these yellow cotton flannel Christian Dior pajamas. Christian Dior! She didn't know who he was; she just had an innate sense of what was beautiful. I, of course, knew perfectly well who Christian Dior was—I was already a devoted reader of fashion magazines such as Mrs. Vreeland's *Vogue*—and I was greatly impressed by these exotic and unusual pajamas. They were lemon yellow with red and green paisleys, and they were unlike anything I'd ever seen. I decided to sleep in them only on special occasions, such as Christmas.

I'm sure the pajamas were Christian Dior licensing—they couldn't have come all the way from Paris to Durham, North Carolina—but I also know that they must have been expensive on my grandmother's salary as a maid. She knew that the occasional taste of true luxury is very important. She was always scrupulous about budgeting and saving, but after her husband died in 1951, she bought herself the diamond ring he could not afford when they were courting. Also after his death, she purchased a sterling silver flatware service for twelve, which we used only on extremely important occasions, such as when the minister came to dinner. Her pleasure in this silverware was not vanity but the true pride of having worked hard to bring something lovely into her life. Since my childhood, I have eaten from silverware far more costly and ornate than my grandmother's; but I have never known a hostess to take such uncomplicated pleasure in its beauty as she did.

I loved to watch her enjoy these things, and when I became old enough and had some money of my own, I took pleasure in spending it on her. When I was living at home during my college years at North Carolina Central University, I used to go to Washington, D.C., in the summertime to work as a park ranger at such places as the Lincoln Memorial. My father, William Carroll Talley, had worked two jobs his entire life—by day, as a mid-grade-level printing press operator at the U.S. Patent Office in Washington, and at night as a taxi driver—to help support me. After six, he didn't have a cocktail hour, and he rarely got to travel, even on the weekends. Other than his Sunday-morning churchgoing and his Masonic Lodge meetings, he took little time off from working. He kept two cars, though: a sleek, sporty car for his playboy life and a cab, all his own. I admired his hard work and dedication, and through them, he had saved enough to pay for my tuition at the state university. However, my grandmother and I agreed that I would have to earn the money for my other expenses. Whatever I earned in the summertime was to be my spending money for the year to come. And of course I saved enough of it to buy myself books and some clothes, the things that a twenty-year-old values. But what I really liked to do with whatever was left over was spoil my grandmother. Each August, before I returned home to Durham, I would visit Garfinckel's department store, which was over by the White House, and pick out two or three pairs of Kislav gloves for her. Garfinckel's was to Washington what Bergdorf's is to Fifth Avenue, and everything it carried was the best of the best. Kislav gloves were considered the finest gloves made, and remember, this was the late 1960s, when no woman's formal outfit was complete without matching gloves. Kislav made hundreds of styles, for day and evening wear: bone-colored wrist-length gloves as soft as chamois, elbow-length gloves in black or white kidskin, shoulder-high evening gloves that could be crushed stylishly down to just above the elbow. They were expensive—around twenty dollars a pair, which was a lot of money back then—but it gave me pleasure to bring home a couple of beautiful new pairs for my grandmother. It was a joy to watch her unwrap them, exclaim over them, and place them carefully in the glove drawer; and the pleasure she took in wearing them was nearly palpable.

Of course, once I began to work in the fashion world, I was able to send her truly extravagant gifts—suits and handbags from Chanel, the finest crepe de chine from Karl Lagerfeld, all manner of classic, well-made shoes. But try as I might, I could never actually manage to spoil her—she had her priorities too straight for that. However lovely a dress I managed to buy her, she always valued the love behind the gift more than the gift itself.

My grandmother's impeccable sense of order, and her pride in the beauty of her home, cultivated in me a real appreciation for the importance of good housekeeping. When, in my late twenties, I came under Mrs. Vreeland's tutelage, I had very little direct experience with the kind of luxury she practically embodied, yet found that I had an innate understanding of it.

Take, for example, Mrs. Vreeland's sheets. Now, in my childhood I had had a true understanding of luxury when I looked through my grandmother's cedar chests, packed with neatly folded, beautiful linens. But nothing in my childhood had prepared me for Mrs. Vreeland's linen closet—an entire walk-in closet, given over to floor-to-ceiling shelves packed with the exquisite linens she had collected over a lifetime. Most of them slept in individual zippered plastic cases. They had little handwritten labels on the shelves: MME. PORTHAULT GIFT, 1965; WHITE SHEETS WITH BRODERIE ANGLAISE; SHEETS EMBROIDERED BY NUNS IN PORTUGAL, 1939. She had sheets in patterns so wild I couldn't see how anyone could sleep on them. She had once seen some sheets that Mme. Porthault had custom-made for Barbara Hutton and spoke rapturously of them for the rest of her life. (Mme. Porthault was, in the middle of the last century, the reigning queen of French linen. She made the tablecloths for the Kennedy White House.) These sheets, apparently, had had the biggest foldbacks Mrs. Vreeland had ever seen, all hand-embroidered with Le Douanier Rousseau's jungle scenes. Mrs. Vreeland raved about the savage tigers, lions, and exotic foliage; she went on about them as someone else might go on about a new lover. But a perfectly made bed was important to her, exactly as it was to my grandmother—and that was how I learned to appreciate the extravagance of her linen closet. Her tastes may have been more expensive than any we had known in North Carolina, but the simple pleasure she derived from them was the same. When Mrs. Vreeland grew older and fell ill, she would still, when I went to visit her, be perfectly turned out, lying on an impeccably turned-down bed. It didn't matter that she could hardly see her colorful sheets anymore; she was happy in the knowledge that the bed was correct in every layer of Porthault.

I realize now that my grandmother and Mrs. Vreeland had similar ways of appreciating luxury, because they both believed in the importance of its most essential underpinning: polish.

And I do mean polish in a literal sense. Once I got old enough to help with household chores, my grandmother taught me not only to clean things, but to make them shine. In the summer I would take all the gliders, chairs, and pots of geraniums, ferns, and sundry flowers from the porch, scrub the floor and the railings down with soapy water and a push broom, and pour bucket after bucket of clean rinse water over everything until I could see my reflection in the pearl gray paint. Lathering up a big plank floor like that was no mean feat, and neither was changing the rinse buckets of cool water three or five times; but when I had finished the task, it made me very, very proud. Polishing the furniture was one of my weekly tasks, as was sweeping the wooden floors. You didn't sweep under a bed in my grandmother's house—you moved the bedstead as far as was necessary to get at the dust and dirt beneath. At Christmas and Easter, we got down on our hands and knees and polished the floors with paste wax; we washed windowpanes, both inside and out, with rags and ammonia. Spring cleaning was the time to embrace the renewal spirit of Easter, with blue Windex in spray bottles and Clorox in buckets. With our cleaning rags and scouring pads we attacked dust and grime in combat mode, making sure that every molding, every window sash, every doorknob gleamed. One of my favorite occasional chores as a child was repapering the cabinet in which my grandmother kept the magical essences, such as lemon and vanilla extracts, with which she baked. I took my time at this task and stopped to open and smell each bottle before I returned it to its place. This was also the cabinet in which she kept our supply of household remedies, some of which—horse liniment for aching joints and the cod liver oil I swallowed, grimacing, every morning—had such pungent odors I made sure the bottles remained tightly capped. I would cover those shelves in bright, festive ginghams—optimistic five-and-dime decorations.

Like any dreamer, I loved to loll, and there were days when I didn't want to get out of bed or dawdled at jobs my grandmother asked me to do. Mostly, I accepted her matter-of-fact attitude toward housework without a second thought. In our family, cleanliness was so close to godliness that we plain had no congress with grime. We cleaned simply because cleaning had to be done. The necessity of an immaculate house was not shrouded in philosophy—it was neither something on which we should pride ourselves nor a burden we should stoically bear, but a key part of good living.

My grandmother thought that preaching belonged in church, so she never sat me down and explained this. Bennie Frances Davis did neither more nor less than set me an example that I could follow without question. Through soap and paste wax, rags, mops, and muscle power, I learned that cleaning can itself be restful, and that a well-kept home soothes the mind and spirit, making it easier to contemplate things beyond the physical and the everyday.

Mrs. Vreeland's home was every bit as neat and clean as my grandmother's, and, while she did little of the work herself, she oversaw it with interest and took real pleasure in the results. With a seemingly endless rotation of part-time workers, she managed to keep house as another might with a live-in staff of thirty. The maids were constantly busy rubbing and scrubbing her furniture and bibelots. The cushions on the couch were always perfectly arranged, with a dent in the center of each. None of her ordinary retainers was allowed to touch her bookshelves, but once a week a college student came to dust and reshelve her books. He tended them as carefully as if they were the stacks of the Library of Congress. I once saw Mrs. Vreeland's French maid, Yvonne, carefully ironing a small stack of five-dollar bills before they went into a black silk evening bag.

A young man came in on Saturdays to see to Mrs. Vreeland's shoes, which he buffed to a meticulous shine. Once the uppers were as glassy as a still Alpine lake, he would polish the soles with a rhinoceros horn. He took care of the soles of Mrs. Vreeland's shoes the way some people look after their family silver. And how she loved it! She really did notice the soles of people's shoes. I came to her house for dinner one night in a pair of pink raw silk Manolo Blahnik Chinese slippers, and as we were relaxing after supper, I crossed my legs. "André!" she exclaimed, her eyes widening in an almost Kabuki expression of surprise. "The next time you come to dinner in those slippers, I want to see the soles polished. When you cross your legs, you must present the same perfection you do in having selected that magnificent fabric for your shoes."

There are people from whom such a statement would be a mark of rampant vanity, of a total lack of connection with the world in which the rest of us live, but Diana Vreeland was as well moored as anyone I've known. She loved beauty, that was all—and unlike most of its devotees in this world, she was less likely to fall into raptures over a beautiful vista or a beautiful face (though she loved these things, too) than over a beautiful example of artifice. To her, the Chrysler Building was as awe inspiring as any cliff overlooking the Hudson, largely because it had sprung from the imagination of a human being who had to coax it into reality through the use of materials as well as dreams. She valued craftsmanship and set great store by both the spark of inspiration and the dogged hard work that brought a painting, a gown, or a well-set table into being. (I don't think she made a qualitative distinction between things that were magnificent because they were art and things that were simply magnificent.) Thus, she was a fan of any lovely thing that required care in its preparation—linen sheets, soufflés, chamber music, a manicured garden. These are old-fashioned pleasures, and they require an old-fashioned investment of time and sweat. The so-called conveniences of the modern world tend to be things that Mrs. Vreeland either lamented during her lifetime (no-wax floors, no-iron fabrics) or would have disliked had she lived long enough to see them (casual Fridays, shabby chic).

Thus, when Mrs. Vreeland admonished me about the soles of my shoes, I know that she was not being faithful to empty form. Rather, she was offering me one more lesson in the ways of living a well-wrought, elegant life. What good does it do, she was asking at some level, to be groomed in the places that are visible to others if the hidden parts of you remain unkempt? I think that what she was asking of me was that I polish myself in every way possible, from the soles of my shoes to the deep recesses of my mind.

At least, this is how I always understood both my grandmother's and Mrs. Vreeland's insistence on clothes being painstakingly cared for. Mrs. Vreeland, for example, had a system for how evening clothes should be prepared when she was going to wear them. If she knew she had a dinner to attend on Wednesday, Yvonne would lay the dress out on Monday, to air. When Mr. Vreeland had passed away, Mrs. Vreeland had converted his bedroom into a dressing room, and in it was a chaise longue, on which the clothes would be carefully arranged on white tissue. Sometimes, if she had events two evenings in a row, two outfits would be laid out, as if having a conversation with each other. This was an important part of her sensibility—and it was almost a Jane Austen kind of sensibility, this notion that clothes would have to be aired for two days before they could be worn. Thus, the kind of idiosyncrasy that makes life wonderful and luxurious.

And to me, it never seemed all that idiosyncratic, because my grandmother had a similar code. Not about everyday clothes—like Mrs. Vreeland, she wore only tidy clothes, but the things she wore to work were always utilitarian, nothing much. About church clothes, however, she had practically a code of honor. On Saturday, when we had finished straightening up the house, we would take out our clothes for the next day—right down to my socks (navy) and underwear (pale blue)—and lay them atop the cedar chests in which the linens were stored. I was used to airing clothes by the time I met Mrs. Vreeland; I'd been doing it all my life.

My grandmother took tremendous pride in our appearance on Sundays. We did not have extravagant clothes, but they were always the pattern of respectability. My suits were always navy blue, my shirts white or light blue, their collars starched until they nearly cut me. I always had a pair of black or Cordovan oxfords for church, and I shined them every Saturday. My grandmother dressed beautifully for church. I remember being in her bedroom when she placed her clothes out the night before, and marveling at all the foundation garments—girdles, corsets, slips, and so forth—that underpinned her Sunday appearance of effortless elegance. She, too, generally wore a suit on Sundays; her favorite, and the one in which I remember her most often, was a simple, black woolen barathea suit with a three-button jacket and a skirt. She must have bought that suit in the 1940s, and she continued to wear it until she died in 1989; it was unassuming, but it was a classic, of which she took appropriate good care. She had a collection of hats, ranging from the subdued to the fanciful, each stored in its own box, and she never went to church without wearing one. Her shoes always matched her handbag. We were so well turned out on an ordinary Sunday that you might almost say we were showboating, except that my grandmother would have dismissed the accusation with a brisk shake of her head. We loved our church clothes and loved the sense of occasion they gave to our lives. When we returned home after church, we changed right out of them before we sat down to our big Sunday meal. I think that was where the luxury came in. Some people love fancy cars, and we loved our beautiful church clothes. We derived pleasure from folding and hanging them up and saving them for their intended purpose.

My grandmother never had to tell me to stand up proud, never had to explain to me or convince me that although we did not have much money, we were the equals of any people in town. I knew this just by looking around me. When I saw the beauty of our home and the many small luxuries with which we were blessed, when I took pride in our appearance on Sundays, I knew my place in the world. Perhaps that's why, when I came to live in the whirlwind world of fashion, I was able to stand my ground and never lose sight of the importance of family, religion, and the other basic values I learned as a child. And perhaps it is why I was able to see Mrs. Vreeland's love of polish and shine as evidence of a deeper philosophy—the primacy of home and the importance of spending time in its service—rather than as slavish devotion to the superficial. Mrs. Vreeland kept her shoes for life, her bags for life, and her friends for life. My grandmother did the same.

The pace of the world has accelerated since my grandmother and Mrs. Vreeland were young women, and it would be unrealistic to think that one could live today exactly as they did fifty or seventy years ago. When I was a boy or a young man, it was pleasant to go for long walks or drives knowing that no one could contact me during my private time, yet I am glad for my cellular phone. As much as I love ironed sheets—as strong as the sense-memory of their texture and smell remains—I don't have time to iron an entire bed's worth weekly and usually find myself sleeping on the same permanent-press sheets that everyone else uses nowadays. (I do love hotels, however, for their crisp linens. It is always a great pleasure to stay at Karl Lagerfeld's home in France, not only because he is a grand and most gracious host and a good friend, but because his laundry maid, Annette, a white-haired woman who wears a pink candy-striped uniform, knows how to do sheets. Annette gives that same care to the tablecloths, tea napkins, coasters of embroidered linen, and one's personal laundry.) Even as someone who never really learned to cook, I cannot imagine having the time to chop wood and stoke the fire in a stove, no matter how much better cakes tasted coming out of a wood-burning oven.

The lives my grandmother and Mrs. Vreeland lived seemed superficially different from one another, but their faith in their beliefs and their ability to bring beauty and joy into the lives of those they loved were very much the same. I am lucky to have known the luxury of a peach still warm from the tree, lucky to have known the luxury of polishing the soles of shoes.

You are not the car you drive, the clothes you wear, or the perks you acquire in your line of work. Neither are you the clothes you do not wear, the perks to which you don't have access. Human kindness is what matters—the luxury of taking the time to say a kind word or to perform a kind deed. That is the only thing that can truly make one's day a day of enrichment.

CHAPTER TWO

Bennie Frances Davis may have looked like a typical African-American domestic worker to many who saw her on an ordinary day. But I, who could see her soul, could also see her secret: that even while she wore a hair net and work clothes to scrub toilets and floors, she wore an invisible diadem. She was one of countless uncredited aristocrats—descendants of slaves, proud and dignified citizens of a place where blood had spilled in the service of freedom. When I watched her go about her work with such nobility and poise, it made me think that the blood of her ancestors had fertilized this land, enabling it to grow some of the truest and most noble Americans. Though her life often may have been hard, my grandmother radiated kindness and love. The sparkle from her invisible diamonds could light up the darkest corner of your soul.

My grandmother—who was born on April 9, 1898—was the captain of our family. I think this may have been the personality she was born with, but certainly a lifetime of looking after seven younger siblings, her own children, and sundry other kin taught her to perform the role effortlessly. She was not the bossy sort of leader who orders people around; rather, she had a soft voice and a shining, gemlike spirit, to which all of us naturally turned. Her immediate family, of course, had no other matriarch once Great-grandmother China passed, but that did not explain why so many nieces, in-laws, and deaconesses at the church were always calling her to ask for advice. Why they did was simple: Because she was hardworking, openhearted, and always right.

The other, more subtle reason why everyone deferred to my grandmother's opinions was that she was a woman of innate elegance and style. I know she never spent much time thinking about her appearance, yet, like all women of legendary style—Audrey Hepburn, Jacqueline Kennedy, Grace Kelly, you name your icon—she had the totally unconscious ability to put herself together in the most perfect, appropriate way. As a result, she always seemed poised, centered, and nearly impossible to ruffle. Bennie Frances Davis's style combined with her practical intelligence and clear moral code to make her a woman at once formidable and eminently approachable, equally a tower of strength and of love.

One image always springs to mind when I think about my grandmother's incredible sense of style, a photograph I still keep in the tarnished gilt dime-store frame she picked out for it. This black-and-white photograph, taken to document the fiftieth wedding anniversary of my great-grandparents, China and Benton Roberson, shows them seated, with their eight children standing in a line behind them. The whole family is posed in front of China and Benton's log cabin, behind which is a dusky, dark sky. The scene is in Orange County, North Carolina, not far from the site of our family church, Mt. Sinai Baptist on Mt. Sinai Road. It is a humble family portrait, from which my relatives look out with serious expressions. These are the people to whom I owe my

Southernness and my sense of place in this world. You can tell by looking at them that the log cabin is theirs, that the land is theirs. The almost regal authority of each individual is evident. What these people had in common, in addition to blood ties and connection to the same land, is clearly a sense of dignity.

My grandmother, the eldest child, stands at the far left of the line of Roberson siblings, the first in the row. She is wearing a chicken-scratch woolen suit, suede '40s pumps, and the elegant pompadour hairdo she liked in her early years. She stands there with her six sisters and one brother who always went by the nickname Buster. (His real name was John Thomas Roberson, and during my childhood he lived just over the way in a town called Apex, with a wife I was fond of, named Callie.) These eight adult children flank Benton and China, who are seated in two thronelike, high-backed cane chairs. Grandmother China is wearing a crepe dress in a dark color, perhaps wine, which she favored, or navy. The dress has a delicate lace collar. Her Eleanor Roosevelt orthopedic shoes, tied as rigid as the tight smile etched across her kindly face, are solid and sturdy. These shoes have always struck me as an apt metaphor for her personality, for of all the people I've known, she was the one who had her feet most firmly planted on the ground. My great-grandfather must have had some white blood somewhere in his family past, for in this photograph, he could almost pass for white. He is wearing a spiffing suit, shirt, and tie, and elegant high-buttoned black boots. This photograph is really all I know of him, for he died in the summer of 1950, when I was not yet two years old.

China and Benton are, of course, old in this photograph, and their children are in various stages of their middle age—some, like my grandmother, with their hair already gone white, others still with the dark or chestnut curls of relative youth. My grandmother is visibly the eldest child, yet none of the younger siblings catches the eye quite the way she does. There is no glaring reason for this—Buster and the six other sisters are as good-looking as she, and they are all dressed in a suitable fashion for an important occasion. But no one else's suit has lines quite as classic as Bennie Frances's; no one else's shoes are so well chosen; no one else has quite so flattering a hairstyle. You can see that the rest of them lack her confidence. As she stands there in her tweed suit, she looks smart and snappy—a woman of the world. But my grandmother never traveled outside of America, and indeed, she'd never been farther than the metropolises of New York, Washington, D.C., and Philadelphia—all places where she went to visit kinfolk.

Bennie Frances Davis was never faddish. Looking her best was part of the natural phenomenon of living, because all of her dressy clothes were for church. People in the South, and black people in general, dress up for church. They do it less today, but when I was growing up, in the '50s and early '60s, it was almost universally the case. No one went to church bareheaded; it was simply my grandmother's good fortune to have discriminating taste in hats. Like all people of style, she understood what she looked good in, and though she might update her clothes from time to time, she was never especially concerned about what was "in" or "out." She was the best dressed woman in her family and the best dressed by a long shot in our church. Right up until the time she died, the women of Mt. Sinai looked up to my grandmother as the most stylish woman of her generation, and all the generations looked to her as a role model for correctness. She had an innate sophistication, never outrageous. It was always a navy blue suit, a black suit, or a checked woolen suit—but it was the *particular* suit, the particular way it hung that made her sartorial choices so noticeable. That one suit I particularly admired was very plain, a below-the-knee skirt and a single-breasted jacket. Nevertheless, it was a classic. She influenced my sense of style in the most subtle and natural way, for it was never a topic of conversation. Because she was the person I spent most of my time with, and she was the person I went out of the house with on Sunday, she was the person after whom I modeled myself. Such silent, unassuming influences often last a lifetime.

At one point she acquired a lime green suit for Easter. This was around the time Mrs. Kennedy was influencing fashion, and it was just the sort of thing Mrs. Kennedy was wearing: a lime green woolen suit. It had three buttons and an A-line skirt; only the color was out of the ordinary for my grandmother. I'm sure the fashion world would say it was an awful suit—a mere rip-off of some Givenchy item, "Lord only knows how it filtered down to *Durham*"—but she wore it with panache. She had beautiful bone-colored gloves to go with it, gloves of the highest quality, and a matched set of neutral handbag and shoes. So although the color of the suit was somewhat shocking, the overall look she created was one of propriety and sophistication. That was the kind of flair my grandmother had.

One of the few times I distinctly remember watching television with my grandmother was that legendary televised White House tour Jacqueline Kennedy gave on Valentine's Day, 1962. We enjoyed the show so much we also read the book that accompanied it. In Mrs. Kennedy, we both saw a light; we were inspired by her clipped diction, washboard-erect posture, youthful elegance, and intensity. Her style was very different from ours, but we recognized a similar interest in creating beauty in one's clothes and surroundings as a way of making sense of the world.

My grandmother expressed elegance in her every gesture. She had that incredible way of packing with tissue paper, like some grand lady. She traveled with hatboxes on buses and trains. And there was no pleasure like the pleasure of going with her to some store like Saks Fifth Avenue or Garfinckel's. I had a limited tolerance for shopping, but I enjoyed watching her admire the goods for sale in these fancy stores and proclaim them, with unerring good judgment, to be of high quality or low. Those trips we took to New York and D.C. are among my most treasured childhood memories—even down to the elegant way the train let off steam.

One particularly wonderful expression of my grandmother's style was the way she wore her hair. Whether because of genetics or because of the cumulative effect of a series of heartbreaks (as a young woman, she lost two infant children; and in my early childhood, she lost her father, her husband, and her favorite daughter, Dorothy Bee, in quick succession), her hair turned from its natural color to snow white when she was still relatively young. I know my grandmother never read a fashion magazine—the only things I generally saw her reading were the Bible, her *Missionary Helper* magazine, and the newspapers, both "white" and "black"—but somehow, on her own, she developed what I consider the high-fashion concept of tinting her white hair with a pale blue rinse. This, after all, was the hair adopted in later life by the late, great Elsie de Wolf, the twentieth century's first world-class female interior decorator and one of the early century's most glamorous women. This was the hair of socialites. It was also what my grandmother intuitively understood to be beautiful.

My grandmother's rinse varied in color from time to time—sometimes it was more a hyacinth or periwinkle blue, sometimes a pale, pale lavender; it got lighter, it got darker, and in her later years she switched to what was known as a "steel rinse," which turned it a silvery pewter color—but it always made her hair sparkle and set off both her features and her immaculate clothes perfectly. My grandmother was proud of her hair, and every evening before she retired, she would come sit on a little bench in my room to put it up for the night. (In my early readings of *Vogue,* I had seen just such a bench covered in fake fur and immediately copied it for our humble home. I was delighted that she liked to sit there and fix her hair.) As she sat in front of the dresser drawers and mirror, she brushed her hair carefully, neatening her side part and reshaping the large ringlets on the back and sides of her head, then she wrapped her head in a triangular head scarf for the night—exactly the kind of head scarf you see in images of slave women as they till the fields. When she went out to do chores such as chopping wood in the mornings, the head scarf would still be in place, protecting the curls. During the week, she kept them tucked up in a silver-colored hair net while she worked. Only on Sunday, the most important day of the week, would her hair be on display in its full splendor.

My grandmother never, ever did her hair at home. In all the years of my life, she never once washed her hair in our own sink or bathtub. Instead, every other week, she went to the beauty salon, where her hairdresser washed and conditioned her hair, put the blue rinse in, and iron-curled it. My grandmother did this twice a month, no matter what. In the wintertime, the curls usually lasted through to her next visit, but summertime's heat and humidity sometimes caused the curls to go limp. But she wouldn't have dreamed of washing and recurling the hair at home—she didn't even own a curling iron or electric rollers. If it went flat or the rinse wore off, she pulled it back neatly into a bun until she could have the problem properly addressed. This is the one true luxury the black Southern woman affords herself: the weekly or biweekly trip to the hairdresser. And my grandmother loved her time there; on late weekday afternoons, when she came home with her perfectly coiffed and newly tinted hair, she was always full of the stories she'd exchanged with other women as they sat in those swiveling, Naugahyde-upholstered chairs. No man or boy ever set foot in that beauty shop, which made me glad when I was a child. I could not imagine anything more boring than sitting through that three-hour ritual.

That blue hair was an integral part of her style. Hair nets were important for maintaining it, and I used to go downtown to Woolworth's with her to buy them. I rarely went downtown with her except when she needed to buy clothes for me, so I have strong memories of those trips to the five-and-dime. The hair nets came in packs of three and cost twenty-five cents.

When, in my young adulthood, I met Mrs. Vreeland, her interest and pride in her hair color reminded me in a marvelous way of my grandmother, though the two women could not have had more different ideas about hair. My grandmother's Lady Mendl hair was special, but also quite subtle; whereas Mrs. Vreeland had her hair dyed to maximum-impact Kabuki black. This was no ordinary color—this was hair lacquered to the blackest black imaginable. Her hair was so black that when she visited someone's home for the weekend, she took black satin pillowcases with her, so that her hair would not ruin her host's sheets. Whatever this hair dye contained, it was denied FDA approval, so Mrs. Vreeland had it privately imported from Alexandre de Paris, and applied every few weeks by Kenneth of New York. He understood her quest for the inkiest, Indian black hair imaginable, and he did a hell of a job providing her with it. I have never in my life seen anyone else with hair so dark it gleamed. (In the months before Mrs. Vreeland died, she slowly allowed her hair to return to its natural white, but it was always impeccably washed and styled.)

Mrs. Vreeland, like my grandmother, never washed her hair at home; if it needed to be done, she went to Kenneth. Of course, she lived a more fabulous social life than my grandmother did, so every two weeks would never do. In an ordinary week, Mrs. Vreeland went to Kenneth twice, but in a particularly busy week she might go three times.

Both my grandmother and Mrs. Vreeland set great store by the cosmetics they used. My grandmother's makeup routine was simple and only for Sundays. She sought not to create an impression of glamour, but to finish her appearance. In much the same way she used paste wax to give that last bit of luster to her well-chosen furniture, her makeup routine provided the polish to augment her natural beauty. She wore only one shade of lipstick, a deep cranberry red, and it was only, only for church. She also kept a box of face powder on the bureau, as well as a small compact in her purse in case her nose should begin to glow; she dabbed the powder on carefully, for a very natural look, on Sunday mornings. The face powder and lipstick were nothing unusual, just what she could buy at the five-and-dime, but she treated them like they were special, and so they were. (As an adult, I would sometimes buy her fancy cosmetics at Bergdorf Goodman's, but I think she always secretly preferred the simple things she was accustomed to, from Woolworth's.) How I loved to sit in my starched shirt and pressed pants and watch her apply the finest layer of complexion-smoothing powder to her pretty face, then line her mouth carefully with that lovely burgundy color. I loved to watch her tuck the little metal tube into her purse, in case she needed to touch up later. The gestures she used unconsciously—placing the lipstick in her bag, or plucking out a handkerchief to wipe her nose—were as pure as a Noh dancer's, perfect in their simplicity and feminine self-assurance.

I often thought of my grandmother when I watched Mrs. Vreeland's raptures over her own cosmetics, particularly her rouge, which she used to smear on her temples and earlobes in order to look as exotic as possible. (Mrs. Vreeland felt about makeup much as she did about polished soles—which is to say that she gleefully strove for and celebrated artifice in its every form.) She would put on this rouge, sometimes with Vaseline on top to make it shiny, and ask me ingenuously, "Is it Kabuki enough?" She loved that dramatic, cigar-store Indian look. Her pleasure in her makeup was as pure as my grandmother's, though the results she achieved might as well have come from a different planet.

The style I learned from my grandmother was plain; it did not draw attention to itself. We considered ourselves lucky to have full hearts, full stomachs, and wardrobes that were out of this world in terms of correctness. My grandmother had the knack for knowing how to make one dime do the work of four; she knew which inexpensive clothes were nevertheless of good quality, and if she wasn't satisfied with something ready-made, she knew how to make it herself. So I always knew that it wasn't the money someone spent that made things special; it was the good taste that went into choosing them. (In another example of her frugal good taste, we would sit every winter around a warm fire, licking the Green Stamps we'd collected in a year of weekly grocery runs and pasting them into S&H books. Before Christmas, we would turn them in for something small but useful, like an aluminum cake dome and plate that snapped tight to keep in moisture. Even to make an insignificant purchase such as this she thought and chose carefully, and her Green Stamp treasures gave us pleasure and pride.)

My grandmother's style also depended for much of its impact on her deft choice of accessories. I can still see my grandmother, dressed in her best Sunday clothes, sitting out on the porch and waiting for her cousin Doris and Doris's husband, Avant, who lived in the elite suburb of Emorywood Estates, to pick us up in their car, which was always immaculately kept. I remember that one year they had a big beige Buick, and at different times they had a red Comet and a blue Comet. Sometimes as we sat there the next-door neighbors, Mr. and Mrs. Coley, came out and bid us good morning as they left for church. They were a childless couple, seemingly with money to burn, and I always thought that Mrs. Coley was the only woman whose wardrobe rivaled the beauty of my grandmother's. My grandmother and I were always outside promptly; we would never want Doris and Avant to come and find us still getting dressed. It sometimes happened that she would turn to me with a concerned expression. "Ray," she would say, "I've forgotten my gloves. Would you please go and take them off the bed?"

I would turn the key in the locked front door and relish the opportunity to retrieve the gloves—so exquisite and luxurious, and at all times impeccable. She washed the warm months' white gloves every week in Woolite, and she stored them in layers of tissue in a special drawer. There was another such drawer for scarves, which were equally well folded and cared for, and a third still for handkerchiefs. I suppose all correct glove-wearing ladies at that time had special compartments for such accessories.

Hats were another item of vital importance. As I said, no black Southern Baptist would have dared to leave the house on Sunday without one. It would have been tantamount to going out in one's underwear. All the ladies of our church had hats to match their different outfits, but my grandmother's collection was both the most varied and in the best taste. She kept her hatboxes stacked neatly on top of her armoire—beautiful hatboxes, some round, some square, some hexagonal or octagonal, covered in papers and fabrics of countless colors and designs. I loved the way the hatboxes looked together, their fine balance between clashing with one another and pleasing the eye with their jubilant visual cacophony. The hatboxes' wonderful variety was a symbol of the riches that lay within. Inside there were summer hats and winter hats, straw hats and woolen hats, hats with wide brims and cloches that hugged the head, hats with feathers, bows, and veils, and hats with no decoration at all. Each was perfect for some particular suit, dress, or occasion; each had its place in the pantheon. I remember the first time my grandmother spent thirty-five dollars on a hat. We were at Garfinckel's, and even though everything in the store was expensive, the price of that hat was shocking. My grandmother's first instinct was to dismiss the hat on that account, but I could see that she really liked it. I was in high school at the time; it was the mid-1960s, and thirty-five dollars was a lot of money. Fifteen or twenty dollars for a hat was considered a reasonable investment.

"I can't spend that," my grandmother said as she fingered the hat on its stand. It was a beautiful, loden green felt fedora, sort of a hunting hat with a curved crown, with two huge, long pheasant feathers curving down from the side of it. It wasn't a loud or flashy hat; it was a classic style and obviously beautifully made. You could see from across the room that it was European. I think it actually had come from Austria. "That's too extravagant," she said.

I, of course, said, "But you should get it! You love it."

"That's too much money to spend on a hat," she said. But she made the (nearly always) decisive error of trying it on. Once she'd seen it on her head, she was doubly convinced of its beauty. She bought the extravagant hat and continued to wear it proudly for years to come.

When I finally met Mrs. Vreeland, I was astonished at the variety of accessories she possessed—but not particularly surprised by the importance she ascribed to them. My grandmother had cultivated in me a love for the elegant glove, the well turned-out shoe, the hat that framed the face just so, the deftly chosen detail that made an outfit special. When I was growing up, we had no major investments, but it was part of our tradition to love fine things like the glazed kidskin gloves and good leather shoes we reserved only for Sundays, along with the special underwear, and my grandmother's lace-up corsets that looked to me, when they lay out airing on the chest, like they'd come straight from the Gay Nineties.

Before I could afford to splurge on the Kislav gloves from my summer earnings, I have no idea how my grandmother amassed such a fine collection of gloves, but she did, carefully budgeting and saving. One could never approach the church door without gloves on. While I'm certain my grandmother never gave a moment's thought to someone as remote as the Duchess of Windsor, her habit of never leaving home without an extra pair of gloves stashed in her bag, in case the pair she was wearing got dirty, was a habit she shared with her.

And there is something I can tell you about Heaven: When a person sets out to make her victory journey home, she had better have the correct gloves on. The writer Fran Lebowitz called me recently, because she remembered overhearing a conversation I had years ago with my close friend Beth Ann Hardison on the sad, sad morning Beth Ann and I were laying out clothes for her recently deceased mother to wear in her passage. "You know, André," Fran croaked in her smoky telephone voice, "I will never forget that conversation you had with Beth Ann, so seriously pondering the question of whether her mother should wear gloves in the casket. That was shocking to me! Jews don't believe in Heaven, you know. Once it's over, it's over—Jews are wrapped in shrouds, buried, and that's it. I guess I always thought that when black Baptists spoke of Heaven, they meant it as a metaphor, an intangible reward for good works. But that day, I realized that you honestly think Heaven is a place. Do you remember the conversation I'm talking about?"

"How could I forget it?" I said. "I told Beth Ann to go out and buy her mother a special pair of shoes, and in no uncertain terms she told me, '*No,* André, I am *not* going to Manolo Blahnik to buy a five-hundred-dollar pair of shoes to put in the ground.' I disagreed but knew how hard the day must have been for her and didn't want to push. 'I understand,' I said, 'but don't you think that your mother at least has to have some gloves? She was such a lady—I am sure she'll want to have crisp white gloves on when she enters the Pearly Gates.' "

"And she acquiesced," Fran remembered, "didn't she?"

"She did. She buried her mother with a pair of white gloves and a small flask of spirits—a very personal touch."

"I still don't understand," Fran said. "Do you think Heaven is an actual place, like Albany?"

"I hope it's nicer than Albany," I could not help retorting. We both laughed. "But in all seriousness, no. I don't think it has a geographical location; and I don't think it's up in the clouds somewhere. But I was brought up to believe in it, and I do not question its existence. If it's nothing else, I know in my heart that Heaven is the memory of love, which never comes to an end."

I thought back on Beth Ann's mother in that funeral home in Brooklyn when my own grandmother died a few years later. On a trip I took to Paris not long before she died, I had managed to buy up the last stock of unworn, vintage Dior gloves from the 1950s to bring home to her. It was in one of those pairs of couture gloves that I buried her; and of course, I tucked a fresh pair inside the coffin, in case the pair she was wearing should become soiled. I gave her a church fan bearing a color image of the Reverend Martin Luther King, Jr., a small tin of her favorite snuff, and a couple of extra handkerchiefs. I selected the hymn "No Tears in Heaven" as part of her going-home services, which were held on a cold March day that I will always carry in my memory. I was glad I buried her with the appropriate accessories, because I knew how proud she would be to enter Heaven with those Christian Dior gloves crushed down to just below her elbows. I know that when I told Beth Ann about those gloves, she smiled, because she knew I was right.

Gloves are missing from the scheme of style in the world today, and I personally regret their demise, as I can think of no more apt metaphor for true elegance. I once heard someone say that Jacqueline Kennedy, as First Lady, wore her elbow-length opera gloves as if she'd been born in them. She always looked remarkable in those gloves.

Fashionable women today will have nothing to do with them! Fran Lebowitz also recalled to me, later in that same conversation, that when she went to Sweden to be with her friend Toni Morrison when she received the Nobel Prize for Literature, there had been quite a scene in Ms. Morrison's hotel room about choosing the correct gloves. She had brought piles of white gloves with her, but also had some sent from New York, and the two of them thoroughly vetted every pair before finally selecting one. (Which were, the images of the event suggest, absolutely perfect.)

One of the few women of style I know who still wears gloves regularly is Grace Jones, the disco star, well known for her rendition of "La Vie en Rose." She wears gloves everywhere, no matter what the weather. Recently the house of Chanel flew her to Monaco by Concorde, so that she could perform under the direction of Karl Lagerfeld. We in the audience were eager to hear her sing, but the star was late. She didn't arrive until close to midnight and did not have time to primp properly before her rehearsal. Grace is a trooper; she flung on her Fendi mink (which was cut like lace) right over her traveling suit. As she entered from stage right, she called out to me, reminding me for an instant of my grandmother, "Hand me my gloves, André!" And then, losing all resemblance to Bennie Frances Davis, added, "I need them for attitude!" The gloves Grace Jones had in mind were leather with outsized mink cuffs the size of two baby elephant ears.

Bette Midler also has exquisite taste in gloves. I recently found her sitting with her husband, Martin von Hasselberg, in the lobby of the Ritz Hotel in Paris, clasping the softest, most beautiful pair of handmade butter-colored, wrist-length gloves, from her vast collection.

I began this chapter talking about an image of my grandmother, an image that showed her upright dignity and incredible, self-assured style. That photograph still sits in her bedroom in North Carolina, left exactly as she saw it on the last day she was alive. I like to be able to go home to the place she loved so well and see things mostly as she left them. Opposite that photograph is a second one that is nearly as important to my understanding of how style transcends race, class, and time. This second photograph sits beside a cherry pink ceramic lamp, which was the pride of my grandmother's living room décor: a fake Boucher love scene, glazed to a sparkling shine in a kitschy, late-'50s interpretation of Fontainebleu taste. (I hope it is clear from the foregoing description that I love that lamp.) In a metal gilt frame that matches the one housing the Roberson family portrait is a formal portrait of my aunt, Dorothy Bee Davis, my grandmother's younger daughter, taken upon her graduation from Hillside High School. You can see from her face that Dorothy Bee is a sterling high school student—she wears the unmistakably bright and self-confident expression of a smart, popular girl. Her lips are huge and sensuous, her eyes also large and almond shaped; she wears her hair in a silken do not unlike Elizabeth Taylor's in *A Place in the Sun.* Actually, the person Dorothy Bee most looks like in this portrait is the sensuous, dreamy Dorothy Dandridge, who was also a Durham girl. She is wearing a pleated organdy blouse, probably made of nylon, and a strand of small pearls with matching pearl earrings.

One can see from this portrait that Dorothy Bee had success written all over her. Right out of high school, she landed what was considered the be-all, end-all job, the first-class ticket out of the lower middle classes: She found employment at the North Carolina Mutual Life Insurance Company home office, in downtown Durham. In my family's eyes, this job was the best a young woman could do. This was years before the television series *The Jeffersons* hit the airwaves, but if you got the job at North Carolina Mutual Life, you were definitely "movin' on up."

All that changed on the Fourth of July, 1951, when Dorothy Bee was twenty-one years old. Her boyfriend picked her up in his car to drive her to an Independence Day picnic up on Mt. Sinai Road, but before they arrived, he lost control of the car—it was a dirt road back then, and easy to slip onto the shoulder, especially going uphill, on the curve—and collided head-on with a telephone pole near the church. He survived the crash, but Dorothy Bee was killed instantly. When I

RIGHT: My aunt Dorothy Bee Davis. BELOW: The Roberson clan. China and Benton are seated in front. Standing, from left, are Bennie Frances, Pattie, Ennie, Minnie, John, Louvenia, Myra, and Mozzella. *(Collection of the author)*

grew old enough to read, I would sometimes extract the yellowed clippings about Dorothy Bee's accident from a hidden-away family album, where my grandmother had pressed them like flowers.

There was never an investigation. Everyone knew that it had been a terrible, terrible accident, that no foul play was involved. I can't remember that boyfriend's name, but he used to come around often. I met him many, many times. He would come to visit my grandmother periodically, to pay his respects and find out how she was doing. He was an extremely nice man.

Very few details about Dorothy Bee's life have remained, except that she was my grandmother's favorite child and that her death haunted my grandmother the way my grandmother's passing haunts me.

I remember her leaving the day she died, and I wanted so badly to go with her. No one remembers exactly why, but on that fateful Fourth of July, while I edged closer to Dorothy Bee, begging to go along for the ride, my grandmother held me back. By all reports I was a well-behaved child, but that afternoon, for the first time anyone could remember, I collapsed into a weeping, wailing fit of bad temper. I know this scene may be one that I only think I remember, having heard the story of it so many times, but I have a strong memory of standing on that porch, my grandmother gripping tightly to both my hands as I tried to squirm free. I believe I can remember that black sedan rumbling off down Cornell Street and the utterly bereft feeling of being abandoned by my beautiful aunt. Once the car was out of sight, my grandmother crouched down to comfort me; I think she may have sensed the tragedy that was about to happen.

Before she died, Dorothy Bee loomed large in my family's mythology, because she was so kind and energetic, and because she had the kind of beauty that brought joy to all around her. My grandmother made no bones about the fact that Dorothy Bee was her favorite child, the one most likely to do her proud. I think that in some ways my grandmother lived through Dorothy Bee, who was so successful and so very beautiful. After she died, she took on mythic proportions. I would hear stories about her goodness and beauty for the rest of my life, and looked toward her portrait with reverence.

One of the chief actions for which she was renowned, not only in our family but in our community, was a small, personal contribution to the civil rights movement. A few years before she was killed, Dorothy Bee was the very first black person to walk into a store called Montaldo's, downtown. Now, Montaldo's was like the Henri Bendel of Durham. In those days, when segregation was still a fact of everyday life, Montaldo's did not have black customers sauntering through the front door. From time to time the back door might have seen a black woman approach, but she would have been a maid picking up a box. When Dorothy Bee got her job at North Carolina Mutual Life, she wanted stylish new clothes, and she decided that the best place to buy them was Montaldo's. She went right in through the front door, took her time browsing, and made a purchase. I don't know exactly what she bought that day, but the very fact that she bought it was legendary in the black community of Durham. This was probably 1950, remember; it was still a long time before Mahatma Gandhi's and Dr. King's ideas of nonviolent protest took root among the African Americans of the South. Dorothy Bee may have made only a small contribution to the struggle for equality, but she did it nonetheless.

I cherished this story when I was a boy, because it showed how important a thing one's sense of self, one's presentation in the world, could be. I liked thinking of her bravery and poise, and I imagined her in her suit (or blouse or merino wool sweater; whatever it was she had bought that day), feeling beautiful not only because what she *wore* was beautiful, but because she had used it to make a stand for her own intrinsic worth and beauty. I cherished all the things that had belonged to Dorothy Bee for much the same reason. When we packed in her three-piece matched set of vanilla-colored Samsonite suitcases to go on a trip, or when I opened the chest of linens, between which sprigs of lavender had been placed, that had been meant for her dowry, I felt close to this person who had known her own worth and conveyed it to all around her.

My grandmother was a good woman and did her best to show me by her every action how to live a decent life. I am glad I had her to look up to, and I try to live by the precepts she taught. Fashion was probably the last thing on her mind, but as someone who has gone on to a career in that field, I find that one of the most important things I learned from my grandmother was that style comes from within. Her taste was classic and proper, but not because she thought one "had" or "ought" to dress a certain way; the way she dressed and carried herself expressed her values and personality, and sat easily upon her. The way she encouraged me to dress expressed my personality in much the same way. Though my clothes were the picture of propriety, I had the occasional bright-colored sweater or tie that emblematized my natural exuberance. She had obviously done much the same for Dorothy Bee, whose clothes, while never outlandish, reflected her youth and vigor.

When I later came to know Mrs. Vreeland, her style was almost the exact opposite of my grandmother's, but it was similar in being such a complete and multifaceted expression of who she was. Mrs. Vreeland could pull together a look from the most diverse elements; she could put on a pair of trousers and a blouse and some wild, exotic earrings, and she'd have a look no one else could make. She put things together in a wonderful manner that truly conveyed her complicated, often irreverent personality. Mrs. Vreeland did not have vaults of fine jewelry, but she could pick a pair of earrings that lit up her face, an outfit, and a room because they were so baroque and dynamic in combination with her expression. My grandmother would never have worn any but the most classic and subdued earrings; and yet both women had equal elegance and refinement in their dress. Having these women for guides has helped me enormously in finding my way in the world of fashion. It has helped me to understand the difference between style and artifice; between that which is deeply, unchangeably exotic and that which merely grasps for attention; between that which is classic and that which is merely dull and uncreative. I could have had no better schooling to go into the line of work I've chosen.

As for my own style, I feel that it expresses my inner essence as much as Bennie Frances Davis's and Diana Vreeland's did theirs. I have learned from their schooling, and found a wellspring of inspiration within. What this means is that since I began choosing my own clothes as a teenager, I've always loved flamboyance and elegant classics. It probably all started with those yellow paisley pajamas, though I have nothing so marvelous to sleep in today. Nowadays, I'll sleep in a Phat Farm T-shirt in size XXXL, or maybe an old Versace silk wrapper, if I feel like it.

When people ask if I have any advice to give about fashion, it's always the same: Follow your own pace, your own instincts, no matter what. You'll get it right. From my earliest days my style has been evolving. As a young boy, I dressed in the classic clothes my grandmother favored, but I can still remember picking out my first serious winter coat. It was a marigold corduroy stadium coat with a rib-knit collar, leather toggle clasps, and a rich, plaid blanket lining. I understood that, coming from one of the better Durham stores, it put some strain on my grandmother's coat budget, but I loved it so much she bought it for me. And until I outgrew it, I wore it with joy and pride. Like she did all of my favorite childhood clothes, my grandmother kept it in a back closet until I was an adult, and then one day, in a burst of spring cleaning, she donated it to the Salvation Army.

As a young man, my style became gradually more outrageous, until it has settled into what it is today, an eclectic mix of the bespoke and the extraordinary. I owe much of my ideal of fashion to the late Duke of Windsor's outlandish plaid suits, which Mrs. Vreeland very much admired (he was a personal friend of hers). She was obsessed with her English background and loved that bold English correctness in a suit. So I have had many classic suits made for me at such proper British houses as Richard Anderson and Welsh & Jeffries. Manolo Blahnik custom-makes my shoes for me, and Karl Lagerfeld designs special clothes for me at Chanel and Fendi.

But the thing that I think most often makes people accuse me of dandyism is my penchant for wearing diamonds. I find that when I have something sparkling around my neck or on my lapel, it gives a definite good rhythm to everything I do. If I go out at night wearing the jewel-encrusted insignia of some fabulous Russian order from A La Vieille Russie, the whole evening falls into place, and I move at my own tempo. I am very, very lucky to have a good relationship with Fred Leighton, my diamond buddy, the Madison Avenue jeweler; he allows me, and other trusted customers, to borrow fabulous jewels for the price of an evening's insurance guarantee. The day of the VH1/*Vogue* Fashion Awards, which I opened along with Cuba Gooding, Jr. (one of my favorite actors), I rushed into Leighton's store. A woman was pondering the purchase of a 1920s diamond tiara in a Greek motif. When she put it down, I picked it up and fastened it around my neck. Presto! The most unusual choker, on a man. I put it on that evening with a coat Karl Lagerfeld had designed for me—a Russian broadtail coat with five diamond snowflakes—and onto the stage I sauntered. I felt no sense of making waves (though I hear some were made), just a sense of following my own beat. At the Vanity Fair Oscars dinner in Los Angeles in 2002, I wore a seventy-six-carat, square-cut sapphire from Fred Leighton, a moghul ring.

The fact is, men have always worn diamonds. Just look at any nobleman's portrait from the eighteenth century. I particularly enjoy portraits of nineteenth-century Indian noblemen: Some of them not only wear diamonds the size of plovers' eggs, but they wear them on ropes and ropes of smaller diamonds. They sport emeralds, rubies, sapphires, and pearls so big they look like they could make a man collapse under their weight. But worn with such rich, classic Indian clothes, turbans, and embroidered shoes, these jewels look correct, elegant. I remember finding in a library book a black-and-white photograph of a dozen Indian aristocrats, including the Maharaja of Baria, in a procession entering the city of Jaipur. The photograph was taken in 1948, which struck me particularly, since it was the year I was born. The men were young, slim-figured, and, in addition to their ropes and brooches of jewels, had huge feathers towering atop their turbans and waving in the air. They were walking in front of an elephant that was every bit as bejeweled as they were. All decked out! Or, as the English would say, "putting on the dog."

That's what I like: *en chien,* as Mrs. Vreeland loved to say, meaning that something was extremely elegant.

When I was in Paris recently, having a fitting for some new shirts at Charvet, Mlle. Colban, the daughter of the owner, made me a wonderful offer. "Would you like to see the bills of the Maharaja of Patiala?" she asked in her light, light voice, almost like something out of a fairy tale. I wasn't sure I had heard her correctly, so she elaborated. "He's dead," she said. "Would you like to see his bills?"

Of course, I said yes—it was wonderful to imagine what a maharaja would have ordered.

"Yes, well you buy almost as much as he did," she said, "but not quite."

I had appointments for much of the day, but later that afternoon I returned to look at those bills of the maharaja's. I was fascinated to be offered such an intimate glimpse into a maharaja's style. As it turned out, the bills were marvelous. On one shopping trip in 1925, he ordered eighteen hundred hand-embroidered handkerchiefs—all for his personal use. He ordered so many shirts that Charvet had to construct special trunks to ship them to him. There were six dozen pairs of beige gloves in Milan silk, and six dozen in maroon, six dozen in gray, six dozen in some other color. But of course, if you have jewels like this man had, you had to have the correct pair of gloves!

Wearing big jewelry and having my own style doesn't always make me friends. I'll never forget going to the White House to photograph First Lady Barbara Bush for *Vogue.* Because it was an important occasion, I wore what was at the time my very best suit—one tailored by Mort Sills, who also happened to make suits for then-President George H. W. Bush. I was wearing a large gold Yves Saint Laurent rose in my lapel. I was in the Lincoln Bedroom, scouting a location for our shoot, when the First Lady appeared.

She looked me over and asked, "What's that on your lapel?"

"It's a gold rose," I said, drawing deep from my reserves of Southern politeness.

"That's a lot of rose," she said, and then did not say another word to me during the entire session.

Despite that, I still felt confident in my choice. I have always known that if you follow your own beat, you might not always be dancing in time with those around you, but you will turn out to be a very good dancer.

I think it's important to remember, too, that dressing up is not for every day. When I go out into the world, I do like to put on the dog, but for a weekend at home, I dress as casually as anyone does. If I have to come into the city on a day when it's raining or snowing, I might wear my Phat Farm velour jogging pants and big parka, because that's what would be practical and comfortable. A person should dress every moment of his life. Dressing up can be fun, but it can also be tiresome, and sometimes you have to be able to relax. Furthermore, I've learned that some things that are wonderful—like having your underwear custom-made at Charvet—are simply impractical for the exigencies of modern-day life. Custom-made underwear has to be ironed every time you wear it, and if you don't have time to do that or a servant to do it for you, you might just as well buy ready-mades in a store. (I still have many of my ties custom-made at Charvet, because they make the most beautiful ties; but even to do that, one has to be willing to invest the time for fittings as well as the money.)

In the fashion industry, people tend to confuse an interest in style with an overvaluing of the superficial. A few people, upon coming to know me, have said, "Oh, before I knew you, I thought you were superficial, affected." They think this because I grew up in the world of *Women's Wear Daily*, and because that is what they think, in their small-minded way, fashion is. Recently I told a friend, Pat Altschul, that I was reading about Louis XIV and Versailles, and she asked me, "Are you reading such things to take on more affectations?"

My answer was to laugh, because of course that was not why. I was reading about eighteenth-century France because of my great appreciation for French history. I relate to the sense of courtliness that flourished in that time—to the grandeur and the traditions, the routines and the rituals, the demands of participating in court life. I also feel that living in our current age of political instability and widespread religious, ethnic, and class hatred, I can relate to the tragedy of the terrible unbalance of those times. (When I read about Louis XIV, I can never forget that while those people were living according to a rigid, often artificial code of manners at court, most of the rest of the country was starving.) These contradictions speak to me. No one interested in style could help being captivated by the curtains, bedspreads, and dresses of Versailles; and no feeling person could help wondering about the myriad underpaid workers who made them. The extravagance of Louis XIV's court provides a fascinating example of a high culture that, through its own excesses, birthed its own downfall, leading to huge changes in society all over Europe and its colonies.

And yet this friend, who is an art historian, could say to me, "Oh, you're taking that up so you can learn more affectations. I can just see you now with a sable-lined dressing gown."

I couldn't help laughing, because that's not really where I get that from. My propensity to show up wearing fancy robes has to do with two things: my physical size (if you are six feet seven inches tall, you might as well wear a beaded caftan) and my intense love of glamorous things. Far, far down the list of things I wish to accomplish on any given day is the desire to affect a certain appearance. Laypeople tend to think of people in the fashion world as so outrageous, but if we are to be good at what we do, we require as deep and thoughtful an understanding of the history of dress as other people need of their fields. No one expects a fiction writer to create worlds without having read great novels, and no one would expect an architect to build without having seen a variety of buildings and monuments. Fashion is the same. It requires the same curiosity and studiousness, and like any other art, does not exist in a vacuum.

For instance, for his last show for Pierre Balmain, Paris, Oscar de la Renta created a Russian tsarina wedding dress with a huge skirt with train and a vest edged in sable, worn with a rich, romantic blouse. The skirt was made from thirty-two meters of floral brocade fabric from the house of Prelle, a French firm that weaves all the gold-shot silk brocades for the walls of restored rooms at Versailles. The hours of work by hand, and the cost of the fabric, caused the tab to soar to one hundred thousand dollars. The original sample was sold to Ann Getty for sixty thousand dollars. Similarly, Karl Lagerfeld once designed a dress for Chanel haute couture, embroidered by François LeSage, that cost two hundred thousand dollars. They sold two of them.

I am suspicious of the idea, which strikes me as popular, that fashion continually "reinvents" itself. No one has to reinvent the wheel—you just keep turning it around and around, recycling the ideas. The couture that was born in eighteenth-century France spread all over Europe and even to Russia, and affected the art of dress, the art of conversation, the art of food, the art of flirting, the art of living, the art of serving up coffee in a beautiful cup. All of that style—some, certainly, would say artifice—connects me to what I believe is important, though what I come from is so simple. The art of serving *café* in a demitasse means as much to me as the art of baking a biscuit; the art of wearing a court dress and wig is as vital to me as the art of being properly turned out for church. It's the same thing. It's the luxury of high style.

I think that one of the reasons people relate to my writing about fashion is that it *isn't* only about what's of the moment—that my knowledge of fashion is steeped in a knowledge of fashion history and history in general. Someone may be writing about fashion and talk about the half belt on the back of a coat without knowing that it has its own proper name—a martingale. Many people don't know that cutting fabric on the bias was not always done, but a daring technique, invented by Mme. Madeline Vionnet in the early part of the last century. Her work revolutionized dressmaking, but many people don't even know who she is. One of the most important things that I learned while pursuing my graduate studies at Brown was the art of research, which is a very important thing to know how to do in this world. I do not think it's affectation to hunger after knowledge in one's chosen field. Rather, I think it's a responsibility.

I have tried to live my life behaving decently, in part so that I don't have to spend too much time worrying about what people think of me. It does always impress me, however, when someone says, "I didn't really know who you were—I thought the façade was all there was." I am not someone who puts on affectations, but some people think I'm very affected. Those who are close to me, however, have always been able to see past the veneer to the fact that my fundamental goal, the thing I strive for, is to be a good human being, for others and myself. To strive for improvement—be that in acquiring knowledge, or learning to do something better than I did it before, or handling something better in my life—is to be a better person. I was brought up around people who not only were good, but were always seeking ways to be better. I saw images of great beauty and style, such as my grandmother and Dorothy Bee, all the time, and I knew that the kind of happiness they brought to all around them was something I, too, wanted to create with my life and work.

Vogue has always been the premiere fashion magazine, the one that stands for quality and good work. I feel blessed to have found a career, and landed in a place within that career, where in my daily work I can convey the pleasures of the appreciation of beautiful well-made things to people from all walks of life, as well as pay tribute to some of the wonderful people who have shaped my perceptions of fashion. When Nija Battle, the thirty-seven-year-old up-and-coming fur designer, died suddenly of an aneurysm just as her career began to take off, I did homage to her life and her Christian values in my monthly *StyleFax* column. Similarly, when Carrie Donovan, one of the women most influential to fashion, an invaluable early supporter of my career, and an old friend, recently died, and when the photographer and fashion icon Berry Berenson was so tragically killed in one of the planes that crashed into the World Trade Center on September 11, 2001, I used my column to pay tribute to their extraordinary careers and humanity. It was an honor to be able to write those pieces, and each of them was written from my heart with love. I received many, many letters from readers who were touched deeply by those articles and by the beauty of the lives they celebrated. I'm sure ladies of fashion read my monthly *StyleFax*, and I hope they find it useful, enjoyable, and instructive. But most of the letters I receive in the column's praise are from ordinary women, working hard at their jobs and at home, who feel that an article has in some way enhanced their sense of the loveliness and goodness of the world. Those letters mean more to me than any gift of worldly value ever could. There is truly no better feeling than to do the work that I love, as best as I am able and in service of the values I was raised with, and to find that that work can resonate as deeply in others as it does in me.

CHAPTER THREE

Bennie Frances Davis and I lived alone and peacefully most of the year—that is, until holidays, funerals, or family reunions caused a wonderful overflow of kin. At those times, people slept wherever they could find a place in bed. (There always seemed to be someplace where someone could squeeze in; no one had to sleep on the floor.) When any of the relatives who had moved "up the road" came down to visit North Carolina, they treated my grandmother's small six rooms as the center of the universe. And when they visited one or two at a time, they were given my bed, a big double bed I inherited from Great-grandma China, and I slept on the couch. (Which I didn't really mind; company was special.) But when a full-scale family holiday was in progress, the sleeping arrangements were catch-as-catch-can. Whether it was a burning-hot summer or an icy winter, my grandmother's bed would suddenly become one big Ramada Inn queen: She slept on the right with her sisters, two of whom slept with their heads toward the frilly-curtained window. People managed to be comfortable under these conditions because everyone was so busy with social family gatherings, church, food preparation, gossip, and long, interesting evenings of talk.

It was very exciting for me when all the relatives came to visit. My mother's twin sisters, Minnie and Ennie, lived in New York, and sometimes they would drive down to visit in Minnie's husband Mingo's car. I would sit on the front porch waiting for them. They would come in a big Cadillac, its flawless paint marred slightly by pollen and dust gathered along the highways. They would have a country ham stowed in the room-sized trunk from when they'd stopped in Virginia on the way down. My Aunt Louvenia would come down from Georgetown, where she worked (for fifty years) for a wealthy white family called the Browns, who also had a summer place in Watch Hill, Rhode Island. Louvenia was a maid, but she always arrived in the most extraordinary, flashy outfits. I distinctly recall her coming down one time in a black cashmere coat and a pair of lavender stiletto heels, with a matching lavender handbag. I loved anticipating the arrival of such glamorous relatives.

Large family gatherings were usually prompted by the occurrence of a holiday—Thanksgiving, Christmas, Easter, or Homecoming, when the founding of Mt. Sinai Baptist was celebrated, the first Sunday in May—but sometimes my grandmother's kin would simply decide to "come home," and those were wonderful, festive times. I had lots of cousins to look forward to seeing: Minnie's daughter Brenda; Louvenia's daughter Thelma; and eventually, Thelma's daughter Jennifer. My mother also had two brothers, Robert and John Albert Davis. The thing I remember best about such events was that whenever the weather permitted, we spent all our time on the front porch.

Front porch life was radiant. Our small house made up in family love for what it lacked in architectural style; but it was always the front porch that remained the center of our social life. Because the porch figured so prominently in our lives and our imaginations, its appearance was of the utmost importance.

Our porch ran the entire length of the house. It was decorated with bright metal chairs and wicker tables; the seat of honor was an old rocker that had belonged to Great-grandma China, which she had brought to the city with her after her husband died and she sold the farm for the absurdly low price of two thousand dollars. I sanded and painted that rocker time and again, and it was always the seat that was most in demand. (One afternoon, long after I had left to go off to college, a white peddler came up and offered my grandmother five dollars for it. My grandmother was polite but firm in her refusal. "No, thank you, sir," she told him. "We wouldn't sell a relic of our family history for five dollars." The peddler went on his way, but when my grandmother woke up the next morning, the chair was gone. We both assumed he had come back during the night and stolen it.)

Back before we had the electrical luxury of air-conditioning, there was no place to be but outside during the summer months, and it was exciting for all the grown-up aunts and cousins to come over and sit all afternoon in our particular patch of shade. I thought they were almost impossibly sophisticated. My cousin Wallace Nunn seemed as dapper to me as a picture in a glossy magazine. He was a bon vivant, always wearing the finest suits and shoes. He was lanky, with freckles and red hair. What a ladies' man! His brother James, the football star, was considered the intellect and the heartbeat of their whole clan of siblings: James, Wallace, Bena, Doris, Georgia, Shirley, and Johnsie. They were the most glamorous and attractive kin. They had style, they were educated, and they had the best jobs, especially the women, most of them employed at that same North Carolina Mutual Life Insurance Company where my Aunt Dorothy Bee had worked so briefly. Shirley, who lived in Jersey City, New Jersey, with her then young and dashing husband, frequently came down for August revival, and she loved staying at her aunt Bennie's. This refined cousin from "up North" was one for whom I willingly gave up my bed. I loved it when she visited, or when my father or Cousin Wallace came down from Washington, D.C. I liked to imagine whoever was coming taking a leisurely cruise down the Interstate. Usually visitors came ambling up our porch stairs in time for an early-morning breakfast spread of hot biscuits, sausages, bacon, eggs, grits, pancakes, country pork, or Virginia cured ham, all swimming in fat and butter. (In those good old days, people ate everything that's now considered dangerous for one's blood pressure and general health. My grandmother and her kin ate bacon, eggs, and sausages fried in fat nearly every day of their lives and lived long, happy lives.) Maxwell House coffee would percolate on the stove all morning long, while we unloaded luggage and tucked it into any available crevice. We took church clothes out to air, while the proud owners took out new hats from their boxes for all to admire. My grandmother and I loved to ogle a pair of new shoes, as well as anything that reeked of the big city, the sophistication of the North.

At night, as I curled up in some makeshift bed, I listened to the lullaby of grown-up talk, as sisters Louvenia, Minnie, Ennie, Mozella, Pattie, and Pete warmed our hearts with their reminiscences and tales. Their talk to me was the sweetest bedtime story, the one I will remember all my days.

My grandmother's sister Myra was, for reasons that were never clear to me, always called Pete. She had a big farmhouse out in the country, which was the other chief scene of our animated family reunions. Aunt Pete's house had a huge country backyard in which chickens walked around freely. Down the lane were barns, still stocked with the last rusting vestiges of farm equipment, though by the time I was young, the family no longer had horses or cattle. (They did keep one aging mule, mostly, I think, out of pity for the creature.) On her porch, Aunt Pete had a rain barrel, whose contents took on the color of its rusty, oil-drum sides. That rain barrel puzzled me, because we kids weren't allowed to dip a ladle into it and drink the water, though the men sometimes did after a rainstorm. As an adult, I realize the reason we weren't allowed to drink from the barrel was that the water drained through a lead pipe from the roof and was used to make those big loads of laundry whiter than white lightning. I suppose it could also have been used as an emergency backup for bathing, in case the plumbing went wrong. As a child I was fascinated, watching mosquitoes drown on the puckered surface of the water, June bugs meet their instant end. I could stare at the water for long stretches of time.

Aunt Pete was married to Uncle Ira Burroughs, who came from a family with a lot of land and who had inherited the plot and the farmhouse. His brother, Veartis, lived across the cornfields with his wife, Miss Louise; their tract of land was also huge. The Burroughs land was like a Kennedy compound without the grandeur or the wealth. The size of things out there—the houses, the barns, the fields themselves—was almost unimaginable to a boy from a small city like Durham. Pete and Ira had one son, James Robert, and Aunt Pete had another son, Eddy Lewis, a love child, who sometimes lived with them and who had a son named Charles. When James Robert grew up, they let him build his own house, small by comparison, on their property, just to the other side of a sprawling watermelon patch. James Robert's was a matchbox modern, ugly as sin, yet it was his. I loved Aunt Pete and Uncle Ira's white clapboard house. Today, that house has been destroyed, and a modern house built in its place.

Twice a year my grandmother and I went out to spend a weekend on Aunt Pete's farm. I liked the place enormously. Aunt Pete always seemed to me like the most affluent member of our clan, because she had that watermelon patch, a matched set of embossed blue velvet, horsehair-stuffed Victorian-style living room furniture, and the biggest kitchen I ever saw. She wasn't as stylishly turned out as my grandmother, or as flamboyant as Aunt Louvenia (the one with the lavender shoes), but Aunt Pete had something no one else had, something that made me think she was filthy rich: In her living room she had a pipe organ, in rich cherry wood with black and white enamel pulls. You had to pedal it with your feet. An organ in the house of one of my aunts!

That was big-time to me. At that time, even Mt. Sinai Church, five minutes up the road from her house, didn't have an organ. It didn't matter to me that nobody knew hell or high water how to play the thing, because I was awed anyway. I never did ask where it had come from.

Some aspects of life on the farm were totally foreign to my everyday life, and I never tired of them. Aunt Pete and Uncle Ira often talked about hog killing, but (perhaps thankfully) I never did get to see them gut a pig. I loved the cured ham that came out of the smokehouse and one day asked Uncle Ira if I could take a peek into the little log cabin, which sat out in the woods, at some distance from the kitchen, and out of whose chimney smoke curled slowly toward the horizon. He agreed to take me in, and I thought it was the most exotic place I'd ever seen. The smell of curing meat was hypnotizing, and I stared through the heavy, smoke-laden air at those big crimson and white flanks of fresh teardrop hams, hanging upside down from the beams in the half dark. That was the only time I ever visited the smokehouse. But I often thought about what was inside it as I dashed down the path that led to the old horse sheds, where that one aging mule still resided and where the rusty old ploughs were stacked up outside.

Down in an open field one day, I discovered a stone grave marker with a name, some dates, and a passage of Scripture faded by time and the weather. When I asked about the grave, some aunt or other told me that in days gone by, when people who had lived on a farm died, they'd simply planted them in the backyard. Some Burroughs had long ago been taken from a cooling board to the back of the property and buried, the spot memorialized with a tombstone. I thought that if there was one grave, there had to be others—perhaps unmarked, or with their stones rooted up by storms and carried off.

At Aunt Pete's, like at my grandmother's, we spent a lot of time sitting on the porch. That was the big ritual, especially in the summertime. Everyone got started early in the day on any work that had to be done, so that once the day grew hot, we could lounge on the porch until suppertime. After supper, we'd go out to the porch again. This was what people did, before there was air-conditioning. I remember Aunt Pete spending some of the hottest hours of the day in the kitchen cooking, so we could eat our supper at five o'clock, get back to the porch at a reasonable hour, and sit there talking till 1:00 A.M. Most of the time, the grown-ups didn't discuss anything special—just church and old-time stories. I'm sure a lot of what they talked about went over my head, but they also spoke to one another about their world—about people who'd died, or people who'd moved up North and not been heard from in a while. They'd talk about things they were doing or some dish they planned to take to a church supper. I was enrapt, listening to them talk, particularly when they talked about growing up or shared stories from the backcountry. Those are good times, when a big family sits around together, talking. And believe me, between my grandmother's six sisters and one brother and all their kin, we never lacked for company.

Other than that everyone turned to their wise sister Bennie Frances for advice, there was no hierarchy among these siblings. As a child, I sensed no rivalries or dislikes among my aunts and uncles—only that they had a long history together full of love, and that I was part of a closely knit family. They were very, very normal people. They weren't extravagant in their needs or desires and didn't go after big things; they went to church regularly; they didn't dance or party, and the only vice my grandmother and her sisters succumbed to was dipping snuff. The men of the family were gentle, gentle giants, saying little but always so central to everyone's lives. They may not have been as flashy or as exciting as the female relatives, but they radiated love.

Sitting out on the porch with my family, the chief thing I learned was how to spin a tale. This was not something I learned by trial and error—it isn't a sport. I had learned early that I really had to respect the grown-ups, so I did not intermingle with them in the way children might do today; I sat and listened. Of course, if they asked me something, I'd readily answer, but primarily, I had the wonderful opportunity simply to observe them. Sometimes my cousin James Robert would sit me on the ground between his knees and massage my little earlobes—a special treat. The cadences of my family's voices and laughter washed over me and deep under my skin, and their stories are still with me today.

(This may sound strange to people of a younger generation, who were probably encouraged as children to seek out the conversation of adults and make themselves the center of attention. But when I was a child, children weren't expected to be outgoing. There were certain things we were told never, ever to do, like to interrupt a conversation our parents were having with other adults, and those things simply never happened. It meant that I derived true pleasure from watching the grown people—a pleasure which I suppose is now lost.)

Many of the stories my family told had to do with snakes.

Whenever I go home to North Carolina, I drive around the various roads that are so dear to my memory, but I almost never walk on them. I have never yet walked down to the end of Mt. Sinai Road. Why? Because once I was walking in that direction, and far, far away you could see something crossing the road—just a shimmer on the pavement. Someone beside me said, "That's probably a water moccasin." And I turned right around and went back to church. I've never had a confrontation with a water moccasin, the poisonous snake that haunts the Southern backwoods, and I don't want to. Even in the churchyard, I pay close attention to where I'm planting my feet. A long time ago, my uncle George was coming down the steps of the church, and I don't know if he stepped on a snake's tail or what happened, but it bit his ankle. If he hadn't been wearing his high-top boots, he might well have been killed, because the snake that bit him was a water moc. I don't actually know anyone who has ever died of snakebite, and I know that snakes are more afraid of us than we are of them. Even so, I don't want to have anything to do with them.

Cousin Ella Richmond, a cousin of my grandmother's on her father's side, was a born storyteller who spun tales with an almost otherworldly skill. It was from her that I first heard tell of snakes lurking outside ordinary folks' back doors in the country. From her, too, I learned the various tricks for ridding oneself of the threat of the Crawling Menace, a predator that instilled in me far more fear than some old Godzilla on television. (Six-foot-long black snakes were common in our parts; city-stomping lizards were not.)

When Cousin Ella, her husband, and her tribe of boys decided to leave the city and move back to the country, she didn't give a moment's thought to snakes—until the day one crawled right through the screen door in her kitchen and sat there, coiled, watching her with its hypnotic gaze. I don't recall how she got the snake out of the house that time, but as soon as the immediate danger passed, she began combing her memory for old folk remedies for snake prevention. From somewhere in the deep recesses of her mind she dredged up this: She told her husband to get a box of sulfur powder and to make a thin white line with it all around the perimeter of their yard, being especially careful about the area by the woods in back of the house. That was where the snakes lived. Her husband carefully sprinkled this white powder around their entire property. Then, with a rag soaked in kerosene, he lit the line of sulfur on fire. I'm not sure if the idea was that the foul odor of the slow-burning sulfur would turn the snakes around, so that they'd skip a fast beat back to the shaded woods, or if it was that crossing the line of powder would irritate the skin of the snake's underbelly, achieving the same result. Whichever turned out to be the case, the snake problem was solved, order was restored, and Ella and her family returned to their ordinarily peaceful existence.

Everyone felt the fear of God when snakes were around—everyone, it seemed, except my grandmother and her sisters, all of whom reportedly thought nothing of picking up a garden hoe and guillotining a creature's head from its body. Stories of snakes in the old homesteads abounded. The women of the family loved to talk—on lazy summer afternoons, over glasses of iced tea—of having crushed snakes. I heard tell of snakes, asleep in shade trees, suddenly dropping to the ground. There was the story of a snake crawling down the chimney, as a small baby lay asleep in the only bed in the one-room, dirt-floored log cabin. In one story, a woman carrying a child woke up to find a glossy old black snake slithering from the fireplace toward her bed and miscarried in fear. The tales that struck me as the wildest adventures were those involving water moccasins; if you saw one creeping up out of a pond or creek, you had to douse it with gasoline. *Now who,* I always thought when I heard these stories, *happens to have gasoline handy in such a circumstance?* I certainly never carried any, but the men of the family told of having to turn around in automobiles, run to the local gas station, come back to the edge of the creek or the woods, and pitch the gasoline at Mr. Moccasin, who would go crawling hell-bent to the nearest water for relief. There was no need to try to light the snake on fire, as one did with the repellent sulfur. Apparently, the fuel itself did sufficient damage to those scary reptiles. Even today, if while channel surfing I come across someone like Crocodile Hunter Steve Irwin grappling with a snake, I have to cover my eyes.

I sat out on the porch (or in winter, by the hearth) listening to these stories hour after hour, from my earliest childhood to my young manhood, and they inked themselves into my memory. Their themes remain with me even to this day. As large as snakes loomed in my family's repertoire of tales, the cooling board loomed even larger. Back in the days before I was born, when people died in the backcountry, the coroner did not immediately come to a rural home. This was well before telephone lines had been run out to faraway places, so while someone went by wagon to notify the correct authorities, the women of the family became the undertakers and prepared the body for the journey home. The women washed the remains, dressed the corpse in a winding sheet, and in the unbearably hot months of summer, placed the dead person on a cooling board—a set of wooden planks joined together, or an old table, if a family possessed one that was long enough—under a shade tree. Once the word got out to the funeral director, he would come along in a horse-drawn wagon with a coffin. In those days, embalming hardly existed, and burial was speedy, economical, and done with respect.

Those strong country people had to do it all. The country women who peopled my early childhood endured everything from birth to death with survival skills that had been passed down from mother to daughter for as long as anyone could remember. Those women could dress a dead person, wash their hands, and then go gather fresh eggs to prepare a feast for the mourners. They could help with the hog killing, the curing of hams, and the making of sausages, as well as contend with vast weekly loads of family wash that had to be pummeled in a pot, rinsed, and ironed by hand; get themselves to church on time on Sundays and sometimes to midweek prayer services, too; cook meals a minimum of twice a day; attend to all of a family's needs; and still go down on bended knee with prayers of gratitude after their weary journey through a day that most of us now cannot imagine having to live through. When the women of my family, in their starched aprons and pinafores, served me food with their blessed, loving hands, I felt as if the food contained the magic ingredients of their resiliency and goodness.

The memories of a wonderful country life, of those vibrant aunts, uncles, and cousins, fill me with a love and optimism that I think pervade the mental landscape of many African Americans (certainly those among whom I grew up). I still live in awe of the dynamic energy that enabled my ancestors to face seemingly any task, duty, or responsibility when they had little to depend on but their belief in Scripture, the grace of God, and the love of family. I think extended family is much of what kept so many of the descendants of poor sharecroppers going. The women of my family survived days of grueling work in the hot weather, when the only break they had was to take a fresh drink of lemonade from a Mason jar or to eat a sweet, ripe tomato right off the vine.

When they had time, they might slice those tomatoes and make a tomato and mayonnaise sandwich, a delicacy my cousin James Robert loved. I can still smell those spicy, fresh tomatoes on a summer afternoon, after all the farming and gardening were done, when everyone sat around in the shade drinking iced tea or lemonade and dipping snuff, spitting it out onto the grass or into old tin cans.

Some of the stories about snakes and cooling boards were meant to convey family history; others, of course, merely to frighten or amuse. Some of the stories imparted practical wisdom—such as the tale about the line of sulfur keeping off snakes. Certainly the members of my family were wealthy in folk wisdom. I will never forget one laundry day when I cut my foot badly on a piece of broken glass in the yard. I was ready to make quite a fuss, but my great-grandmother simply stopped the bleeding by scooping up a handful of fresh red earth and applying it to the open wound. She calmly went back to the work at hand, leaving me to contemplate my foot with amazement.

I realize now that along with all the other wonderful things they taught me, my family indoctrinated me into all kinds of superstitions—some of them quite wonderful. One of the topics about which my grandmother could truly wax fanatical was pests in the house.

Daddy longlegs spiders were a big nuisance: They would crawl into the cracks of the house, and you could wake up any morning, in any season, and find one looking down at you from an invisible web while you rubbed sleep from your eyes. The broom was my shotgun when it came to those beige spiders, but I didn't fear them as I feared the yellow-and-black ones that spun webs in our neighbor's yard. As for mice, I can only say thank goodness we were not plagued with rats like those I so often see out taking the air on the evening streets of New York City. Just as she whacked the snakes with a garden hoe, my grandmother dispatched the field mice that invaded her home. She always kept a brick of yellow cheddar in the icebox for macaroni and cheese, so there was always some available for baiting mousetraps. I would hear the traps crack down on their victims during the night, and in the morning, my grandmother would pick them up and fling the dead rodents into the fire in the wood-burning stove. (Once we converted to an electric stove, she had to resort to the less dramatic method of disposing of them in the garbage bin outdoors.)

At some point, my grandmother believed she saw an earwig near her four-poster bed. Neither of us—nor any of the aunts, who were, of course, rapidly consulted—had ever seen an earwig, so we were not entirely certain what it looked like. However, Grandmother's family was full of stories about earwigs causing total deafness, so you can believe we pulled her room apart from top to bottom. We pushed everything into the kitchen—chests of drawers, end tables, her wardrobe, that trunk full of Dorothy Bee's never-used linens—in order to scour the room, and went over and over her bed, mattress, and box spring, but it was all in vain. The earwig hunt went on for four days and nights, until we finally just gave up, hoping that whatever she'd seen had crawled through some slat in the wood or one of those gaps in windows that seem to exist though no one can ever see them. When we were done, we repeatedly thrust the brooms into zinc tubs of scalding water, just in case the insect invader had nested in their fibers, but we never saw it.

The unsolved earwig caper seemed like the worst bug-related incident I could imagine, until one day I whacked a furry caterpillar off my neck after it had fallen out of the broadleaf sycamore. I hardly felt that uneasy sensation of something crawling on my neck before the jerk of my hand brought it spiraling to the ground, dead as dead can be. The hives it raised on the back of my neck itched like crazy. My grandmother and her sisters all agreed there was only one thing to do—calamine lotion. For some reason we didn't have a bottle at the time, so she went over to our neighbor, Mrs. Addie Coley, to borrow some. Those hives lasted for over a week, and you wonder why some people have phobias about worms, snakes, and bugs.

Even the caterpillar-inflicted misery paled, however, the next summer, when Aunt Pete invited my grandmother and me to spend the entire week of August revival with her. I was excited about this because it was to be the longest I'd ever stayed at her magical house. As good as the prospect of good company was, the fact that Pete's blackberries had come ripe all of a sudden was another attraction. She said that if we would pick them for preserves, I could eat as many as I liked while I worked. Of course, as any boy would, I jumped at the opportunity and ate myself silly on the sweet, bumpy berries, dreaming all the while of my grandmother's delicious preserves.

But nothing—nothing!—had prepared me for the agony of the chiggers that had quietly decided my testicles would be a more hospitable environment than the blackberry bushes they called home. Have you ever had a colony of chiggers take up residence in your balls? I couldn't see them, but they made me want to rip my private parts to shreds. The temptation to scratch ate up my imagination and many of my waking hours. It was agony trying to sit through revival meetings, and Grandmother and I slipped back to Durham, where I went through a bottle of soothing pink calamine in two or three days. I could hardly sit, let alone ride my red bike. And when I tried to ease myself into a pair of undershorts, it felt like I was easing into a bed of needles. I endured the days of torment and felt, once it was over, that I had achieved a victory. Out on the porch we continued to share the story of those chiggers for years. I never again went to pick berries in those dense bushes back by the smokehouse.

Bugs, like snakes, were always discussed with a mixture of humor and dread, but the one menace that was never anything but serious was an electrical storm. The way our house shut down in those storms continues to live vividly in my memory. My grandmother and great-grandmother feared electrical storms because they believed they were expressions of God's anger. If, on a hot summer afternoon or evening, a storm unexpectedly crackled against a gray sky, our life automatically went on hold.

My grandmother called these rages of nature 'lectric storms. "God's not happy with somebody," she would say, shaking her head. The very ebb and flow of the house and the people who lived in it stopped at the first flash of lightning, the way you can push a button on a VCR and the image immediately goes blank. Chores were left till later, and once we had an electric stove, it was turned off (its heating coils gradating back to black), our supper left to simmer; televisions, radios, and record players were turned to OFF, as if the clapping thunder and flashing bolts meant that the doors of Hell were cracking open. The telephone was forbidden—if someone had the bad luck to be in the middle of a conversation when the storm began, the party on the other end of the line was told in a decisive manner to "call back when the storm is over!" Then the receiver was slammed back into its cradle. My grandmother, you see, believed that lightning storms would cause death-inducing electrical currents to run through the box, the receiver, and straight into your brain. If we were outside, we rushed inside. In bad storms, we pulled all the window shades right down to the sill. Each family member took to his or her bed or a sofa. Since we had no air-conditioning back in those days (and would have had to turn it off, even if we did—air-conditioning is, after all, electrical), my grandmother would take her church fan with her to get a little breeze going as she lay atop her impeccably dressed bed. No one really spoke—if it was necessary to say something, one said it softly and succinctly. Until the storm passed over, we lived in that stillness one experiences during silent prayers in a church sanctuary.

Once the storm passed, and the thunder rolled farther and farther away, we did not break into song like the Negroes do in those bad racist Hollywood musicals of the Old South with Shirley Temple or whoever. Nor did we meet one another on the porch, clasp hands, and break out in prayers of thanksgiving, having feared for our very lives. But the calm after a storm always gave us a sense of renewal, an affirmation that God was finding all well in the lineup of things. Once a storm subsided, our silent hearts felt refreshed. When the storm ended, drops of rain beaded against the window screens and left crystal pearls on the velvety leaves of the red geraniums.

Life ceased during storms, but it slowly blinked back to normal and went on. As Mama began to stir the pots, turning the heating rings on the stove back up again, and as I went back to my baby blue and white record player or the television set, we still felt the prayerfulness of those moments. All her life, my grandmother could be heard saying, "Thank you, Father, thank you," as she went about her business after an electrical storm, not because, I think, she truly thought something ill would befall us (barring electrocution via the telephone), but because she was thankful that the world now seemed at peace. After a storm, I always had the pleasant feeling that we could communicate to one another without utterance; that I could tell from her eyes if she were pleased or displeased. We always held mental dialogues—our closeness to and understanding of each other was that ingrained—but it was after electrical storms that I truly thought that to articulate an idea or emotion would be, quite simply, out of place and unnecessary.

Life after a storm began again with the smell of nature washed clean, a smell as invigorating and reviving as any I have experienced. When I was a young man living in Paris, I loved the smell of the chestnut trees in the spring after an afternoon storm because it reminded me of those times at home, and of my family, with all their foibles and superstitions. Everything, you see, was right as rain after a 'lectric storm.

CHAPTER FOUR

The soothing power of old-time Negro spirituals is a luxury that has sustained me throughout my life. There are certain songs that uplift my spirit and carry me back to my home. This is because church was one of the most formative experiences of my childhood and continues to be the foundation of my life today.

The reason for this is, of course, that it was the support and bedrock of my grandmother's life. She did not have an easy time of it in this world. As the eldest child in a family of modest means, she was looking after children from her earliest memory, and when she grew up, things didn't get easier. She gave birth to stillborn twins as a young woman—babies who, though they'd never seen the light of day, had to be laid together in a coffin and buried—and, when she was an adult, she lost her father, her favorite daughter, and her husband within the space of a few years. When her mother died less than ten years after that spate of tragedies, she was surrounded by sympathetic kin but left with no one in her immediate family but me; and I was too young to give her much comfort. From 1952 until the day she died in 1989, she did everything all by herself. Yet she never complained and remained the large force holding her entire family—all those sisters and brother Buster—together. She had so much faith in God, and as a consequence, so much faith in herself. Her faith gave her the inner resources to be resilient when faced with any kind of adversity, any sort of situation. She just kept getting up every day, going to work; getting up, going to work; and these rituals of household cleanliness, of work, and of churchgoing kept her going.

We went to church nearly every single Sunday of my life.

Mt. Sinai Road, on which Dorothy Bee was killed in 1951, was named after our church, which was founded in the early 1870s by former slaves. The story goes that they had worshiped in a white church but eventually asked the property owners in the area to donate land for them to build a church of their own. The land was granted to them by the white citizens of Orange County, and the church went up during Reconstruction. Some of the descendants of the people who founded Mt. Sinai still belong to the church today—the Barbees, the Hendersons, and the Robersons feel, in many ways, like part of my extended family.

The church is set on a beautiful tract of land. I don't know how many acres it is, but it feels vast. The old cemetery—where generations of my kin are buried—is not snug up against the church as cemeteries so often are, but perhaps five or six hundred yards down a verdant, sloping hill. When I was growing up, Mt. Sinai Church was faced in clapboard and painted white. Inside, it was all plain, gleaming wood. There were no stained glass windows then, only panes of clear glass, but there was a bell tower with a rich-sounding bell, which used to peal for funeral processions.

When I think back on my childhood, I realize that churchgoing was its focal point and center. At the time, however, it didn't seem like anything special. It wasn't as if my grandmother made a big deal out of our preparations for going to church; it was simply what we did. I wasn't particularly awed by the power of the sermons, or swept away by the music, or uplifted by beautiful religious art. I wasn't looking forward to gossiping with friends, because of course that wasn't allowed. I felt good when we went to church, because it was the correct thing to do, a weekly ritual that helped us to know our place in the world. I sat attentively and did my duty and knew that this was right. Sunday was the one day of the week when we were guaranteed to see family. My grandmother talked on the telephone to her sisters during the week, but they were all busy, between their jobs and their families, and almost never made midweek visits. So I looked forward, not to seeing any family member in particular, but to being with the whole clan.

Mt. Sinai was a rural church, so it did not sponsor many events during the week, such as the lectures and classes one might attend at a more urban congregation nowadays. This was surely part of the reason Sundays took on so much importance; because we had only that one weekly contact with our church. Sundays were, mind you, not the only days on which we worshiped. Grandmother sometimes told me stories from the Bible or Jesus' life. For years, before church, I went to Sunday school at First Calvary in Durham, because it was within walking distance of our house, which meant that I could be back at the house in time to go to Mt. Sinai with everyone. One summer I also went to vacation Bible school, but I preferred to be home during the summers, so my grandmother didn't make me go back. For a while I sang in the choir, and I occasionally attended missionary society meetings with my grandmother.

After church on Sundays we generally all went our separate ways; my grandmother and I would go back to our house for an early supper, and the various aunts and uncles would similarly retire to their own homes. Therefore, it was a truly special occasion when we all got together to share a meal. When we had the huge family gatherings, for major church holidays or revivals, it was even more special still. It took surprisingly little, in terms of money, to sleep, feed, clothe, and bathe all those people who came to stay with us, sometimes for two weeks at a time. And somehow—certainly by God's grace!—we managed to get out of there, with relays in the one bathroom, in time for church on Sunday. Our family gatherings, where covered dishes and picnic hampers were filled to the brim with good eatings, were hugely important to us and one of the most important was our annual church Homecoming Day. Homecoming, like all large church holidays, provided a wonderful opportunity for humor, drama, and the display of respectability. After the morning service, we would all go outside, where the pastor and his helpers would have laid huge, rough planks out on sawhorses under the trees. The families divided up, and the women, wearing freshly starched, patterned aprons, would cover those wide boards with crisp, hand-embroidered tablecloths, some bedecked with fruit, others with sprays of blossoms, oak leaves, or ivy. Each family brought a basket or more full of food, which was laid out in a loving display on the impromptu buffet tables. The minister said a blessing over the food, paper plates were distributed, and everyone began to make the rounds, heaping their plates. As one walked from table to table, aroma after delicious aroma rose from those makeshift cardboard picnic boxes (or the trompe l'oeil wicker tin hamper my grandmother used, with additional cargo boxes for her famous cakes and pies). Pyrex dishes of macaroni and cheese, fully seasoned turnip greens, fried chicken, biscuits, sweet potatoes, potato salad, and cabbage were laid out on those open-air banqueting tables, for everyone to enjoy. There was always good food on the table at my grandmother's house, but at Homecoming there was a wonderful variety of different dishes. As much as I loved eating the food, I loved watching the grown-ups go around smelling, tasting, and talking about it in an atmosphere of celebration.

I particularly recall one Homecoming for what happened to Cousin Ella Richmond. Ella always seemed to be living with some dilemma at hand. That Homecoming Day, when the food was brought up from the hampers and placed on the tables, silver-haired Cousin Ella simply couldn't wait for the prayer to be finished before she snuck a taste of someone's golden lemon pound cake. As the minister was concluding his blessing, a wild, banshee howl rose up out of Ella. I am sure I wasn't the only one who assumed she was having one of those out-of-body, speaking-in-tongues religious experiences, which were rare in our neck of the woods—Mt. Sinai Baptist was as restrained, refined, and dignified in our style of worship as any white Episcopalian congregation. What, I wondered, could have caused Cousin Ella suddenly to spin out into religious orbit?

She had trapped a wasp in the ivory prison of her teeth; and having met with the threat of extinction in Ella's mouth, the wasp went into defense mode and stung her tongue, which swelled to an unbelievable size. All the young cousins laughed like crazy, though really, it was no laughing matter.

Another important church event was the August revival, which lasted from the first Sunday in August to the next. Guest ministers would come and preach in the evening, when it was dark in the country in a way it never was in Durham, and when the lightning bugs and June bugs were out. The crickets and other insects sang as those visiting preachers treated us to their grandest subjects and best rhetorical strategem. Revival was an inspiring experience—the whole affair had a holiday atmosphere, which was heightened for us children by the fact that we ate our festive, main meal of the day at about ten o'clock at night. That meal was called a repast. Our family's repasts were often held out at Pete and Ira's farm, which for me, made them seem even more special.

People were converted in large numbers during revivals, though of course, they were converted during ordinary Sunday morning services as well. Conversion could change a person's life completely, and at our church the ceremony was conducted as a solemn affair. People were imbued with the Spirit of the Lord, but this generally didn't cause any of the showier potential outbursts of religious feeling. If a person truly wanted to be converted and join the church, there were certain rules he would agree to accept and live by (the simple precepts of an honest, Christian life, which, I have learned in my travels around the world, are pretty much the same for good people of all religions and creeds), and he would be baptized to signify his entrance into the church community. Baptism was the ceremony of greatest significance in one's religious life, to be undertaken only when one was certain one was ready.

Nowadays people are baptized at Mt. Sinai as they are in many churches, in a small pool behind the altar. But when I was a child, people were baptized by full immersion, so the church maintained a baptismal pool down at the bottom of the woods behind the cemetery. The pool was, I think, full of rainwater; it didn't seem to have either a man-made or a natural source, but was simply a concrete pool with steps leading down into it. I don't know where the water came from, but it always had a murky, yellow appearance.

I made up my mind to join the church during the revival when I was twelve or thirteen, which was a momentous, life-altering decision. Many of us had chosen to join the church at that time, so the minister thought we should all be baptized together on a certain Sunday in September. I was eager to become a member of the church—it was something I wanted for myself, as well as something I knew would make my grandmother proud—but I confess that I spent much of the intervening month worrying about the ceremony itself, because, you see, I was deeply afraid of both the cemetery and the baptismal pool. I am not afraid of cemeteries in general (though I suspect I am not the only person who wouldn't go walking through one at night), but there was something sobering to me about walking through the place where all my ancestors had been laid to rest. As for the pool, in snake country, a stagnant pond is one of the things to be most deeply feared. I did not tell my grandmother about my worries, because I didn't want her to think I didn't take the ceremony seriously.

The morning of the baptism, I dressed carefully in my best suit and was nervous and proud as we headed off to church. Those of us about to be baptized lined up for the processional and were led, slowly and quietly, down through the dreaded cemetery and into the woods before the 11:00 A.M. service. The members of the congregation held flickering candles as we passed, which, in my state of mind, chilled me. My grandmother was there, looking on with pride in her eyes, and it was our beloved Reverend Perry who, when the time came, dipped me in the pool. I will confess that the only thing I could think of, once we had passed through to the other side of the graveyard, was a refrain that went something like this: *I'm going to be dipped and I'm going to see a snake; I'm going to go under and there'll be a water moc.* Of course, that was not the case—you're underwater only for a split second—but when it didn't come to pass, I was as relieved as I'd ever been in my life that far.

I do laugh sometimes when I think of the terror I conjured up in anticipation of what turned out to be a not-at-all-frightening event. But on a more serious level, I realize that my fear made the experience of baptism doubly important to me. For in addition to symbolizing my rebirth into the church, in a more private way it symbolized my rebirth as someone who could grapple with fears in an adult fashion, which I think is one of the most important things a sense of faith gives a person. Joining the church meant joining the tradition that had kept my grandmother and all her ancestors going through times of joy and times of tribulation. For me, in a literal way, it meant learning to trust the love, support, and understanding that sustained me.

The rite of baptism asks the participant to enact a symbolic death and rebirth—the laying aside of the former life and the generation of a new person with the joy of God's love in his heart. I sometimes think that this is because death is in some ways the defining moment of our lives, the one thing we know with certainty will happen to each of us. Death may not be the reason we turn to our faith on a daily basis (we have plenty of minor crises for that), but faith is perhaps the only thing that can help us to face it bravely. I remember once, in an issue of *Nest,* there was an article showing the funerals of famous people—Jimi Hendrix, Abraham Lincoln, President John F. Kennedy, Martin Luther King, Jr.—and someone told me that they found it distasteful that Joseph Holtzman would publish an article about death. I was puzzled by this comment; I told the person I thought the article was a masterpiece for showing how in the celebration or memorializing of a human being there can be so many different styles. Death is a hugely important part of our lives and our culture. I believe that my experiences of death as a boy, in the context of my and my grandmother's faith, were some of my most formative life experiences.

When my aunt Dorothy Bee died, I was only four years old, too young to understand what was happening and too young to participate in her memorial services. I don't know who they left me with while they went to church, but I stayed at home. (This was unusual in those days, before people relied heavily on baby-sitters. Whenever people had to go somewhere, the children went, too. When I was slightly older, this meant that even when there was a funeral for someone I had hardly known, I had to go if my grandmother went. I found these experiences both frightening and fascinating. Children really don't understand those things very well.)

After Dorothy Bee died, women filled up the house. I can see them now, surrounding my grandmother, who, behind a wall of wailing women, lay on the front-bedroom bed. A coffin had been rolled into the living room. The table with the two photographs—Dorothy Bee's high school portrait and Benton and China's anniversary image—had been shuffled aside to make room for the coffin. At the time, I had no idea what the large object contained. The grown-ups had decided that I must not be allowed to see a dead body or to learn anything about death. No one had bothered to explain to me why Aunt Dorothy Bee never came home from the picnic, and I never saw her extinguished light resting in that simple casket. What I do remember is women,

women and aunts, Aunt Pat, Aunt Louvenia (who was secretly my favorite), standing around the front-room bed, fanning my grandmother. These women crowded so thick around my grandmother, it was hard to break the line of them. Yet I was determined to ease between some of those skirts and stockings and get to my grandmother, who, I remember, was wearing a knife-pleated blue skirt with a diamond pattern. In my young mind, I thought she was being harmed by all those women, who seemed to be holding her down as she cried.

Is she in pain? I wondered. *Are they hurting her? What can I do to stop these women from clawing at my grandmother?*

"Stop it! Stop it! Leave her alone!" I screamed, but nobody moved away. Confused, I continued to scream and to try, with little success, to penetrate the wall of women.

Now, of course, I think, *There she was, being consoled, and I, with no understanding of what was going on, was trying to stop that vital process.* As I grew older and this was all explained to me, I came to understand that had my grandmother let go of me, on the front porch on that fateful Fourth of July, there might have been two coffins in the living room that day instead of one, and two coffins rolled up the aisle of the church: one for the beautiful lost daughter and one for me.

The first funeral to which I felt any true emotional connection was Great-grandmother China's in January 1960. Our entire clan took up living at Aunt Pete's for the three days leading up to China's funeral. (In those days, funerals were always held on Sundays after morning services. In the '70s, more modern ways took over, and services could be held any day of the week.) After being embalmed and dressed, China's body arrived in its casket at Aunt Pete's house on a cold, cold, rainy Saturday night, in time for the all-night wake.

None of the adults slept during the wake; they stayed up all night talking, laughing, crying, and preparing for services the next day. Children were put to bed at their usual time, and during China's wake, most of the children, wearing flannel pajamas, were lined up like clothespin dolls in big old-fashioned beds in a bedroom next to the living room. I was terrified of what was in that casket. When Great-grandmother China's body had been placed in the living room by the undertakers, one of my aunts had told me to go into the living room to see my great-grandmother, who had been positioned on the slant, on the other side of the pipe organ, for viewing. I loved Grandmother China, and remembered her, then and now, as a wonderfully giving and caring person. She had many great-grandchildren but managed to make each of us feel uniquely and specially loved. But I was terrified of her cold, dead body. I was frightened that she might reach out and grab me or admonish me for some hitherto-undiscovered sin. And now her body lay between me and the living room.

The cold seeped into my bones that night, and so did the fear that kept me from sleeping. I lay awake on a bed shared with a boy cousin, listening to the grown-ups talk and trying not to panic about my great-grandmother's corpse. I don't know how much time elapsed—it seemed like hours—but at some point that evening, one of the aunts called out from the kitchen, "Ray? Could you please bring me my snuff? It's in a Railroad Mills tin. I left it in the parlor."

I shuddered at her words. How, I wondered, could she ask me to go into that room alone? I pretended I was sleeping and didn't answer my call. After a while, whoever had asked for the snuff went in to fetch the tin herself. The next morning, Grandma China was driven off to Mt. Sinai, where she was to be funeralized and buried in the family plot.

As we prepared to go off to the funeral that morning, a chilling rain came down loudly and heavily, and I heard a grown-up say, "Old folks say it's a good sign, putting someone in the ground and it's a rain." I tried to get as close as I could to my grandmother, in her black cashmere coat, but I was kept from her protection by protocol—she was the eldest child, and I was just one of many grandchildren and great-grandchildren, no guest of honor. I panicked at being unable to get to the person with whom I felt most safe, because I had been shaken by the night I'd just spent. I also remembered how I could not get to her when the women had tried to console her during the wake of her beloved daughter. I felt true terror that cold, rainy day, when I learned that I was supposed to ride to church in a car far, far behind the black limousine in which my grandmother was the first to be seated. Somehow I thought that when Skippy Scarborough's father called her name in the processional lineup for the cars, she would automatically take my hand and shuffle me through the sisters to be next to her.

When I look back upon it now, I can see how foolish I was. At the time, though, I was a scared, left-out child in a situation I had never been in before—attending the funeral of someone I loved. After the fear I had suffered the night before in contemplating the snuff tin, I selfishly wanted to be next to the person I knew best.

I was pushed into a car with other young people and felt alone as I watched the long line of cars snake up the wet, muddy road on the way to the main unpaved one. I didn't dare show my fear.

When the church bells began ringing and the coffin disappeared into the church, I considered running and cutting into the processional to catch up with my grandmother. At that point, as they were marching in, I could still see my grandmother, but she was beside her next-eldest sister, Mozella, who wasn't all that nice. I knew that to trespass on adult doings would bring sure punishment. And even if by some chance it didn't, to bolt to the front of the line when the processional included my own mother and father would surely have caused a scandal.

The thing I remember most vividly about the funeral itself was that when we walked down to the grave site, the open grave was covered with a green canvas awning that the rain beat upon with a deafening sound.

After the funeral, the ushers piled us back into the cars to return to Aunt Pete's for the repast. For some reason, the cars carrying the nieces, nephews, cousins, grandchildren, and great-grands arrived ahead of the two cars with the sisters and one brother. I stood out on Aunt Pete's porch, watching the rain patter into the rain barrel, waiting to see that big, fin-tailed Cadillac come up over the hill bearing my grandmother.

It was already getting dark when her car turned into the drive. She was the first one out of the car, and as soon as she stepped up onto the porch, she reached out, still wearing her black gloves, and took my cold, cold hand. She hugged me to her side; her wet cashmere coat seemed as cozy and welcoming as the mountain of quilts on my bed at home. We walked through the front door of Pete's house together. I was now the man by her side and at last felt at ease.

As I grew, funerals sadly became an increasingly common part of our churchgoing life, much more common than weddings, because so many of my cousins were already married by the time I was coming up. From that moment on, no matter how solemn the occasion, I simply moved up to my rightful place beside Grandmother and asked no one for permission. It was understood between the two of us. It was not necessary to put my name on the list for any processional; when her name was called, I was always right there beside her.

I believe in God. I believe that God is present in many forms, and I believe that we should try to reflect godliness as much as possible in the way we live. That's certainly how I saw my grandmother do things. She did not have the advantages of a wealthy upbringing or a fancy education—I think she went to grade school, but no further, and she almost never read for pleasure—but God and the Son of God kept my grandmother going right up to the very day she died. I have found that church people, and church attendance, have been much of what has kept me on the straight and narrow thus far.

When I go home to North Carolina now—which I do at least once a year—Mt. Sinai Church looks different. It's been fully restored and now has a brick façade. It has been modernized so that, for example, we have a beautiful dining room facility instead of eating outside on planks like we used to do. Even the road heading out there is different now. It used to be a dirt road, but now it's paved. There are houses much closer to the church than there used to be, though there aren't any right up against it. The cemetery is unchanged, and all my wonderful aunts—in fact, nearly everyone on my grandmother's side of the family—are now buried there. My father and his kin are buried in Red Mill Creek Church cemetery, up in Roxboro, where his family was from. I don't mean to sound morbid, but visiting one's family cemetery can give one a strong connection to history, to place. As an adult, it's a sad but wonderful thing to be where your ancestors are buried in the earth. I often drive there to commune with dead loved ones.

I still attend church, partly out of a sense of duty to my grandmother. If she were alive, this is what she would want to see me doing; so when she looks down on me from Heaven, I want her to see that her teachings were not in vain. When I go to church, I feel recharged, whether that's through the minister's words, or the songs the congregation sings, or simply being there. Going to church is the best way I know to connect to the world of people who believe in God, to become part of their community, which is one of the only communities I really want to be a part of. Church gives me a sense of grounding and well-being. It feels like the place I should be. I think some people go to a weekly therapy session, support group, language lesson, or cooking class, and I go to church. For me it's the best place to be in the world, and Scripture is the deftest tool for shaping reflection.

I try to be friendly and polite with the people at church, but I do not go there to make friends. I think that one's spiritual life is essentially a solitary thing. What I like about my current church is that Abyssinian Baptist is a church of tradition and history, and its pastor, Dr. Calvin O. Butts III, is a dynamic speaker. The choirs move me through the power of song. And every week when I go there, I feel like I'm going back home, because in my youth, church was my second home.

The store I set by churchgoing is one way in which my life is significantly out of sync with what people assume it would be. When people in the fashion industry get to know me, they are sometimes surprised to realize that I don't necessarily have what one would consider a normal life in the fashion world. I do not make a habit of trumpeting how important church is to me. I don't go around bellowing, "I go to church every Sunday!" But people find out, because people find out things whether you trumpet them or not. And they realize that going to church keeps me connected to the values I was raised with and connected to tradition. So often in the modern world, people feel rootless because of the stress and isolation of living in an urban environment. My brief weekly visit to church keeps me grounded. If I miss a Sunday, I tend to feel off-center for the rest of the week. It also, quite simply, makes me happy to go to church. I feel uplifted by the sermon, the prayers, and the ministry of song.

It's important to connect to one's sense of ritual and tradition. If you've grown up in a church, that's one good way. And of course I don't think it's the physical building that makes it so; it's an intangible quality. I feel like nothing bad can ever happen to me in church. It provides me with a safe environment in which to think meaningfully about my life. I always know what's going to happen there, and I look forward to that repetition, continuity, and tradition.

I do not think I would have been happy had I spent my whole life in Durham, in a more rural environment and on a smaller stage. But I know many people who, in finding their place as I have done, have completely given up their connection to their pasts and their homes. I believe that this is a mistake, as so many of them seem to have, in that way, bypassed happiness as they rushed toward where they thought it might lie. When I think of the people I have admired in my life—my grandmother foremost among them—I see that one common theme, one thing I admire in each of them, is that they were fortunate in being content with their lives. They didn't have the wanderlust to get out of their natural sphere. I certainly did, and I think my wanderlust has brought me a fair measure of happiness, but I don't know that getting out to see the world is *intrinsically* important. The older I get, the more I realize that many of those who are truly content have not lived incredibly broad or sophisticated lives. They base their happiness on faith, home, tradition, and values.

We live in a culture that privileges wandering. Children are not encouraged to stay at home, or near home, once they reach young adulthood; they are supposed to move into their own apartments, and make their own way in the big cities. For some of us this is the only possible road to happiness. I know I could never have lived my dreams if I'd been unwilling to move out of my grandmother's house. But as someone who has made his way in the bigger world, I recognize the importance of a connection to history and home. Once you've traveled the world, it's good to go back to your roots. So many people try to block the past out, but I don't ever want to forget mine. Ever. Everyone thinks they have to go out in search of new experiences, to hone their way of looking at things. In truth, the real trick would be to learn new ways of seeing the flora and fauna in your own backyard. When I read in 2001 of the death of Eudora Welty, a great American writer, I noted that all the obituary writers mentioned how remarkable she was for being able to create an entire universe though she never left the house she grew up in. Hers was a rare gift; but ideally, we could all figure out a way to attain that breadth and clarity of vision, even if it seems like what we were born with isn't much to look at.

I love what I do, but I think there are many pockets of emptiness and shallowness that come from its being such a jet-set industry. I agree wholeheartedly with Voltaire's idea of the importance of cultivating one's own garden, whether that's a rose garden, an apple orchard, or a few sandy square yards that might someday be worked into a vegetable patch.

In 1951 my grandmother's husband dropped dead of a heart attack on the sidewalk on his way to work; only a year later, her favorite daughter died. Yet Bennie Frances Davis continued to be a lighthouse to her family, guiding and leading us with strong beams of love. Against the swirls and eddies of crushing tides, her special light still shone. She continued on, for that was all she knew how to do—continue on, through happy times and sad. And her faith withstood those terrible, gale-force storms.

Once Dorothy was gone, Ray had to take her place. After the death of her favorite, she fed life into me. In return, I pray that the love and admiration I gave her helped to assuage the losses of her husband, her daughter, and a decade later, her mother. From that moment forward I remained the center of her life, and for me she was the source of unconditional love until the day she died.

We lived on love in that house—on love and faith, which I believe are inseparable. With those to sustain us, our spirits were as free as the red cardinals that flew around the house all year long.

I still possess Mason jars of canned tomatoes and green hot sauce that had not yet been eaten when she died in 1989; I keep them as relics of her rich life and of the way her memory is preserved in mine. From the cake batter she made to the loads of laundry she washed, everything my grandmother did was an expression of prayer. And every page turned in the Bible, every word of grace at table, every prayer uttered, aloud or in silence, was an expression of her unfailing belief in God's grace and mercy.

A haven of safety from the outside world—that was my grandmother's home to me. Springtime blossomed even in the granite-cold winter nights, because our plates were heaped with servings of wonderful food, our beds stacked with vivid-hued homemade quilts, and our bodies kept warm by well-stoked fires. In the four decades that my grandmother's life guided mine, there was nothing safer or more sacred for me than closing down all the portholes and resting securely in the care, concern, and faith of her marvelous home, where the one great refinement was love.

Nothing I could write could say it better than one of the old spirituals they sing in church:

Precious memories, how they linger,
How they ever flood my soul!

In the stillness of the midnight
Precious, sacred scenes unfold.

Let the choir begin that refrain on any given Sunday, and tears well up in my eyes. Those Sundays we spent together back at Mt. Sinai Baptist Church; that sea of hats, piled with artificial flowers or wrapped in gossamer bows; those undulating waves of paper fans, all bearing a color photograph of either Dr. Martin Luther King, Jr., or the exterior of Scarborough & Hargett, our local funeral home; Cousin Ella's high tenor voice swelling over the entire choir on some sweet, familiar hymn; the emotionally overcharged prayers of Brother Charlie Baldwin, who eventually opened up a twenty-four-hour prayer chapel in a small house adjacent to his own. I long for all these things most Sundays, and I cry silent tears for days past and for the old-time religion of a missionary church in Orange County, North Carolina—a religion that now seems gone.

Sometimes I feel like I will never feel springtime fully again, since I cannot watch its sun rising, coloring everything blue and gold, from the safety of my grandmother's enveloping love. I think often of that wall of sheets flapping in the wind or of those Mason jars of damson and peach preserves fossilized in walls of hard sugar. (A spoonful on a hot biscuit: ecstasy.) I remember the honeysuckle vines on our white picket fence; the wild rabbits rushing to some garden party in our rows of cabbages; Easter eggs being dipped in vegetable colors on Easter Monday afternoon. What I remember and cherish most is it being just the two of us, my grandmother and me.

I am thankful that I joined the Abyssinian Baptist Church in Harlem, in August 1989, one mere week prior to the death of my mentor and friend, Diana Vreeland. My grandmother, who had already gone home to Heaven, would have wanted me to be in this church family, for what a wonderful family it is. On Sunday mornings, Dr. Butts in the pulpit, wearing his grand gray robes with crimson edges, reminds me of those Orange County Sundays in the country church of my youth.

Dr. Butts and I have never had lunch or a long phone conversation. We communicate in silence, in the realm of our spiritual connection. Sometimes he speaks to, or of, me from the pulpit in his sermon, which lets me know that his concern and care are there.

Like my father, he is a man of few words, a beaming smile, and a handshake as strong as a vise. He has street-style elegance, that same certain strut in his walk, a kind of staccato bounce to his gait. He is dapper and looks every bit the urban bon vivant, although he is a sober and spiritual man. His suits are bespoke, his shoes spit-shined till they gleam like mirrors. He causes his congregants to stand up with correctness and dignity. Sometimes in the lonely hours, when the slender evidence of my life's achievements blurs into doubt and despair, I picture the face of Reverend Dr. Calvin O. Butts III, and I feel, from his gaze of approval and strength, that a light is shining on me. The beacons who lit my way in youth may have passed to the next sphere, but I am thankful my grandmother taught me where to seek guidance. If I can never go home again, at least I am certain of my spiritual family and church home.

CHAPTER FIVE

I remember my grandmother getting down from the bus every Friday afternoon and walking toward our house with two heavy brown shopping bags containing our weekly groceries, one bag to each hand. She never learned to drive, so she repeated this weekly ritual rain or shine, like it or no, until she was retired. (After she retired, cousin Johnsie drove her to the supermarket every Friday, until Johnsie's death from breast cancer.) When I heard the bus purr to a stop, I would head off down the street to relieve her of her burden. We would talk on the way home, and together we would put the groceries away. Some vegetables, fruits, and meat; onions; perhaps some staple we'd run out of, like oatmeal or flour; a couple dozen eggs. But the things my grandmother could make from these simple, inexpensive ingredients were astonishing.

My experience of the family gatherings of my childhood—the reunions, the Homecomings, the repasts for occasions happy and sad—would have been very different if the women of our clan had not been such excellent cooks. Everything we did as a group revolved around good food, lovingly prepared and enjoyed at leisure. Every family gathering and every quiet Sunday centered around a meal; my birthday celebrations were less about presents than about a delicious dish cooked in my honor or a special homemade cake with candles from the five-and-dime. I think this is true in many hardworking families. There may never be enough money for an extravagant gift or vacation, but there is more than enough skill with baked goods and roasts to make up for it. My grandmother came from a family of gifted cooks, and she herself was magnificent in the kitchen. I should emphasize, however, that neither she nor any of her kin was showy about these culinary skills. Cooking was important—the daily, weekly, and annual routine was a main ingredient of my grandmother's and her sisters' lives—but it was nothing to gloat over. Gloating, you see, would not have been *correct,* and the Roberson women did everything correctly, from cooking to cleaning to arranging a funeral. Their faithful, joyful observance of ritual clearly brought happiness to them and to everyone around them, as it imbued even the simplest activity with meaning. And it is a privilege to carry the memory of all that wonderful cooking with me through life.

Until I was ten years old, Bennie Frances cooked on that monstrous wood-burning stove, so large it took up what seemed like a third of the kitchen. When company was coming, she might have all eight burners and the oven going at once, but even when she was only boiling water or making toast, it cast a fearsome heat. That stove was dangerous for a child to be around, so I was never allowed anywhere near it. I had no experience helping in the kitchen. I think that if "Keep back from that stove, Ray!" had not been my grandmother's mantra, I might have learned to cook. As it is, I was frightened off and today can no more bake a biscuit than I can fix a car. I sometimes think this is a sad outcome for a man from a family in which such wonderful food was always on the table. On the other hand, I think my grandmother's concern for my safety is part of what taught me to revere her skills. As a grown man, I am still awed by the love and labor she expended on vegetables and meat. And I remember clearly what a reward it was for her to call out, "Thank you, Ray!" if I gathered up some kindling or buckets of coal for her while she stood over the sink, tearing up a chicken for baking or frying. Custard pies, Argo starch, spittoons, jars, dipping snuff, horse liniment, mustard plaster, chitterlings—all of these kitchen things were important threads of the rich fabric of my childhood life.

As with all the women of her family, my grandmother's aptitude in the kitchen was innate. She did not cook from recipes and in fact did not own one cookbook. She never wrote one thing down, not even if she asked one of her sisters how to make some particularly enjoyable dish. If someone explained a recipe to her, she knew how to make it thenceforward and could modify it to suit her taste. I have memories of her occasionally calling up Pete or Louvenia to clarify an instruction—"Did you say to heat it to three-fifty or four hundred degrees?"—but other than that, all her cooking was done according to an intuitive understanding of what was right. Like most cooks, she measured ingredients out by teaspoons, tablespoons, and cups, but as for how *many* cups of flour, buttermilk, or water something took, how *much* butter or seasoning, that information she kept in her head. Bennie Frances Davis did not experiment with the cuisines of different regions or nations, or bring desserts to the table on fire. With minimal fuss, she prepared a variety of foods simply and well, so that my experience of eating in her home was that food was something intrinsically wonderful, to be savored rather than fretted over.

The women of the Roberson family practiced a style of cooking that had come down to them from slavery times, called "dump cooking," which is a pithy way of saying cooking by instinct. The secrets of dump cooking were all kept in the well-organized drawers, cabinets, and pantry of my grandmother's kitchen. She didn't need anything fancy. Her pots and pans were cast iron and aluminum, and she cooked in the same half dozen her entire life. (I still have most of them and love to think of the delicious meals she could make with those time-worn implements. The old black skillet, smooth with age, and her nickel-colored aluminum pots, slightly dinged and slope-bottomed after so many years of use, strike me as some of the most elegant objects I possess, because they pay homage to my grandmother's uncomplicated way of living. They still sit in the kitchen, where they remind me of the marvelous things she could prepare.) She did not have to run out for fresh cilantro, truffle oil, or leeks every time she wanted to prepare a dish. She kept a large tin canister of flour and another of sugar; she fried things in lard or vegetable oil; and her spice cabinet was stocked with basic, flavorful ingredients such as good cayenne pepper and ground sage.

The smell of my grandmother's kitchen varied from day to day, but it was always tantalizing. In my early childhood, this was partly because of the smell of the wood-burning stove, which, as you know if you have ever cooked over a Boy Scout campfire or eaten an apple-smoked ham, imparts a delicious aroma to even the most mundane dishes. But Mama's cooking would have smelled good even if she'd done it over a kerosene flame in a cast-off metal drum. The bread dough rising in a sunny spot by the window; the bacon slowly crisping in its own fat; even the steam rising off a pot of green beans could spark my imagination and set my stomach rumbling. The extracts of lemon and vanilla my grandmother used in her frequent baking were part of the backdrop of my day-to-day experiences as a child; cakes and pies announced their presence to my eager nose long before they made their grand debuts on the sideboard. In my grandmother's house it was always biscuits releasing their perfume of butter, or butter melting on biscuits—two of the most wonderful smells I have ever known. (And on Sundays, she made an extra pan of biscuits—twelve of them!—solely for me to enjoy. I sometimes finished the whole batch before they grew cold.) Always having such delectable scents rising from a mixing bowl, bubbling on the stove, or seeping out of the oven made me feel very secure as a child. Though, like most children, I sometimes found the world outside my door imperfect, I never sensed that it was overarchingly ugly or threatening. The minute I returned home, my grandmother's thoughtful words calmed any mental agitation I'd suffered during the day, and the warmth and aroma of her kitchen soothed my senses. (I often miss the smells of her house and her cooking, but one of the things that makes me miss them the most is the smell of New York City in the summertime. As someone who grew up around pound cake and biscuits, I can't imagine anything more jangling to the nerves than the odors of frankfurters and sauerkraut, wafting over every street corner, admixed with the stink of bus exhaust.) The potpourri of smells in her kitchen—from stove-top corn bread to stewed dumplings in butter—permeated my life.

Every summer when the peaches came ripe, she would go out to the peach trees, pick all the fruit, cut it up by hand, and can it or make it into preserves. She did the same with our damson plums, and, that one time, with those hard-won, succulent blackberries. This was truly a labor of love, because the North Carolina summers were brutally hot, and we did not have air-conditioning. Though it might be ninety-eight degrees in the shade, my grandmother would put a big pan on the stove—a pan as large as the top of an end table—and boil those vats of sweet fruit down. I couldn't imagine how she stood there patiently stirring in the sugar without collapsing from the heat. In addition to making the preserves or preparing the peaches for canning, she had to boil and prepare the jars, and the cleanup afterward (with which I helped) was quite a chore. At the appropriate time she also put up tomatoes, green beans, carrots, and sweet relish. All of this seemed to me a relic of an almost pioneer lifestyle, yet she did it seemingly unaware of the labor involved. She enjoyed canning and preserving, and the pleasure we both took in the products of her labor clearly justified the means for her. To her, this was all just normal. It was part of her living.

My grandmother cooked with a sense of occasion even when there was no occasion to speak of, when, for example, the two of us ate a quiet meal together on a weeknight. Sundays *were* considered occasions, so we had a more elaborate dinner then, and any kind of family function was accompanied by prodigious quantities of food. One thing about a black Southern family: No matter why people are getting together, they will be well fed. Baking was to her what bridge is to the leisured lady. With her giant glass rolling pin (sadly now lost in some move), in the blink of an eye, she could roll out enough biscuits to last from breakfast to supper.

The dishes my grandmother favored were uncomplicated, but they set each other off in wonderful ways. On an ordinary night, we might have a single simple dish, such as baked chicken, meatloaf, or her incomparable macaroni and cheese, accompanied by lima beans, corn, okra, or some other vegetable that complemented and highlighted the main course. Usually we also had some of her homemade biscuits or bread. Another common dish when I was growing up was chicken and dumplings: chicken, chicken stock, and dough rolled into little dumplings. My grandmother had a cousin, Bessie (now long since passed on), who would sometimes come to church with a pan of chicken and dumplings for my grandmother to take home. We never knew when such a heartfelt, homemade gift might come our way, but some ordinary Sunday, there it would be for us.

On a Sunday, my grandmother liked us to have a bountiful and special meal; but rather than cook more complicated foods, she would prepare multiple dishes. For Sunday dinner, it was never one meat or one main course, one vegetable. If my grandmother wanted to prepare stewed beef for the Lord's day, she would bake or fry chicken as well. I can still see her quartering a chicken and leaving it to soak on a Saturday afternoon, so that she could simply roll it in seasoned flour when we came home from church and drop it into a boiling pan of fat. If we had okra, we also had sweet potatoes, green beans, or lima beans; corn on the cob in the summertime or creamed corn in the winter; or well-seasoned collards or turnip greens, boiled with a ham hock for flavor.

Potatoes might be baked, boiled, mashed, roasted with a chicken, twice deep-fried for a crispness no fast-food chain can approximate. A Sunday breakfast included sausage links or patties, thick-cut bacon, and ham either smoked by Uncle Ira or brought from Virginia by some relative traveling south to visit us. Sometimes I split my grandmother's biscuits in half and buttered them, but sometimes I couldn't resist eating them straight out of the baking pan. Either way, I ate them with great pleasure, and as often as not running with puddles of blackstrap molasses. She also thought nothing of whipping up a pan of corn bread, and did so with as little fuss as someone else might heat a can of soup. Sometimes she baked corn bread in the oven, and sometimes she fried it in a skillet on the stove; either way, the result was delicious. In today's world, fresh biscuits and corn bread are rare luxuries, but in my grandmother's, they were very much part of the routine of our lives.

Another of the beauties of Sundays was that there was always more than one dessert to choose from. Frequently my grandmother made Jell-O into which she put peaches and orange slices and, to my delight, turned it out jiggling from the aluminum Bundt pan onto a plate. Along with the Jell-O, Mama might make some variety of pie, with a homemade Crisco crust—peach pie was probably my favorite, but she also excelled at cherry, blueberry, and apple pies, sometimes with hand-cut latticework crust atop the fruit. She often made custard pies, such as egg or coconut, and sweet potato pies and puddings were also Sunday favorites.

My grandmother's true genius, however, was for cake baking. In all my life, every cake she produced was level, fluffy, moist, and perfectly flavored; and every type of cake she made was great. There was a devil's food cake and a richer German chocolate cake, her famous lemon pound cake, a pineapple cake that everyone in the family raved about, and, my own favorite, her coconut cake. To make it, she bought a fresh coconut from the market and enacted a whole ritual: drilling a hole with an ice pick so she could extract the milk, hacking up the coconut, and shredding and washing its tender meat. The coconut cake was a layer cake with white icing that turned even the quietest supper into a grand finale.

At a family gathering, my grandmother's cooking was truly monumental. The sideboard often looked like it would collapse under the weight of all the pies and fruitcakes, the sweet potato pudding, the coconut cake. The turkey she cooked at Christmas was a major, major thing—nearly as big as the oven itself and roasted until the skin was crisp and brown, though the meat was tender. We had a Christmas tree, but it wasn't the center of our celebration; that huge turkey was. Food was the next most important thing to church and family; and of course, it had a great deal to do with both.

Every year around Thanksgiving, my grandmother prepared her special Christmas fruitcakes. This was something she had done annually with her own mother, and I have memories of her making those cakes with Great-grandmother China when I was very young; mostly, though, I remember this task as belonging especially to my grandmother. She would make the cakes, with rum and sliced apples, wrap them in cheesecloth, and store them, unsliced, in a cool part of the pantry until Christmas Day. I loved the smell of the fruitcakes as she made them and as they ripened in their dark corner. Their fragrance when she at last cut into them was magnificent.

In junior high school, I discovered Truman Capote's wonderful memoir, *A Christmas Memory,* I was astonished at how much it reminded me of my life with my grandmother. We were both happy thenceforward when, every year, an adaptation of *Christmas Memory* was televised. (Because we did not have a color television, I always thought the movie was in black and white. A few years ago, I was shocked to see it in full color! Somehow, the movie did not have the same emotional resonance that it had had in my memory, when so much of its beauty was left to the imagination.) What a privileged childhood Truman had with his unconventional aunt Sook, who sent fruitcakes to strangers, even to the president in the White House! It was only by chance that I came across Truman's precious memoir, and yet I felt that he had written my own narrative—the story of a life that was sometimes lonely yet also extremely rich. Truman's book expressed perfectly the way my grandmother and I had our whole world together, the way things were understood silently. Our spoken conversations were very important to us, but the silent ones mattered just as much. Although I was a child and she was an adult woman, Mama and I had a deep understanding of each other. I was able to look up to her in everything without having to look up to her in a forced or specific way. I had never seen a relationship like ours described anywhere and was profoundly thankful to Mr. Capote for having written about one.

To this day I cherish this small book, and I try to read it every year sometime between Thanksgiving turkey and Christmas Eve, for in some ways it seems like my life growing up with my grandmother. From the first time I read it, I saw that this was a rare and special portrayal of the love that can bond two people together, even if they are of vastly different ages—something that much of the world seems to find it difficult to comprehend. My grandmother and I, like Truman and his aunt Sook, were happy with each other in a simple, unaffected way. I felt like the message Truman's memoir sent out into the world was much like the message I often wanted to send from me and my grandmother, when I was growing up: "Listen, we two are on a journey together, hitched to the same dog cart. Do not break our hearts, and we won't interfere with anyone else."

It wasn't until 1959 that my grandmother's huge cast-iron stove was hauled out to the backyard and taken away on a truck. Much less appealing (though easier to work with and maintain) was the gleaming white enamel electric range, which obviously saved my grandmother a lot of labor. She was excited about her new purchase and learned to use it with the same consummate skill with which she'd managed our former behemoth. But I truly missed that old stove. It had meant a great deal to me, as a small child in a world unpeopled by men, to sit in the glow of the woodstove's fire. Mama's cooking remained phenomenal until very near the end of her days, but for more than forty years now, I have missed the heat, the sound, and the smell of the way she cooked in my earliest memories.

My grandmother was one of the best cooks I've ever known; I know now that, because my grandmother's generation had grown up in hard times, when food wasn't always abundant, in childhood my life revolved around food. There was no escaping it! What else would we have done on Aunt Pete's porch than sit around eating or talking about what we might eat? The variety of food was incredible, and so was the amount of time that went into preparing and consuming it. But no one ever seemed fatigued by what I can only call the incredible *duration* of all that food. How could they have been? Food was of tantamount interest and importance, and came in enough varieties to stoke conversation for years on end.

My uncle George, for example, was a hunter, so in his deep freeze he had rabbit, squirrel, and all kinds of meat that seemed exotic to a young child. When he brought such trophies home fresh from the hunt, the women of the family skinned them skillfully and without complaint. My grandmother and all the women in her family drew the line at preparing coon meat. Coon was tough and difficult to eat, so women steered clear of it, but Uncle George was fond of his coon. He used to hunt the creatures at night by lantern light. (According to his daughter, my cousin Doris Armstrong, coon meat was somewhat more palatable if cleaned and cooked by their neighbor, a Mr. John Pratt.) Uncle George will also live forever in my memory as the man who first fed me—and showed me how he made—the incredible luxury of home-made ice cream. He had one of those old-fashioned ice cream makers that require sweat and strength to turn the crank on top, as the cream, sugar, and flavorings tumble around in their own container inside a bucket of salt and ice. I lived for his fresh lemon or vanilla ice cream, served in fancy colored glass bowls out on his porch.

And in truth, it wasn't just our family that was obsessed with wonderful food. Our next-door neighbor, Mrs. Addie Coley, was the biscuit and crescent roll baking empress. Her rolls were lighter than snowflakes, and when they broke apart, revealed thin membranes of butter between their perfectly flaky layers. She would make a batch of these incredible rolls, wrap them in a rose-colored linen napkin, stick them in a basket, and show up on our doorstep to present us with them. She always said she did this on a whim, for the pure joy of baking, though doubtless she also did it for the gratifying experience of seeing our excitement. This was one of my favorite childhood moments, when Mrs. Coley would come over with her covered Parker House rolls or a few slices of a cake she'd baked. Sometimes Mrs. Coley's rolls arrived not as a surprise but on request. If my grandmother was expecting a special guest, such as our church pastor, Reverend Alston, or the Sunday afternoon missionary circle, she might go out to the porch, lean over the railing, and call out to Mrs. Addie, asking if she might be willing to whip up some of her rolls. Mrs. Coley always obliged, for she understood what a big thing it was to have one of those meetings at one's home or to have the minister to supper—which, for us, was like having the world's biggest celebrity come over. In those situations, Mrs. Coley's rolls were the caviar to my grandmother's menu.

(Mrs. Addie and her husband, Mr. Birch Coley, were, in untold ways, ideal neighbors. Until he became infirm, he tended our yard, clipping hedges and making sure it all looked neat and pretty. In his own backyard, he had topiary bushes, which were the walls to my secret garden.)

Mrs. Coley, by the by, was the first person on our block to have a double-decker electric oven with glass doors. What a treat it was to stand in her kitchen, watching her cakes turn golden brown, as she sat peeling potatoes or preparing deviled eggs!

Mrs. Vreeland was one of the most sophisticated people I ever met, but her taste in food was as bland as could be. Though she had been raised in France (with a nanny named Pink—the whole nine yards), she preferred simple English food. Shepherd's pie was a perennial favorite, as was Stilton cheese, as were different kinds of salads, never overly complicated. Garden peas were a big favorite of hers, fresh from the pod with a little bit of butter, pepper, and salt. She liked all kinds of porridge for breakfast or lunch. And though she did not particularly have a sweet tooth, she might occasionally want sliced fruit or some kind of fruit crumble or pie, such as a small piece of apple pie with ice cream. The idea that someone so worldly might have such a limited palate was new to me. Stranger still to me was the fact that not one morsel of this food did she ever cook herself. A cook came every day and had absolute dominion over Mrs. Vreeland's kitchen. If Mrs. Vreeland had to speak to Cook in person, she would do so in her dressing room, but most of the time she called her on the telephone from her bedroom or bath, or left some detailed note scrawled on yellow legal paper in bright green ink.

Once, late at night, after a long, entertaining evening of reading and gossiping, we found that we both craved a snack. Cook, however, had long since gone home. Mrs. Vreeland, sitting in her red Georgian dwarf armchair, which flanked her huge boxcar of a chintz sofa, was puzzling over what to do when I suggested, "Why don't we go make ourselves something to eat?"

Mrs. Vreeland's face lit up with a sense of impending adventure. "Good," she said. "Marvelous! Let's go find the kitchen."

The two of us ventured out, laughing, on a mock hunt for that most mysterious of rooms. Mrs. Vreeland's kitchen was, indeed, a place that time had forgotten; for all the money and care she had put into the extravagant décor of her "garden in hell" seraglio, she had never changed anything about her kitchen. The gas stove was the old-fashioned kind, with wide expanses of white enamel to the left and right of the burners and a warming drawer for bread or pies. It, the refrigerator, and the porcelain double sink were exactly as they had been on the day she moved in. Her kitchen was as neat and clean as a hospital, but she hadn't wasted one nickel on the kinds of things people today can't seem to live without—professional refrigerators, convection ovens, pasta makers, bread machines, and the like. Off we went into this uncharted territory in search of something to eat.

We went into the pantry and retrieved the peanut butter. Mrs. Vreeland was wild about Skippy smooth, to the point where, when she later became ill and confined to bed, I remember her one afternoon sitting up like a queen and spooning it elegantly from the jar to her mouth; she must have had a truly intense craving for it. We found strawberry jam in the fridge and white bread in the bread box. We searched through all the cabinets until we had tracked down two dessert plates and a couple of butter knives. We successfully made sandwiches and brought them out to her living room, where we continued laughing until dawn, talking about everything from Mick Jagger to Karen Blixen.

New York in the '70s was a fairly wild place, and the evening Diana Vreeland and I tried to find her kitchen certainly wasn't the most unusual night I passed in those years. I will talk more about the heyday of disco later; but while I am on the topic of food, it seems worthwhile to relate the story of the strangest dinner spread I've yet encountered. This undisputed champion of weird meals was served to me one night when Halston invited me to join him at his Paul Rudolph town house for dinner, just the two of us. Understand that Halston was a sociable fellow, the center of his own clique, and nearly impossible to talk to alone. He was always surrounded by people: his lover, a Venezuelan amusingly named Victor Hugo; Diana Vreeland and Martha Graham; and a whole posse of girls I referred to as the Ultraettes, because they favored the Ultrasuede clothes Halston was designing at that time. This evening promised to be just me and Halston, his dogs, and the huge Marisol Escobar ebony-wood fish sculpture that towered beside the fireplace. I looked forward for days to this rare opportunity to speak with him in a tranquil environment, uninterrupted by other people.

That evening, dinner was served right on time. It consisted of: one baked potato loaded with sour cream and caviar for each of us; frozen vodka in small, chilled glasses; and an absolutely huge heap of white powder—cocaine. The coke was piled up in a neat mound on the coffee table, right next to the food. Tiny sterling silver straws were lined up alongside it, the perfect utensils to complete the mood of impeccable chic. It was the first and last time in my life I ever saw so much cocaine in one place. Halston consumed the chilled vodka and the cocaine and talked; I ate the potatoes and listened. The caviar turned out to be all mine.

When I went home late that night in a taxi, I wondered what Halston would do with all the coke he hadn't sniffed. Would he throw it away? Maybe seal it in a Ziploc Baggie and store it in the stainless steel Sub-Zero refrigerator, so Victor could have it later? Or did he leave it out for his servants to clean up and wonder about (or partake of) the next morning?

It was a strange night indeed for me when I realized that a respected friend might consume nothing but drugs for dinner. I was constantly exposed to drug culture in the '70s—there was no escaping that it was all around me in the fashion world—and I was no naïve country boy about it. But it was a part of those worlds in which I never participated. I had not been raised to turn to substances for amusement. My grandmother may have enjoyed dipping her snuff, but I had hardly ever seen her drink. Most of the alcohol she consumed could be accounted for in the tiny sip of Communion wine she took (and which she passed to the other church members the first Sunday of each month, in her role as the chief of the deaconess board, and all dressed in white). The only other alcohol I ever saw her drinking was ghastly, cheap Manischewitz, which she purchased in the supermarket and stored in the fridge. She said that a glass of wine from time to time was good for the blood, and she may have been right, but I thought my blood would have to be in poor shape before I chose to treat it with that particular tonic. She had no other vices—she certainly never drank a beer or, Heaven forbid, a rum and Coke. Once she confessed to me that she had done a terrible thing: On a whim she had played the numbers, gambled. But that very same night she had a bad dream, and she knew that it was God speaking to her, punishing her for her misdeed. After that, she promised God and herself that she would never play again. Other than an eggnog with a sip of whiskey at Christmastime and her daily dip of snuff, I never again knew her to have any vices.

I will always remember that wild evening at Halston's and will remember it fondly, in no small part because it made me realize how lucky I am to have been raised by and around people who loved to eat, and took their food seriously without ever being sanctimonious about it.

CHAPTER SIX

For me, school was never much of a pleasure, but it was a responsibility I took seriously. I worked hard enough to do as well as I had to. Beyond that, I preferred not to give school a moment's further thought. I loved learning but had discovered early on that my education took place as much out in the world as in the classroom. Perhaps the one thing I learned in school that proved infinitely valuable to me in adult life was touch typing, which enables me to write my *StyleFax* column almost as quickly as I can dream it up. Other than that, I knew that my education was important and tried not to worry about it more than that.

I tried to make myself fit into whatever categories I was supposed to fit into, but I didn't spend much time aping the other students or wondering why they did or didn't like me. I didn't really yearn for other kids' companionship and tended to go straight home when the school bell rang. When I walked through our front door, my great-grandmother was always waiting for me, and I was allowed to play or watch television before supper. Afterward, I did my homework, perhaps watched *The Ed Sullivan Show* on Sundays, and went to bed.

The truth was that I didn't have many playmates. There were friends on my block, but they weren't all a day at the beach. Even if they had been, I'm not sure I would have spent much time with them, because I've always been the kind of person who doesn't necessarily want to go outside to find entertainment. One of the things I most looked forward to doing after school was spending time with my grandmother, even if we weren't doing anything special. I preferred being at home; I *loved* being at home. I loved the warmth and protection of it, and the idea that no threat to my ideas or identity could ever come to me there.

You see, the boys on Cornell Street could be fun, but they made life hell. I was different, and while I did not go around broadcasting my interests to the other kids in school, children do have a way of preying upon those who aren't exactly like them. The nine Smith brothers and Bruce Weaver and his brothers often found ways to torment me. They always had a reason: If it wasn't because I was unlike them, it was the fact that my father gave me extravagant gifts. When I think about those gifts now, I realize that my father, who wasn't always able to express his emotions in words, must have wanted to buy beautiful presents to help safeguard the love of his faraway only son. It touches me to think about the care with which he chose things for me. At the time, I was simply glad to be able to enjoy the spoils of only-child-hood. When I was eight or nine, my father bought me my first bicycle, fire engine red, packed it into the trunk of his car, and hauled it down the Interstate. I couldn't have been more proud of it, or felt more special when I rode it around, thinking of how my father had saved to give it to me. That bike stayed under our porch until I was an adult. One year, my dad brought me a beautiful Mamiya 35-millimeter camera, which I still treasure. And when I decided to join the high school band, he took me downtown and bought me a snare drum. (Later, when I tired of band practice and long hours learning different beats on the drum, I gave that snare to my friend Peter Joyner, but I later retrieved it when I realized how it would have hurt my father's feelings that I had given it away.) I never especially enjoyed or had a real aptitude for sports, so after a time my father quit hoping I might grow up to be a basketball star and stopped giving me sports-related gifts. Before that time, he did once give me a baseball mitt, which I treasured. And I took avidly to the roller skates he bought me; I enjoyed the solitude and isolation they afforded me, the freedom to daydream, and the feeling of gliding that must be one of the closest things we humans can experience to winged flight.

When I was still in grade school, he gave me what I considered the best present ever: a full Western town, complete with buildings, small figures, and an overland stagecoach. That town and my electric train set (also a gift from my father) were my favorite toys; both allowed me to enact scenarios and imagine stories. Nothing could touch that Western town, with its cowboys and horses! I still watch *Gunsmoke* reruns with glee.

Seeing me play with those toys all the time, my grandmother must have deduced that I had a real liking for cowboys and Indians. So when I was around nine, she bought me the very special Christmas present—a fancy Roy Rogers costume, complete with guns and a holster. This would surely have been one of the most magical gifts I'd ever received . . . if only I had not somehow discovered it, a few weeks before Christmas, hidden in a box behind the living room sofa. As soon as I'd opened it, the walls of my childhood fantasies came crashing down around me. I had abruptly ended that chapter of my life in which I could dream on Christmas Eve of Santa Claus. There would be no more imagining Prancer and all those other reindeer traipsing all over our rooftop. I felt sick contemplating that present. I rewrapped it as quickly as I could and shoved it back behind the couch, but that couldn't change what I'd seen.

This was coming of age. After that, Christmas, for all its pleasures, no longer gave me quite the same anticipatory delight. Because religion was so important in our house, we still sang beautiful hymns like "Silent Night," but for me there wasn't much joy in it. When Nat "King" Cole came over the radio singing "Please Come Home for Christmas" that year, it made me sad in a way it's difficult to remember as an adult, because that year my father, working double time, wasn't making it home for the holiday. All I wanted was for him to walk through the door, and that yearning, combined with my disillusionment, made it a grim holiday.

Imagine the pretense of sheer astonishment I plastered across my face when I pulled the wrapping off that box on Christmas morning! There were the clothes, the tooled leather holster, the realistic-looking guns, the ten-gallon hat, the spurs—everything a little boy could desire, and an extravagant gift. But it was hard work trying to feign happiness. Eventually, I managed to convince my grandmother that I was pleased. When we were finished with our presents, I put my costume on and ran outside to show it to some of my friends on the block, Bruce Weaver and Reginald Hinton.

They complimented me on the gift at the time, but less than a week later, they figured out a way to torment me for receiving something so grand. One afternoon, they dug a hole a few feet wide and deep in a neighbor's yard, filled it with mud, and covered it with grass, twigs, and fallen leaves. They then invited me out to play cowboys and Indians. They were the Indians, and I, of course, was Roy Rogers, in my spiffy new gear. We chased each other around the neighborhood hollering, and after a time, they contrived to chase me down the path toward their booby trap. I fell hard into the hole. When I stood up, everything on me was covered with mud and there was a huge gash in my new trousers. In a single instant, my Wild West gear was stripped of all its value and became instead a vehicle of shame. I was confused and humiliated watching those two gleemasters roar with laughter.

I had worn that cowboy shirt and pants only two or three times, but when I went home that afternoon, I cleaned them, folded them up, and put them away, never to be worn again.

We had a cold winter that year, and one day in January, school was called off on account of snow. It was the perfect day—bright sunshine and no wind, so children could enjoy being out in the winter wonderland. I cherished those rare days when my grandmother didn't go to work and stayed home to keep me company. In the morning I went outside to build a snowman and found that the abundant snow packed perfectly. In one of those bursts of creative intensity that seems to pass in the blink of an eye, I created a perfect, three-lump snowman, with two chunks of coal for his eyes, a carrot for his nose, and a long coat made of chips and flakes of black coal. The neighborhood boys, friends and foes alike, peeked over from time to time to see how my work progressed, and I believed I could see their awe at the speed and sureness my hands had suddenly acquired in building this wonderful snow sculpture. Around noon, my grandmother called me in for a lunch of her homemade chicken vegetable soup and crackers. The kitchen was cozy with the heat of the stove. After lunch, I took her to the front of the house, intending to show her my beautiful morning's work. But when I returned to the front yard, I saw that my snowman had been tumbled to the ground and squashed. I immediately turned to Bruce, who said he'd had nothing to do with the destruction; rather, Reginald Hinton had waited like a fox to steal into the yard when I went inside. That was really the last straw between me and Reginald. I no longer wanted to talk to him.

My father lacked the ability to grasp my situation and always said he thought that Bruce and Reginald were nice boys. Whenever he'd come to Durham with one of his wonderful gifts—an entire set of World Book Encyclopedias, bound in shiny red imitation-leather cardboard, or my first television set—he would say, "I hope you'll share it with the other boys in the neighborhood." I could never explain to him that Bruce was the only one I could ever forgive long enough to invite over. Meanwhile, my father wondered why I didn't play with the other boys more. But the snowman incident made me remember that both Reginald and Bruce could be dangerous, and as much as possible, I avoided them for the next few years. As adults, however, Bruce and I continue to be friends. I still manage to see him almost every year when I go home to visit; one year, I ran into him in Paris, on the Rue Faubourg.

"Hey, Ray!" I heard a familiar voice shouting. When I turned around, I was shocked to see him.

We were really happy to see each other, which was doubtless why he ribbed me so. In the first five minutes of our conversation, he chided me for not being married yet and professed disbelief at seeing my hair go gray. (His was just as silvery and had been for some time.) Bruce seems not to remember any of the bad times we had as kids; he's the kind of optimist for whom the best times shine through. For my part, I gladly forgive him his pranks, because he's grown into such a kind and trustworthy man, and a very good friend. I have not, however, forgotten those incidents.

Sadly, Bruce and Reginald were not the only banes of my elementary school existence: There was also Kenneth Green. Kenneth was the worst kind of duplicitous—smart, sociable, and good-looking. He had a real knack for getting other kids in trouble. Once, during vacation Bible school, we were tossing balls at recess against the brick wall of my uncle Lewis's church. Kenneth kept egging me on to throw the ball higher, until finally I threw it high enough to break a stained-glass window. Then Kenneth vanished, as such people will. My uncle and his wife, Aunt Noonie, who was a schoolteacher and had a personality I can only describe as ice queen, made such a big fuss about the broken window, I thought my family might turn against me forever. For two weeks, I believed I had ruined my life with disgrace, though the window was fixed almost overnight. I truly loved my uncle Lewis. He was a kind man, a barber, and he drove absolutely the biggest, flashiest car, a '57 Chevrolet with enormous fins, and had the biggest house and the best china. Aunt Noonie was imposing, but Uncle Lewis was one of my favorite relatives, and I couldn't bear the thought of him being angry at me. One interesting fact about this incident: Although my grandmother regarded churches and their property as highly as she regarded anything, she never punished me for this flagrant misdeed. She knew that I had been punished sufficiently by Aunt Noonie's disapproval.

As I mentioned earlier, I could not go to Sunday school at Mt. Sinai because it was too far away; I went to First Calvary, Kenneth's family church, which was up on the corner of Moorehead Avenue, near Kenneth's house. Theirs was a large two-story house, in which Kenneth lived with his mother. (It was hard to tell if Kenneth had ever had a father, and if so, where he'd gone.) One morning as we stood outside the church, waiting to go in to class together, Kenneth handed me a small parcel, a neatly wrapped square thing of shiny plastic. "What is this?" I asked, unable to figure out what the mysterious object could be.

"I don't know," he said. "I was thinking you might show it to the teacher—maybe she'd know."

So I stuck the little parcel in my pocket.

After we had finished our lessons for the day, I walked up to our Sunday school teacher and asked her if she knew what was in the package. When she said she didn't, I asked if she would mind opening it and telling me. The teacher unwrapped it, and her face went blank with shock because—as I'm sure you've guessed—the thing Kenneth had given me was a condom. The teacher got up from her desk, and escorted me home and through the screen door to talk to my grandmother about how I had acquired this foreign object and why I thought it was an appropriate thing to introduce into the classroom. In referring to the condom, she used the term that was considered correct at the time—a merryweather.

My grandmother knew that I wasn't at the root of this caper, and when I told her and my teacher that Kenneth had put me up to asking about the parcel, they both believed me. I was not punished, and Kenneth received his due reprimands. For weeks he went around wearing a decided scowl and kept promising to "get" me. I kept my distance and never sat next to him in Sunday school again. He still knew how to get me, though, and once in grade school I got so angry at him that I threw a textbook at him, right in the middle of class, which struck him squarely in the back of the head. Mrs. Alston took me into the cloakroom and beat the palm of my hand with a ruler, which, though not ideal, was much less humiliating than having it done right in front of the class.

Boys really were trouble in my neighborhood, there was no getting around it. A friend of mine knocked up one of my cousins while we were still in high school, and she had to have an abortion. It was perhaps the biggest of those silent scandals, such as cancer or divorce, that no one in my family talked about but which I and my teenage cousins knew about in almost lurid detail. Around that same time, there was a much older boy, practically out of high school, who lived down the street. He had a fancy secondhand car and was the star of the First Calvary choir; he stuttered when he spoke, but he sang like an angel. He started out early on his life's journey. He, too, got a girl pregnant while still in high school, but he did right by her: married her and got a decent job working at Duke University. I didn't hear of him again until a few years later, when my grandmother greeted me at dinner with the shocking news that he had killed a man.

"Truly?" I asked. He seemed as mild-mannered as any man I knew.

"He came into work early one morning carrying a revolver and shot one of his co-workers stone cold dead, just like that."

It was horrible to think about. "Does anyone know why?"

"He must have gone sour over something that'd been said, or maybe something having to do with his wife. He just walked into work, aimed, and fired."

I followed his trial with sadness as well as interest but could not help thinking it just that he received a long prison sentence. When he finished doing his time, he moved away and changed his name. No one has heard of him since, but I do remember once, when I was home visiting from Brown, that my grandmother was having a telephone conversation with Willie Mae Thompson, who was a cousin of hers by marriage, and an expression of wonder passed across her face. She repeated his name into the telephone and hung up only a few minutes later.

"Has there been any news of him?" I asked.

"No. But Willie Mae says her husband still misses the sweetest sound he ever had the experience of hearing—the sound that emerged from his throat, more beautiful than a nightingale's song."

All of this is not to say that I never had any boy-bonding experiences. There were years, for example, when I belonged to the Cub Scouts, but I confess that the thing I truly cared about was the uniform: that sprightly yellow kerchief, the hat. I was also crazy about the furniture in den leader Miss Katherine Shaw's living room, the first pseudo–French country furniture I'd ever sat upon. (It certainly hadn't come from Durham, but somehow, as if by magic, she had acquired an entire suite of woven cane-back chairs and a settee.) Miss Shaw's house was an expression of tasteful style. It was a pale mint green on the outside and was the first house that I recall having what seemed at the time like something truly extravagant: wall-to-wall carpeting. This carpet was beige and so thick your feet sank into it when you stood up to walk to the silver tray of milk and cookies she'd placed on a side stand. Those same "friends" who'd dug the hole and tricked me into tearing my Roy Rogers outfit were the other den members.

I've heard from other men that their Cub Scout days were full of adventure, but ours were fairly placid. When we went on "field trips," Miss Shaw didn't need to accompany us, because all we did was go to the ballpark down the street, opposite Lyon Park Elementary. She and the other neighborhood women could peek out their windows to see that we were fine. One of the Scouts was a few years older than the rest of us, and he always took responsibility when we went out to wander. We usually went on walks in the woods, often stopping to look for tadpoles in a stream. We would bring empty Mason jars and fill them up with murky stream water full of tadpoles swimming every which way. I loved hunting for tadpoles.

This older boy was all animal magnetism; he looked like a young, black Ricky Ricardo, with dark, dense, wavy hair that lay flat to his forehead. He was as handsome as any of the conked-hair soul singers we all loved to watch on *American Bandstand* or the *Ed Sullivan Show.* I was afraid of him and tried to avoid him exactly as I avoided the daddy longlegs spiders in the corners of my grandmother's house. You see, he had already physically come of age, and his awareness of the difference between his body and ours, and of the discomfort this caused the rest of us, became a prime topic during these woodland adventures. On one such outing, when, of course, we had no adult chaperone, he decided that our regular tadpole hunt would be replaced by his own personal demonstration of masturbation.

He unzipped his trousers and went at it furiously. This in itself made me wince, because it seemed as if he must be inflicting pain on that part of himself, which I knew only as a conduit for pee. We were all, as you can imagine, simultaneously repelled and fascinated by his ministrations to himself. I remember that he had his feet anchored on a rock, and that he produced a little goo, which looked like what happened when my grandmother was boiling Argo starch on the stove and neglected to lower the heat in time. I could only think of how the gooey white substance that emerged from his exposed sex—which seemed to us little boys to be of an abnormally large size—looked like what my grandmother dipped my white church shirts and blue church underwear in. I realized, as I watched him finish up, that I was basically indifferent to him and all those other Cubs, that I hated those exploratory field walks and would rather have been at home cutting out pages from *Vogue* or *Harper's Bazaar.* But it was, of course, at that moment that he decided to try and get a rise out of me.

He gathered his few drops of excretion into one of our empty Mason jars and handed it over to me. "You should take that home and drink it," he said. "It's like milk."

Does he think I'm that dumb? I wondered. But I was afraid of being humiliated in front of the group, and for some reason thought that the best way to avoid that would in fact *be* to play into his game. "What should I do with it?" I asked. "Put it in the icebox?"

They all laughed at me. All I could think of to do was to hurl the jar at his feet, where it broke into several large, clear chunks. The boys were all still laughing, so I ran away, thinking that in a matter of minutes they'd show up in a pack behind me and beat the daylights out of me. Nothing doing. They were too happy to stay there laughing. I stopped running when I realized they weren't going to hurt me.

When they caught up to me at an ambling gait, all he said was, "You're not a man, André. You should have drunk it, so you could become a man."

That afternoon remained a secret between me, him, and the other Cubs. But verbal scars can last as long and hurt as badly as physical wounds, and I never wanted to go back to the Cub Scout meetings. I retired my uniform, folding it up neatly and sticking it in the drawer with my Roy Rogers outfit. Miss Shaw would often stop by on her way to church and ask why I didn't come to den meetings any longer. Every time I came up with an excuse—I had too much homework, or had been sick with a cold, or had been up to my ears in household chores. She always expressed her desire to see me at meetings again, but I didn't want to go back after what had happened.

Another only child might have taken some solace in the company of a pet, but we never did get a cat or dog of our own. Instead, I surrounded myself with a universe of imaginary friends to whom I spoke frequently in my head. Most of them were girls.

We did have a stray cat for a while, whom I called Betty. She was a tuxedo cat with a black nose and yellow eyes, and she ambled back and forth between our house and Mrs. Addie Coley's, accepting handouts and back scratches from anyone willing to provide them. And at Easter, my grandmother always selected a baby chick from the five-and-dime and brought it home to me. They were frail little things resembling nothing more than cotton balls dyed yellow and blue, my favorite colors. I kept them in a shoebox, which for some reason I stored on the lid of the toilet tank, back behind the seat. I distinctly remember one Good Friday when a pale, feathery hatchling fell into the toilet bowl. I suppose he must have been trying to fly, or had at least been hopping around; at all events, he landed in the water and practically drowned. When I discovered the nearly weightless body floating there in toilet water slightly yellowed from the dye on his feathers, his dark eyes seemed lifeless. I lifted him out, ripped a piece of Alcoa aluminum foil from the roll, and placed the poor, half-dead chick on the heating elements of the electric oven. Our oven, unlike Mrs. Addie's, didn't have a glass door, so I just left the oven door open, and watched the heating coils go bright red. By the time I realized that this might not actually be the healthiest thing for the chick, it was too late; its yellow body, shriveled and matted, no longer moved. Grandmother came into the kitchen from the porch, and when she saw what had happened, said not one unkind or scolding word. She understood that this was my first true confrontation with the loss of a living thing, and she was very gentle with me as we buried the dead chick together.

At the time I thought I would never want another chick, but by next Easter, I was eager to have one again, so my grandmother brought one home, this time in bright blue. One afternoon before Easter I took the chick out on the porch to play, and Betty the cat came by and snatched it up in her mouth. I went screaming after her, chasing her the whole length of our yard, into the Coleys', and all around the secret garden, with its elegantly clipped box hedges. Around and around we went, Betty way ahead and never letting go of that chick, which she held tightly in her needle-sharp teeth. Somehow I thought to grab a broom, and as she ran up a tree, I raced up behind her and whacked her on the spine. That caught her attention; she dropped the chick, looked at me with a shocked, pained expression, and tore off down the street. The chick was long since dead, and Betty was never seen on our block again.

I cried for hours, and intermittently for days and days. I gathered up the little blue body and cried over that. I took it to our own backyard, dug a hole, and gave it a full burial in a fresh, clean shoebox. There were no more baby chicks after that, no more little-kid pleasures like Easter egg hunts. The death of those two chicks changed my life every bit as much as had my discovery that there was no Santa Claus. I had dreamed of those two chicks growing into the chickens I loved and which I would see walking around my Aunt Pete's country yard, gobbling up corn kernels and chicken feed outside her huge kitchen.

Luckily, I was good at entertaining myself with other fantasies—all kinds of dreams and ambitions. My grandmother was very good company, but there is something intrinsically lonely about being an only child in a world where most people have siblings or at least two parents instead of only one. I didn't have another kid in the house to trade stories with at night or after church, or more than one tired parent to look to for entertainment, so I learned early on to turn to books for much of my adventure life. This made my grandmother very, very proud. When I would go to spend weekends with my father in D.C., rather than take me to the ballpark, he would take me to the Library of Congress, where we would amble through the reading rooms in search of knowledge. It was there that he introduced me to the works of the great Frederick Douglass and there that he might sit on a Saturday afternoon, catching up on black history while I plunged into whatever topic was dearest to my imagination at the time.

Books were my world. I loved everything about them—the musty, disintegrating smell of volumes that hadn't been opened in years and the heady aroma of a brand-new art book with glossy illustrations; the brightly colored graphics on paperback jackets and the faded red, orange, or green spines of library bindings; the sticky-smooth plastic on the books one could take home and the rough, goatskin feel of the revered books in the reference section. There was nothing like taking out one of my schoolbooks (barring the mathematics and biology texts, to which I never did take a shine) or hunting something down by Dewey decimal in the library and delving into a whole new world.

One of my favorite times to read a book was when I was traveling on a bus or train. There were all those uninterrupted hours and the gentle rhythm of covering ground to help keep me within the walls of my fantasy world. Twice a year, my grandmother and I made the trek to Washington, D.C., where we visited my divorced parents and did our seasonal shopping in the big department stores. I cherished those trips as much for the journey itself as for the visits. On one such trip, when I was thirteen, my grandmother sat by the window while I sat on the aisle, and we rolled up I-95, with delicious deviled eggs, fried chicken legs, biscuits, and pound cake packed neatly into a clean shoebox. I selected *Madame Bovary,* and it was thus that, on the Interstate, I became acquainted with one of the great masterpieces of all time, one of the books that has most influenced my ideas and aesthetics. It was a joy beyond measure to be safely next to my grandmother on a Greyhound bus and simultaneously to be in Flaubert's world of drama, intrigue, and beautiful prose.

When I got to high school, I parlayed my love of books into my first job, a student librarian at the school library. My grandmother could not have been more delighted when I came home to tell her I'd been hired. And I loved shelving books, helping other kids find them, recommending books when asked, even stamping the due date on the card inserted into the back page pocket. Being around books all the time like that gave me tremendous joy. They were, after all, one of the surest means of escape from the everyday. Movies were pretty much off limits. In those days, Jim Crow still reigned. We had to sit upstairs in the balcony, segregated from the white audience; so the only times we went were those rare occasions when Cousin Willie came by to escort us to the Carolina Theatre in downtown Durham. Willie had what I considered dreadful taste in films—with him it was always some horror flick, like *The Fall of the House of Usher.* All I wanted to see was glamour: Jean Harlow, Bette Davis, Carole Lombard, Katharine Hepburn, and Elizabeth Taylor.

These women, you see, were already vibrantly alive to me through the pages of *Vogue,* which, since the time I turned eight or nine, had reliably provided me safe passage into the exotic world of the international jet set. While other boys may have been out practicing their fastballs or trying to break track records, I was on the couch, enrapt in the pages of the world Diana Vreeland had invented, a world of fantasy, style, and exquisite fashion.

I am not sure quite when my interest in fashion began, a moment in which I spied a fashion magazine and thought, without any cues from anyone around me, *Perhaps that would be the thing for me; I think I'll have a look at it.* I do, however, know that this interest was cultivated and refined through *Vogue,* as well as through the *New York Times* fashion pages, which, at that time, did not yet reproduce photographs but contained marvelous sketches of the latest styles. At some point in my formative years, I simply realized that I really liked *Vogue* (which I first saw in the school library), and it became one of my Sunday rituals, after church and dinner were finished, to walk across town, across the railroad tracks, to the Duke University campus, and to spend my pocket money on a thick stack of magazines. (As a child I spent lots of time walking around the city; thanks to my fear of snakes, I would never go alone for a walk in the woods. Even today, although I love trees, I would much rather look at them from my house or out a car window than go walking or, God forbid, bike riding in a deeply wooded area!) Only the *Times* came out weekly, but in those days, most magazines came out twice a month; there was a January 1 issue of *Vogue* and another on January 15. (This persisted, at *Vogue* at least, until 1971.) It was a big thing for me to go out and buy these magazines; I anticipated both the walk and the reading all week. Not only because I enjoyed looking at the images, but because I was fascinated by the way the magazines described the clothes, the music, the people they spoke of. I loved reading the *Boutique* and *Observation* pages. These pages pictured all the with-it young people—Halston, Berry Berenson, Loulou de la Falaise—in the very hippest locations, such as Paraphernalia or the Electric Circus. They were always photographed wearing the most fabulous things in these face pages. You'd see men in beautiful clothes in the *Men in Vogue* pages. *Vogue* especially had a distinct and worldly style that seemed innately right to me and to which I had an immediate connection. It was visually inspiring, and I felt that it was possible to live an entire life of the imagination through the pages.

I don't know if any of the boys in the neighborhood knew about my secret passion (I certainly didn't go out of my way to tell them about it), but I do remember that once, as I was walking across the railroad tracks, a handful of pebbles hit me, which some white boys had thrown from a passing car. I entered the main gates of Duke's East Campus, on my usual route to buy my weekly reading material. The gravel that had scraped at me could not diminish my pleasure in the heft of the big, fat Sunday *Times* as it swung in a black plastic bag from my hand, nor could it deny me the many hours of entertainment that newspaper would provide.

I was a true convert of fashion by the age of twelve. I was reading everything I could get my hands on—scrutinizing those fashion sketches in the *Times* and drinking in images classical and modern, traditional and daring with the same eager eye. John Fairchild's classic book *The Fashionable Savages* was my correspondence course primer. One afternoon, searching through my beloved card catalogue at the public library by the bus depot, I stumbled upon the card for his book, which looked intriguing. When I took it down from the shelf, I realized that it was my passport into the world I had only dreamed of. I read it so many times I practically memorized it. There in its pages were C. Z. Guest (now a long-standing, wonderful friend and a true inspiration), wearing her flawless Mainbocher and photographed by Tony Palmieri. There, too, was Jackie Kennedy—whom Mr. Fairchild so correctly called Her Elegance—dressed perfectly for evening in a strapless gown and perfectly for day in a wide-collared coat and hat. There was Mlle. Chanel, in her impeccable suit, with her strong opinions about the female form. These women and their images fueled my imagination, as did those in many other books, notable among them

Marilyn Bender's *The Beautiful People,* which is surely one of the best books ever written on the culture of fashion.

But *Vogue:* Somehow, I just knew that *Vogue* was the pinnacle of everything for me. I knew who Diana Vreeland was just as I knew who all the beautiful people were in the 1960s. The people in the pages of *The Fashionable Savages* and the magazines came to seem like my classmates, role models, and friends. So you see, I knew Mrs. Vreeland years before I met her; she was my mentor even when I was a teenager. Not only did I admire her work, I read every profile of her I could find. I loved poring over the pages she created, the fabulous, often shocking ways she paired images. Even now, if you are lucky enough to be able to view a copy of her coffee-table book *Allure,* which she wrote with Christopher Hemphill (under the editorship of none less than Jackie Kennedy Onassis), the way she paired images seems revolutionary. Only she could put Irving Penn's blunt, abstract pictures of lips and fingernails into the same milieu as Edward Steichen's wispily evocative early twentieth-century photographs of Poiret mannequins, or put Anna Magnani's smile with Maria Callas's grimace, and have the dream logic of her composition be at once so evocative and so clear. When I was in high school, I remember vividly that Mrs. Vreeland went through a phase of doing lots of fantasy photo shoots for *Vogue.* She would have Vanessa Redgrave dressed up like a Romney portrait, or Greta Garbo as Queen Christina.

That sense of grandeur rubbed off on me; I intuitively connected with it, and it fired my imagination. So when you see me now coming out of a party in some extravagant Galliano-Dior coat from Paris, or carrying a Fendi Russian sable muff big enough for a child to sit in, that's something that just comes from my childhood. That was the way I was, and that was what I loved. I had a loving, nurturing home to grow up in, but in many ways I had to make my own world. And it was a world of the imagination that I created. I only shared my world with my grandmother, and only as I approached adulthood did I find myself able to share it with certain carefully chosen friends. In high school, it was pretty much all mine. In my teenage years I was also listening to lots of the wonderful music that was changing the world at that time—Marvin Gaye, for example, and Laura Nyro—but something was more influential, at the very base of how I saw things, and that was Diana Vreeland. From years of observing, following her lead, I think I learned everything I know about fashion, decorating, and, this was one of her favorite words, *splendor.* I must simply have had an innately acute visual sense, because in the same way that some kids gravitate to horses or NASCAR racing, looking at things was what I related to. I loved looking at pictures, at people, at the living rooms in my aunts' houses . . . I loved beauty in its every form, high or low, and from my earliest childhood that found its expression.

Another of my great pleasures was to watch television: *The Carol Burnett Show* and my absolute favorite, Julia Child's cooking show on Channel Thirteen, the local PBS station. These shows carried me far beyond my daily life in North Carolina, into a world of humor, glamour, and best of all, French cooking. As I mentioned, we did not have a color TV; this was all still the black-and-white era, and viewed on a relatively small screen. I loved everything about Julia Child—I loved her kitchen, her accent, the clipped and musical way she said, *"Bon appétit!"* It was fascinating to watch Julia Child stuff a chicken or tie up asparagus. Once my aunt Pat sat there with me and couldn't believe I would choose to watch Julia Child pull a threaded needle through the skin of a hen. This *amazed* her, but I don't know why; after all, she had sat around with our extended family on many long, lazy summer afternoons, filling my head with crazy stories about cooking as much as about any other part of life. She herself had told me about a time she'd cooked eel for an Italian couple she'd worked for. She had never cooked eel before, and when they told her to fry it, she dipped it in batter, tossed it in the skillet, browned it, and figured that was that. She served the fried eel for lunch and put the leftovers aside under cover. The next day when she arrived for work, she uncovered the eel and found it wriggling out of its fried coat! Mind you, my interest wasn't in actually learning to *cook*. No, it was the style of Julia Child's cooking I was interested in and her remarkable Frenchness, via her California roots.

My grandmother thought nothing of this. As long as I took an interest in the world around me, she didn't care to designate some things as suitable and others as off-limits. (She herself didn't watch much television. I don't recall her having a favorite show, and if she had the TV on, it was usually while she was talking on the phone.) She'd be in the kitchen, putting the finishing touches on our Sunday dinner or laying it out on the table, and I would be in the living room, watching Julia Child. This became part of my Sunday ritual every bit as much as church and the magazines. Around six in the evening Mama and I would have a light supper and perhaps some more cake; then we'd watch Ed Sullivan together at eight, and soon after, I'd retire to bed.

You see, Mama never once questioned my hobbies. If I liked watching a faux French lady cook on television, that was fine. If I wanted to sit there looking at *Vogue,* that was okay, too. (At the time, I was also looking at *National Geographic,* also because the photographs so encouraged me to dream, and I don't remember her ever suggesting that one might be more suitable reading matter than the other.) She allowed me to do anything I liked, as long as it didn't harm others or myself. She understood that the images I was gathering through magazines and television were helping me to define what would eventually become my world.

"Well, what do you want to be when you grow up, Ray?" Cousin Avant asked me one Sunday after church.

"Oh, I don't know," I told him, a child's pat response. But I *had* thought a lot about my potential future career as I pored over my collection of magazines, so I decided to go ahead and tell him. "Well, okay. I'm going to be a fashion editor at a magazine!"

His mute response was a dazed and disgusted look, in which he furrowed his brow until it was as wrinkly as an old man's, shrugged his shoulders, and walked out of my room. His rudeness stung me, though, as you know, if it had any effect on what I eventually chose to do with my life, it was to spur me on. Still, I felt as if he'd betrayed me by asking for a confidence and then shrugging it off. I thought about his reaction as I sat on the edge of my bed and looked out the window, and I realized that his opinion didn't matter much to me, not in my heart. But after that incident in my bedroom, I decided to keep my dreams more firmly to myself, and I never discussed them again with any but my female friends until college. (You can analyze this, if you will, but I think such responses are common among people who don't live according to the expectations of others.) Like a tortoise, I retreated into my carapace. I spent more and more time with my fashion magazines, which I stacked neatly by title and month.

By that time I had also begun to clip out images from *Vogue* and other magazines and thumbtack them to the walls of my inner sanctum, so that I could literally be surrounded by them. The room I am talking about was not my bedroom, into which anyone could come, but a smaller room just off it, which my grandmother had painted a pleasing, strong hot pink, and into which I invited almost no one. That hibiscus pink wasn't a color I'd asked for. I never even had the impression my grandmother had given much thought to that paint before she had slapped it up. I could imagine her standing in the paint store some time during my early childhood, saying to the clerk, "All right, pink for the little room, and beige for my bedroom, and gray for my mother's bedroom," and that was that. (Even if she had cared about such things as color schemes, children simply weren't consulted about such topics in those days. Your room was whatever color your guardians painted it, period.) In any event, the little shocking pink room was all my own, to do my own thing in. All over the walls of that room I pinned up a kaleidoscope of images I'd torn from the pages of *Vogue* and the Sunday *Times* fashion supplement. I loved the models from *Vogue,* especially the black models Naomi Sims and Pat Cleveland, who gave me my first inklings that a black person could have a place in the world of high fashion. The model Jean Shrimpton was all over the magazine then, as was the divine Penelope Tree. Richard Avedon was taking many of the photographs, and even at that young age, I was stunned by the clarity of his composition and put many of his images on the wall for inspiration. The words in the captions were as luscious as cake, and I couldn't believe how beautiful the people were. I loved to read about the discotheques in New York City. I remember reading about the famously with-it Peppermint Lounge in those pages and stuck a picture of it on my quiet, small-town wall, little knowing that I would someday dance on its polished floor. I learned about the fashionable boutiques of Paris and New York seemingly as quickly as anyone who lived in one of those wondrous cities. The people and how they lived in their houses—all of that seemed magical, part of a different universe and also, somehow, part of what I had always, always known. Those were the days when much of *Vogue* was printed in stylish black and white, the stark, formal beauty of which I appreciated. But I was also fascinated by the colors in *Vogue,* the fabrics and textures, the accessories and the cosmetics. The magazine, in short, touched me deeply. I took the images that spoke to me most directly and surrounded myself with them.

Only one of my male friends in the neighborhood was ever allowed into that secret room: Sam Morrison. Sam and I became friends in junior high and managed to grow steadily closer as we matured, building one of those friendships that last despite all the changes that take place on the way to adulthood. By the time we got to high school, Sam and I were both beanpole thin, like two hearty bamboo shoots towering over a crowd of houseplants. Sam wore his hair in a neat, cropped Afro style, while I always got the correct, traditional cut my grandmother favored. By the time we were sixteen, Sam had his own car, and not just any car, but a smart red MG, possibly the most exciting vehicle on the road in the early 1960s. He was the only person in our high school class who had such a status car, and I always felt proud to be chauffeured by him. Having Sam for a friend meant that even if I was considered an oddball, I was shielded from other people's scorn or inquiries. He was a popular boy, a member of the sedate Jack & Jill set. (Jack & Jill was—and is—a national association for upper-crust black teens; anyone who belongs to it seems sure to have impeccable manners, perfect diction, new clothes every season, and lots of friends.) On my own, I didn't have much opportunity to mix with those kids, except at school events; and while I knew that I didn't really want to be part of their social universe, I sometimes couldn't help feeling left out. My association with Sam meant that however much of an outsider I was (and, of course, at a deeper level, wanted to be), I also had leave to hang around the sophisticated insiders.

When Sam wasn't busy taking me places or squiring girls around town, he'd come over to my house. We could sit together for hours on end without saying a word, which, I have come to realize, is one of the marks of a true, abiding friendship. Sometimes we would listen to Laura Nyro, Nina Simone, and Patti LaBelle, and sometimes we would talk or work on our homework, either together or individually. Sam never understood my attraction to *Vogue.* He didn't give much thought to the pursuit of luxury or to the sparkling world the magazine portrayed; he had a much more practical turn of mind. But just because he didn't understand it didn't mean Sam minded my walls of magazine pictures. We were good enough friends that he could accept that I was different from him and love me anyway. I felt exactly the same about him and his Jack & Jill life—it may not have been exactly what I wanted, but I was glad that he enjoyed it. As an adult, it's good to have friends who are outside of my professional sphere; they remind me that the gilding and artifice all around me, however wonderful, are not the only things on earth.

I know that as a child and teenager, I made a fool of myself as often as any kid, but if my grandmother even knew about my antics, she never let on. I wonder, for example, if she noticed what a plumb fool I was the day, in high school, I watched the Beatles step off their plane for the first time in New York City, and later appear on *The Ed Sullivan Show.* I sat on the living room floor screaming just like the kids in the footage behind the gates at Idlewild. My grandmother glanced in to see what I was doing, but she went right back to talking to one of her sisters on the phone. February 1, 1964: my fool phase in overdrive. As the Beatles stormed the American airwaves, I secretly went out and spent my allowance on two black Beatle wigs, one for me and one for Peter Joyner, who was equally obsessed with the rock and roll sensations. My grandmother must have known about my frivolous purchase, but she would never have chastised me for it. She had faith that I would outgrow such ridiculousness.

CHAPTER SEVEN

I never knew him well, deep inside, but I always, always knew that my father loved me. He visited as often as he could, usually bearing gifts, and I understood that when he couldn't visit, it was because he was working those two jobs to help support me. I wished he could be around more, but when I sat down to think it through, I understood his reasons. And unlike so many children who, for whatever reason, end up living with people who aren't their birth parents, I was blessed with a stable home in which I always felt surrounded by love. So I felt my father's absence more as a dull ache than as a searing pain. As an adult, I had the blessed opportunity to get to know him, both as a parent and as a friend, and to spend time in his company. When he died in 1993, I was very sad but also thankful not to have had the crushing sadness that comes when someone dies before you come to appreciate fully who he is.

My father was born on October 5, 1924, to sharecroppers in Roxboro, North Carolina, and his life growing up was Tobacco Road. A log cabin lit by candlelight; the same galvanized tub for laundry and bathing; a one-room schoolhouse through the ninth grade; spittoons homemade from old tin cans—these were the things he knew as a child. Like me, he grew up not regretting the material things he lacked but appreciating his large family's closeness and commitment to religion.

Talley, as everyone called him, worked hard his whole life. Like most good taxi drivers, he had the knack for turning almost any fare into a lesson in human nature. As a child, I would sometimes spend much of a visiting weekend riding up front with him on a day of long hauls and was amazed at how he could soften the hearts of the most tightfisted non-tippers. He treated boisterous drunks with quiet respect, and if a child was being yelled at by a nervous mother, he might give the kid a shiny nickel out of his own pocket. Old ladies were his favorite customers. He was very fond of his aunt Jennie and my grandmother, so the frail old ladies who rode in his cab were treated like royalty. When young couples got hot and heavy in the backseat, he would stop the car and lecture them on manners. He probably touched the hearts and raised the hackles of more people than I'll ever imagine. And all the while, he struggled through the same difficulties as so many black men who work hard just to tread water when it often seems as if the whole system is designed to keep us down. Before his son, however, at least he maintained the appearance of a man who'd always held his head high.

My father was every bit the hepcat, to put it in the terms of his time—especially to me, growing up in a house of proper Baptist women. As a young teenager, I was always proud and happy to walk beside him. He had a rapid, springy gait, and at any given time, he looked dapper. His shirts were always laundered at the Chinese laundry, and his shoes freshly polished—no worn heels or chipped toes. His wardrobe, although Spartan, had a certain elegance: white shirts with short sleeves in summer, long in winter; slim, dark Velcro-tab pants with boot-cut legs; and the kind of short stacked-heel boots that zipped up the inside of the ankle. He favored a simple single-breasted jacket for a suit and an unassuming thigh-length overcoat. If the temperature went up to a hundred and five, he would still not have allowed himself to be seen in shorts.

He was a great dancer. I can remember him making up special dances in his little bit of spare time and showing them to me with glee. I keep a photograph of him, dressed in black tie, on his way to some Masonic Lodge ball. In this image, he is a real urban man, every inch the stud, ready to parade around the ballroom in search of some brown sugar. He was a women's man through and through. When, during his decline, his doctor told him he'd need to be placed in a nursing home with a dialysis machine, the first thing he told one of my cousins was that he was worried he'd no longer be able to have sex on a regular basis. She told me about this later, saying, "I told him, 'Talley, when was the last time you had sex, anyway? You don't need to worry about that anymore.' "

No longer being able to be a ladies' man must have come as a disappointment, but he always handled disappointment gracefully. He never once complained that he wished I'd become a sports star, though I knew it had been his dream for me. And as much as he loved driving, when I failed to take to it, he didn't try to force me. One day when I was seventeen, he took me to a quiet, paved road on the outskirts of D.C. to begin giving me lessons in his cherished bottle green Ford sedan. His explanation of how the car worked made my palms sweat, but I still managed to move the car about a hundred yards at a snail's pace before my hands turned to stone on the steering wheel. I remember looking out from under the wide straw brim of my National Park Service hat (I was working as a ranger for the summer) and saying weakly, "This is not for me." My father did not utter one chastising word. He simply drove me back to the apartment I was sharing with a friend. I stayed up all night playing Eddie Kendricks's "Keep on Truckin' " on the record player and did not learn to drive until I was fifty.

The year before Talley died, I had a last few great moments of bonding with him. I remember sitting beside him as he lay in bed, and watching his face light up as I told him something few people know about the actor Sylvester Stallone, with whom I had recently become acquainted: that although he is self-taught, he is better read than most college graduates and takes pride in his personal library. I related that on Sly's shelves I'd seen the complete works of W. E. B. Du Bois and Frederick Douglass, two of America's greatest black thinkers, and my father was deeply impressed.

"Do you remember," I asked him, "how when I was a boy, you pointed out to me that Douglass said, 'Truth is of no color'?"

He nodded, delighted that our early visits to the library had made such an impression. Later I brought him an autographed picture of Stallone on a polo pony and once again had the pleasure of seeing my father's unself-conscious, wide smile.

He eventually died of brittle diabetes, with which he'd been diagnosed during my boyhood, and which had been exacerbated by a lifetime of eating junk food while driving the cab. (As long as I knew him, he stopped into a diner every morning for breakfast, and ordered a large cardboard cup of milky coffee, and two doughnuts.) His decline was tragic to watch. His beautiful caramel brown skin turned dark from liver failure, and his body grew frail despite what seemed endless hospitalizations for blood transfusions. The last of many times I took the shuttle down to D.C. on receiving an urgent call from the Veterans' Hospital, I found him in a small, narrow room, in the bright sunlight of a spectacular spring day, lying curled up in the fetal position, his head turned to the wall. The rumpled sheets were wound around his lower body. When I saw him lying like that, turned away from the sunlight, I knew he was ready to give up.

No one knows what happened to his assets during his decline. He had had a wonderful collection of cameras—Leicas, Hasselblads, Nikons, Rolleiflexes, and Mamiyas among them—as well as some darkroom equipment he'd shared with his best cab-driving buddy. There were also albums upon albums of his skillful, telling photographs documenting important family events as well as the moods and scenes of the place where he was raised, but somehow the photos all disappeared by the time he died. Before he was hospitalized, he'd desperately needed a new car, so I'd sent him a check to buy one, but he got so ill he put the money into an account, in my name, to pay for his funeral expenses. By the time he died, everything he owned was gone, except for that car money and a huge color television in a wood veneer cabinet. My cousins and I agreed to leave the television to his favorite nurse.

I received the call notifying me of his death on a stopover in New York on a Los Angeles–to-Paris flight. Anna Wintour went to great lengths to make the airline patch her call to me through to a private phone in the business-class lounge. Luckily I had not yet boarded for Paris and was able to return to my Chelsea apartment in London Terrace, exactly as I had done when my grandmother had died five years before.

The next day, with the money he'd put aside, I set about providing him with victory services that befitted my respect for his long life of labor and sacrifice.

My first stop was at Bergdorf Goodman. I bought him a good black Italian suit of silk and mohair, a crisp white shirt and gray silk tie from Charvet, cotton lisle socks, and the best underwear and ribbed undershirt I could find. I bought him fine white Italian calfskin gloves, because he had been a Mason, and Masons must be buried with gloves on. He loved Polo cologne, so I bought him a new bottle, as well as a flacon of Van Cleef & Arpels; I thought he would like to be sent off with fresh new scent in the side of his coffin. We blacks in the South love it fashionable. All of this I sent by FedEx to Scarborough & Hargett, the family funeral home that was taking care of driving the body down from Maryland in a hearse. I ordered the same make of coffin I had ordered for my grandmother—his a platinum silver, while hers had had a pale blue cast—and the same kind of vault, and made certain that my father's Masonic apron was handed over to Skippy, the undertaker who had buried everyone in my family since Dorothy Bee and before her. A beautiful wreath and blanket of Casablanca lilies were ordered from Robert Isabel, the *Vogue* in-house florist, and shipped air freight to North Carolina. I flew down the next day.

Once all these arrangements were made, I never went to look at my father in his coffin. I did not want the memory of his beautiful tan skin and big, wonderful smile to be replaced by the memory of an empty shell, pumped up with embalming fluid, a wan smile positioned by the able embalmer.

My cousin Georgia went to see him, though, before they laid him out for his wake. "He looks great, Ray," she reported to me. Georgia also reported that my mother had gone to the funeral home and had said of him, "Talley looks nice. I can tell André had something to do with all these details. That gives me great comfort." I was glad I had finally done something to please her. My mother and father had barely been civil to each other since their divorce, but when she had decided as an older woman that she wanted to go back to Durham to retire, he had driven her and all her belongings down Interstate 95 without hesitation.

My father's funeral was a somber one, at Red Mill Creek Baptist Church in Roxboro, half an hour away. Because the Masons were taking charge of the service, I remained in the car until they were ready to begin. I entered the church alone and sat by myself in the front pew.

I was happy to see how much kin—including many Talley relatives previously unknown to me—showed up for his homecoming services. I thought that the Masons seated to the left and right brought appropriate pomp and dignity to the proceedings, with their splendid clothes and their a cappella choir. The pulpit and choir loft were hung with a Victorian swag of deep crimson velvet, though this country church had only enough congregants to hold services two Sundays out of any month. One of my father's Masonic brothers read out the personal farewell I had written to William Carroll Talley and had had printed in the program.

When the beautiful service ended, the casket was driven in a white hearse to the far side of the church graveyard, just on the edge of the woods. I had maintained my composure during the funeral—my grandmother's and Mrs. Vreeland's had taught me to keep a dignified air no matter how full of turmoil I felt inside—but at the graveside, the Masonic rites caused in me a great, surging emotional charge. I felt my mouth opening wide, about to moan or howl. My cousin Doris, who had been standing behind me and had seen many of her loved ones go down into the red North Carolina dirt, psychically received a silent André alert. When my jaw began to drop, she swiftly came up beside me and gently swept the palm of her left hand under my chin to close my mouth. As odd as this gesture may seem, I knew it was a gesture of love; she was giving me a moment to regain my composure. Her subtle move probably went unnoticed by most around me, but it kept me from giving in to an overemotional reaction that I would have felt uncomfortable about later on.

When my father's vault was lowered into the ground, it looked slightly askew, and when I asked the gravediggers' foreman why that was, he said it was because there was no way to get the last rope out from underneath it. I had to accept that this was so, but then he began lowering a sheet of plastic onto the lid of the vault.

"What are you doing?" I asked.

"The plastic helps to keep the vault watertight," he said.

"Please don't put it there," I said. "My father is not going to the dry cleaner's." I knew it was the custom that we're all buried in these expensive coffins and vaults, but who's to say that water, worms, and decay won't seep in over the course of five or fifty years, or history? Sometimes I think we should all be buried in cardboard boxes, so we could biodegrade as God meant us to. Or be cremated, which is the way I want to go out.

Finally, everyone, except me, retreated to the church basement for a light repast of fried chicken, potato salad, collard greens, and sweet potato pie. Even the gravediggers were fed.

Seven years later, I was sitting one morning on the wraparound terrace of Karl Lagerfeld's new home in Biarritz, having just succeeded in filing reports from the Paris couture. As I looked out at a cloud-filled, Vermeer sky, I thought about all that my father had not seen during his sixty-nine years. I had just witnessed some remarkable fashions—Viktor & Rolf's brilliant, crazy garments covered with real or embroidered Swiss cowbells, Jean-Paul Gaultier's Eiffel Tower dress, of tulle, chenille, gold lamé, and electric lights—and I thought, what would my father have thought of all this? I had also walked across the Pont Alexandre III, which had been regilded sometime in the not-too-distant past, and which has those wild allegorical statues of gilded, naked women with horns and horses, and thought of how my father had never had the opportunity to see Paris. And I love Paris so much and would have loved for him to see it. I would have loved to take him for a cup of chocolate in a French café, or explain to him about the workmanship behind those beautiful French grosgrain ribbons—so different, in silk, from the nylon Japanese ones—or the handmade silk camellias at Chanel. I would have loved to show him this marvelous place where values seem so much less superficial than they do at home, where not everything is about your weight going up or down, and where style is not about faddishness. I would have loved to take him to the Père Lachaise Cemetery, to see the graves of Proust, Colette, Oscar Wilde, Delacroix. I would have loved to introduce him to a society in which being black was less of a barrier to success. But as I sat there on the terrace, I realized that he had at least had the opportunity to see all this through my eyes. He had worked hard to give me the opportunity to be in this wonderful place, doing a job that I love. Every time I saw something wonderful and conveyed it to others in words, I was, in part, doing that in honor of William Carroll Talley. When he died, his only son was not a nobody, and I know he felt largely responsible for that. So if I continue to walk on that beautiful bridge across the Seine every year, alone, it is in memory of the trips he never had, the photographs he would have loved to take.

He was proud of me, proud every time I sent him an article I'd had published in a magazine, and proud when he saw me on Jennie Becker's *Fashion TV* show from Canada. He was proud that I was educated, as well as that I grew up to be the sort of person he'd hoped I would be.

He did not live to see the *Mona Lisa,* or to see Venus Williams win Wimbledon and her father wiping away tears of joy as she leapt into the air with her victory trophy. He left little. But the small acts of kindness and sacrifice he performed every day, like many a good father, live on in the mind of his son and in the minds of many people he touched.

I do wonder sometimes, if William Carroll Talley had been around more in my childhood, if I would have turned out exactly as I have. In his absence, I was raised and influenced almost entirely by women, in a world of women's values and women's concerns that has clearly shaped the man I have become—someone in an industry whose stars may often be male but whose audience is mostly female. When I say that I was raised by women, I do not mean it in the sense that my grandmother, and in early life my great-grandmother, brought me up. I mean that they themselves were supported by, surrounded by a network of women—my grandmother's six sisters, various cousins, Mrs. Coley and the other neighbors, and the deaconesses and other women of the church. Everyone I turned to for guidance was female, as was everyone who ever scolded me for not doing what was right. For Heaven's sakes, even my Cub Scout den leader was a woman! And people wonder how someone from my background ended up in the world of fashion.

As I have said, my grandmother taught me not by lecturing but by example, so she certainly never sat me down and told me to value the strength and fortitude of the women around me. But I saw how well they kept their homes, fed their families, and steered us all through difficult times, and the lesson was not lost on me. From my earliest childhood, I knew that the people looked up to older women—women of courage, strength, humor, faith, and above all, capability. In addition to the real-life role models all around me, the people who fired my imagination—Emma Bovary, Diana Vreeland, Aunt Dorothy Bee, Pat

Cleveland, Anna Karenina, Aretha Franklin—were all women, too; and it was my great good fortune to know two girls my own age growing up, Lana Love McClary and Anne Bibby, who were also very inspiring. Their influence on me built upon my grandmother's solid foundational teaching, so I want to pay them their proper due. As much as anyone in my childhood besides my grandmother, they helped steer me to become the person I am by encouraging me to be me.

In my teenage years, I didn't attend many parties, so I honed my dancing skills on my grandmother's bedstead. Like the pages of *Vogue,* that was a place where I felt free. How I loved my make-believe partners on Saturday mornings! I finished up my chores as quickly as possible so I could dance, while my grandmother stood in the kitchen, preparing Sunday dinner or stirring one of her delicious cakes.

American Bandstand was my dancing school, and it influenced me profoundly. It's hard to imagine that anyone of my generation escaped its sway; that show, which aired from Philadelphia, broadcast the Motown sound to the whole country. That was where I learned of the Marvelettes, the Supremes, Marvin Gaye, Gladys Knight and the Pips, Smokey Robinson and the Miracles, Stevie Wonder, and the Temptations. Their music filled my head morning, noon, and night. Most Saturday afternoons—once I had dismissed all pretense of Cub Scouts, field sports, and other forms of boy bonding—I spent with the *AB,* the radio, or my own record player, for which I had a collection of 45 rpm records purchased with any pocket change left over from my weekly magazine run. I danced so fiercely and so hard that my cousin Avant, the husband of my cousin Doris, had to come over and glue the wooden joints of Mama's bed frame together. Not satisfied that his work could withstand my dancing, he took industrial wire and wound it from post to post around the bottom of the bed, to keep the whole thing from collapsing. My grandmother never said a word about the bed, except a "Thank you" to Avant and didn't seem to notice the ugly metal wire that was wrapped securely around the frame to keep the bed upright.

From Mama's bed and *American Bandstand,* I slowly made my way out onto the social circuit. But to a young black man from the wrong side of the tracks, it was the Jack & Jill Club that seemed surrounded by a ten-foot fence. Still, I outshone all those well-heeled young men in our senior year of high school, when I was chosen for the particular honor of escorting my friend Lana Love McClary to the most glamorous event anyone we knew had experienced.

Lana lived four doors down from us, at 1023 Cornell Street, in a much bigger house that she shared with her mother and father, Mary and Benjamin, her aunt Naomi, and her grandmother, Olive Love. Like me, Lana was an only child, spoiled by her parents, aunt, and grandmother, but not spoiled rotten. Rather, Lana was the ideal teenage young lady; she took all the attention they lavished on her and truly made something of herself. She had a gift for playing piano, and she devoted herself to an assiduous practice, as much as four hours a day on the weekends, one hour a day after school, and a weekly lesson with the best teacher in Durham, a Mrs. Spence who lived all the way across town. All that discipline paid off for Lana: She went on to win first prize in a state championship concert recital contest. She was rewarded by her parents with the privilege of going on the local teen dance show, Channel Five's *All-Black Teen-Age Frolics,* one Saturday afternoon in our sister city of Raleigh. And after much ado, she and her family agreed that there was only one young gentleman upright enough to be her escort on the show: André Leon Talley.

That Saturday morning, Lana went off to the local portrait studio, where she was photographed in her candy pink lace and organdy party dress. I put on my best navy blue Sunday suit and black shoes: so correct. We went on television that afternoon with a bunch of other high-school kids, but in our minds we were jitterbugs of the first degree, two of the fanciest people on earth. And we knew all our friends back in Durham were watching us. That afternoon, I felt both special and free in a way I never had felt in public before.

Shortly thereafter, in May 1966, Lana was my ticket to another night of dancing that helped propel me on my way out of Durham and into, it seemed to me, the stars. Lana's parents, grandmother, and aunt, you see, gave her a wonderful gift that spring before we enrolled in college: They opened up their beautiful home for an after-prom dance. Weeks before the event, the McClary women invited me to join in the fun of planning, and together we pored over invitation designs, the music, and the decorations. Early that Saturday afternoon, I went over to help shift furniture from the living room and dining room to the back halls and spare bedroom, and to roll up the rugs. The same pink dress Lana had worn to the dance show was hanging up to air, and the whole house breathed a festive atmosphere.

I had been greatly looking forward to the prom, because the two most important girls of my wonder years, Lana and Anne Bibby, would be in the same room in all their splendor. (Anne Bibby was my true love in high school, but she never knew it; it never crossed my mind to tell her.) And as it turned out, I was right to have invested the event with so much anticipation. Forty years later, when I look back on it, I see that evening as a fleeting instance of great magic. Anne Bibby is still as bright in my imagination as she was that evening. For the event, Anne and her mother had purchased the finest white silk ottoman faille to make a simple, stunning sheath of a dress, cut on a Givenchy couture pattern, which Mrs. Bibby had found in the sewing department of a pricey store downtown. Anne's mother had true chic; she managed to make even a nurse's uniform look regal, her white shoes and stockings immaculate and trim. The large house the family lived in also seemed to me the epitome of style. They had windows that went right down to the floorboards—something I had seen only in movies or in magazines.

Anne Bibby's glow could illuminate an entire room. She was tall and broad-shouldered, with wide-set eyes and fair skin. When her ample mouth smiled, she showed off her gleaming, white teeth. She wore little makeup on her fine-pored skin, and most of the time she wore her hair ironed straight, in a sophisticated, society lady flip. On prom night, she had it pinned and sprayed up into a fashionable dried helmet like Jackie Kennedy's. Her voice could be bold and efficient for her cheerleading duties or as soft as a wind chime. Her laughter was raucous, and her tapered fingers looked like they came right out of a Dürer etching. I loved those long fingers—to me, they always embodied elegance. In short, I thought she was the most beautiful girl on earth!

I managed to get along with some of the boys in my class, but Anne and Lana were my two most special friends. We all spoke the same language, especially about fashion, my true and otherwise private passion. So you see, I was frankly awed by the bateau neckline of Anne's gown, its wide, shallow opening from shoulder to shoulder hitting her collarbones perfectly, and the back plunging in a long, square cut all the way down to her waist. This daring front-to-back neckline left Anne's perfect spine exposed nearly to the small of her back; and Anne, our homecoming queen, was the belle of the ball, as always. I, meanwhile, was my usual wallflower self. I had friends, but along with the few other shyest people in my class, I went to the prom alone and hung around the periphery of the dancing area, far from the lights and streamers that sparkled from the gymnasium ceiling on those brave enough to dance.

As I was sitting in the first row of folded-up bleachers, one of the smartest guys in the class, William McLaughlin, sidled up to me. "Hey, André," he said, "do you want to dance with me?"

The question threw me for a loop, and I sat there frozen in fear. *Why did he ask that?* I wondered. *Out of boredom? Politeness? Because he didn't know what else to say?* My only response was to sit there in dignified, terrified silence, which was how I usually responded to situations that caused me anxiety or discomfort. I knew for a fact that William was too much of a jock to get out there and cut a rug with me. Even if he'd meant the offer seriously, it would have been the scandal to end all scandals had it actually come to pass. Now, looking back on the event as an adult, I think William might just have been trying to express some kind of admiration for me, but at the time, I was too confused to think about it clearly.

Right then, Anne Bibby must have had a psychic intuition that I was in need of help, because she paused in the center of the dance floor, sought me out with her eyes, and began walking toward the bleachers in that white Givenchyesque gown. As she approached, I stood up and moved toward her. When we met at the edge of the dance floor, she asked me to do her a very special favor. Not a funky chicken or a boogie-woogie, but . . . "André, I think I'm glowing. Would you mind powdering my back?"

She took a pale puff predipped in face powder from her purse, handed it to me, and turned three-quarters away. I stood there for a moment with the puff in my hand dripping loose face powder. She wanted me to touch her back, her cool, perfect back! Right there, where everyone could see us! Her dance card was full up with the stars of the football team, practically waiting in line to take a spin with her, yet she wanted me to stroke her back with the misty powder, which flew up in little clouds.

"Of course," I said, as calmly as I could. "Anything for you, Anne." As I complied with her request, I felt as if a chilling breeze were striking me in the face. It was the single most erotic moment of my high-school life. And I knew that this intimate moment with the homecoming queen meant more than any twirl around the dance floor. The whole rest of the evening I kept dreaming of her beauty and perfection, of the way she'd reached out to me with a hand elegantly gloved to the armpit in a white, glazed kidskin glove.

Of course, the evening went on; dancing started up again, and Anne turned, smiled, and was off in the arms of yet another super jock, some bosom pal of her big brother Billy. As the music rose up to the ceiling, over the heads of the coupled students, I turned back to my bleacher, where William McLaughlin still sat and where it seemed that everyone had witnessed my special powder moment and seemed dazed by it. There everyone had stood—varsity athletes, popular girls, her friends, my friends, people we hardly knew at all—with their eyes bulging, as I sewed up in memory one perfect moment of connection. I will always remember that moment on the dance floor as one of complete acceptance. When Anne handed me that powder puff, it was a sign of an affection that lasts much longer than the memory of the lusts, bumps, and grinds most teenagers take home with them on prom night.

After the prom there was a series of special after-prom dances, between which we all motored dutifully in our mostly borrowed cars. At a swanky restaurant someone's parents had rented out for the first post-prom pass-by, Anne and I bumped into each other on the dance floor. In that private room, she asked me to dance—and did we dance, me holding her hands in her white opera gloves. By the time we at last arrived at Lana's house around three in the morning, Anne and I had fused our dancing talents into a truly gleeful last-dance frenzy, and I felt as if my life had changed for good. From wallflower to happy dance partner—it was a huge transformation for me, all wrought in a single evening and through one person's graceful, joyful friendship. It is a true sign of both Lana's family's respect for her and of how much she deserved it that evening, that the adults of her clan were nowhere in sight. It must have been difficult to sleep in those back bedrooms that night, but that was at least what they pretended to do, for the sake of the kids' night of fun.

Lana and Anne both continued to be my friends and muses once we went on to college, which we all did the following autumn, after Anne and I both ended up spending the summer in Washington, D.C. Anne was staying with relatives, mostly as a vacation before she went off to school. I had come up to D.C. to spend time with my divorced parents and to go the rounds of the government agencies, looking for summer work to help defray my expenses the following year. I found a job with the help of my father, who took valuable vacation days from his own job in order to stand in line with me all morning and make sure my applications were both properly filled out and delivered to the correct hands. His patient presence beside me both assuaged my impatience and impressed the employment officers, because he was so clearly a man who wanted his son to find high-paying, honorable work. I ended up working those first two summers as a ranger in the national parks, and the next two in government offices.

Together, on weekends, Anne and I explored the nation's capital, saw movies, and, most important, shopped! It was at Garfinckel's that I introduced Anne to the luxury of Kislav gloves. (Which I had learned about, of course, in the captions of *Vogue.*) That autumn, I returned home, where I continued to live, while Lana and I both attended North Carolina Central University (NCCU), which was right in Durham; Anne traveled south to attend Spellman College. I'll never forget how she came home from Atlanta that Christmas wearing a navy blue military cape—unheard of in our neck of the woods. Anne's mother had ordered it in white, but Anne sent it away to be dyed blue and lined with a special paisley fabric, some of which I also used to cover the chair cushions in my hot pink sanctuary.

That Christmas, the Jack & Jill set had many dances, to which, as usual, I was not invited. But I remember how Anne drove up on her way to one of them. She had two of her gal pals with her, Debbie Watts and Ethel Richardson, and a favor to ask: Could she borrow my grandmother's black glazed, crushed Kislav gloves? She remembered them vividly from the summer before. My grandmother did not like to lend her personal clothing, yet she allowed me to be able to contribute to Anne's sartorial splendor with the loan of the gloves. Anne drove off to the party, to dance the night away with some handsome, beefy boyfriend, while I retreated to my pink-walled room, with Nina Simone, Laura Nyro, Diana Vreeland, and my dreams.

Even when I was attending lectures or studying for exams, much of my time was spent in dream scapes in which Anne Bibby featured as the primary landmark. Most of these were based on events that had actually transpired—from the prom to her appearance as homecoming queen out on the football field. I played that event over and over in my mind, savoring particularly the memory of what she wore that cool autumn day: a speckled, hunter green bouclé tweedy coat with a matching dress, the whole thing loosely belted with a leather thong and finished with her very expensive court shoes. The most impressive thing she wore was then, as always, her almost horse-scale enormous grin. Anne had bought the outfit especially for her appearance at homecoming, and everything about it pointed to intrigue and glamour. The outfit had come, you see, from Montaldo's, that same candy-pink store on Main Street that my aunt Dorothy Bee had so brazenly entered so many years before. Times had changed since Dorothy Bee's act of defiance, but not that much. To give you some idea of what kind of black lady would have dared to go into Montaldo's, even in those days, she would ordinarily have been none less than the wife of the president of the state university. Or, to make it clear, to shop there a person had to have both chutzpah and a whole lot of cash—Johnnie Cochran bucks, in today's terms of wealth. The place was unofficially off limits to colored folk, rich or poor; on the rare occasion a black had the audacity to walk in and look around, she was eyed suspiciously. Not even the Jack & Jill sophisticates went in there to browse. The Dukes (of the Duke tobacco dynasty) shopped there, and it was the one place in Durham where you could find some of the clothes you pored over in *Vogue, Harper's Bazaar,* and *The New York Times* fashion section; or, if you couldn't find the originals, then very similar styles. I don't know how well-off, financially, Anne's parents were, but she had her homecoming suit from Montaldo's, and you couldn't get any better than that.

Anne and her mother had for me, in the words of my favorite writer, Gustave Flaubert, "a complexion of wealth; the veneer of painted antiques." Every wall in every room of their house was painted oyster gray, even in the kitchen. To this day, I continue to copy that style, and the walls of my house in New York are still painted that same shade. Anne's older brother, Billy, was a bully and a football hero. In those days he constantly harangued me, for no reason other than that he was bigger and older. Rude, raw, rough, and also quite the man about town, he had none of his sister's polish. He was the first person to label me an outcast. I was as afraid of him as I was of the snakes in those back-home tales my aunts and cousins told. I didn't want to be near him, and somehow, it seemed that whenever I went to visit Anne, he was out joyriding or doing whatever it is that bullies do. (Luckily, he got all that wildness out of him. The last report I heard of him was that he was one of the head honchos of the Durham Fire Department.)

The summer we spent in Washington, D.C., I waited until I found a job and then took Anne out for one big date. I was glad Billy wasn't around to chaperone.

The date was a dress-up affair, me in my bleeding madras cotton blazer, best navy alpaca trousers, a white shirt, and black shoes. She wore a pale pink sheath, street length, and, of course, long beige gloves crushed down beneath the elbow, even on such a warm summer evening. If Anne and I weren't yet one hundred percent certain of who we wanted to be, we both certainly knew who we wanted to look like. We had very defined opinions on all things sartorial, as well as on anything French, particularly those things that came from Paris, and the French styles espoused by Jacqueline Kennedy, who was by then a widow. Those dazzling gloves, with a patch of perfect skin exposed—to me, Anne had crossed over to the level of a *Vogue* model. The club we went to that night to hear music is a blank in my memory, as is the jazz artist's name; dinner is a vague blur of heavy silver and white linen. Everything disappeared that night except for her smile, her dress, her Norell perfume, and, of course, those gloves.

After dinner, we taxied home. There were no teen gropes or fondling, no hands up under her slip. Anne was too perfect for that; I would never have done anything so vulgar. But she did manage to remain my friend for life.

Lana, meanwhile, continued to be my bosom pal as we made our way through college. Anne was off in Atlanta, but Lana was just four doors down, and she knew how to sew, so we had plenty of fun designing our looks. The streets of Durham, then as now, were conservative, but Lana and I created fashions for the streets of our imaginations. She didn't care what length other people's skirts were, or what colors other people thought matched; and I didn't care if I was the only man in town wearing sailor pants. We enjoyed our clothes, and we lavished as much attention on them as we could.

During college, I acquired the habit, when I had some spare money, of going down to Baltimore, to a Middle European tailor there, whose name I have, sadly, forgotten, who custom-made pants. He had a tiny little old-fashioned place that he worked out of, and he didn't care who you were or whether he liked what you wanted. Whether you were a young black college student or a Baltimore man about town, you got good service, and he made what you asked for. Whenever I got a check, down I'd go on the bus and get him to sew up the wonderful fabrics I picked into the bell-bottom trousers I favored at that time. I had them made in every kind of fabric, every sort of color, for day and evening—you know, beautiful worsted wools and that sort of thing, just extraordinary fabrics. If I felt particularly cash-happy, I might get two or three pairs at a time, and one time I got him to custom-make a navy blue suit for church. He sold his own fabrics, but I liked to pick my own and bring them to him. Sometimes it seemed like I was having just truckloads of these pants made. That was my regular *de rigueur sortie*—to go to Baltimore to have my pants made for school. I loved that. Lana and I were certainly sartorial outcasts in college—I wouldn't be surprised if some of our classmates considered us freaks—but we were happy. We knew who we were.

Meanwhile, I still had my grandmother, Anne Bibby, and Anne's mother continuing to epitomize high standards. To me, they were taste at the top. And of course, from the pages I still raked over Sunday after Sunday with an ever-refining eye, I mined my future and learned much from Diana Vreeland. The books and magazines I read then inspired me to get out into the world, to follow my dreams and desires, even if I didn't know exactly how they would play out. I will always be grateful to them for that. But I know in my heart that all the words and images in the world—all the beauty, all the style—would have meant nothing to me if the people who raised me and shaped my tastes had not been such models of strength and style, and if they had not encouraged me so sincerely to hew to my own ideas about how I wanted to live my life. My life has certainly had its enchanted moments, but when people marvel that a boy from a black family of little means in Durham, North Carolina, could have risen as I have to the top of the world of fashion editorial, I feel blessed. I know that the women there had as much fortitude and panache as any women I've seen in Milan or Paris, just as I know that some of the most fashionable women in New York are not the socialites but the women of the Abyssinian Baptist Church in Harlem. My life since leaving Durham has in many ways been an exotic adventure, but it is still the plain good taste and solid values of the women who shaped my youth that matters to me most.

CHAPTER EIGHT

On November 28, 1966, Truman Capote hosted his legendary Black and White Ball in honor of his friend Katharine Graham of *The Washington Post.* I managed to "attend" the affair the following March, when Diana Vreeland ran a lavish spread devoted to it in *Vogue.* There was Truman Capote, whose writings I already admired, in all his social glory. I learned from *Vogue* of his friendships with such remarkable women as Lee Radziwill, C. Z. Guest, Babe Paley, and Marella Agnelli. When I looked at the pictures of his sumptuous party, I felt as if I could actually walk around that world. It felt as real to me as Durham; in some ways, more so.

In the meanwhile, my life as an undergraduate was much as it had been in high school. I was living off campus, and it was a state college, so tuition was low enough that my father could realize his generous dream of contributing to most of my education. I worked during the summers, but I didn't have a job during the year. During the school year I took classes during the days; evenings and weekends I worked on papers and other school-related projects and talked about them all with my grandmother. In the time left over from those responsibilities and church, I indulged my fashion fantasies with Lana. My college years were a turbulent time for America, and especially for African Americans, but I was blessed to feel that little of that strife encroached upon my immediate sphere. In April 1968, during my sophomore year, my great idol, Martin Luther King, Jr., was gunned down. When I heard the terrible news of his death, I was deeply saddened. During those times of tribulation, televised images of men and women being sprayed by fire hoses and bitten by police dogs gave me and my grandmother unease. We followed current events closely but tried not to discuss them too much. We did not want to dwell on negativity when we were so lucky to have a life of relative ease in our own city.

One time I had a frightening experience of racism. The scene: Along with hordes of other college students, both black and white, I was walking alongside a Georgia highway, hoping to hitch a ride home to North Carolina after a Jimi Hendrix concert. It was a hot summer day. All of a sudden, a redneck Georgia highway patrolman set his lights spinning and his sirens blaring, and pulled his car up to a screeching halt alongside me. He got out of his car, looked me up and down, and without saying a word, kicked me in the butt, got back in his car, and drove off. No one around me knew what I could possibly have done to provoke him; his reaction had clearly been simply to the color of my skin. This incident upset and angered me, because I knew that if I had been walking in the same place alone or at night, anything could have happened—I could have been shot. I kept walking, praying silently to return home safe and well. My prayers must have been heard, because soon thereafter, a van of white New England college students pulled up and offered me a ride. They took me all the way through South Carolina and left me off very close to home—on a dark, unlit highway outside Durham at two in the morning. As their taillights sped away from my sight, I just put one foot in front of the other and prayed to God that I would see my grandmother. She didn't hear me let myself in through our unlocked front door near dawn. And I never told her of my humiliation.

At the university, of course, my color didn't matter. For the first time in my life, I was passionately interested in what went on in my classes—in *all* of them, now that I was allowed to leave math and science behind after fulfilling the basic requirements. I had always been a good student out of duty, but now, inspired by my professors, I excelled in my academic work. The fervent francophilia I had developed in high school led me to become a French major under the able tutelage of Dr. Irene Jackson—who was not only an incredible teacher but something of a celebrity in my eyes, because she was the mother of the first black mayor of Atlanta. Dr. Jackson believed strongly in my scholarly abilities, telling me that I had something unique to contribute to French studies. Her encouragement assisted my natural aptitudes, and in my junior and senior years at NCCU, I truly began to shine academically. And when Dr. Jackson saw what I was capable of, she encouraged me to apply for a scholarship to pursue graduate studies at Brown University, in Providence, Rhode Island.

Of course, I had heard of Brown, as I had heard of all the schools in the Ivy League, but I had never really considered going there. It was far from home, and as far as undergraduate studies went, I was more than satisfied with the education NCCU had to offer. I did, however, find that the academic life appealed to me as a possible path. As much as I dreamed of the world Diana Vreeland and Truman Capote inhabited, academia provided possible career options that seemed both fulfilling and secure; I could easily imagine myself living a quiet life as a tenured professor at a respectable university or private school, taking the same pleasure in my students' learning that my professors took in mine. The university seemed like a safe environment to me, a sure route to a life of honest work and suburban security. Of course, when I think back on it now, I realize how quickly it would have snapped my twig, but that's the benefit of age and hindsight. So at the beginning of my last year at NCCU, I applied to Brown's Ph.D. program in French.

To my tremendous surprise, I was not only accepted by Brown late that winter, but also offered a full scholarship.

I thought long and hard before sending a reply to the admissions committee. I had never left home for longer than a summer vacation—which I had always spent in the company of family—and I found it difficult even to imagine living so far away from my grandmother and the home I'd always known. This fear of the unknown, and clinging to what I loved, was something to reckon with. Yet despite my trepidation, I understood that this was the opportunity of a lifetime, one that I might always regret if I declined it. And my grandmother, though she knew she would be sad to see me go, was so proud of me and so strongly in favor of my accepting the offer, that I sent a happy "yes" to Providence, and thus took my first real step away from everything I'd known in my life that far.

After another summer working in D.C. and saving money, I prepared to set off on this new adventure. As I packed my few possessions—really just books and clothes—I tried to concentrate on the positive, to look forward to the life ahead rather than mourn what I was leaving behind. Nevertheless, when all my family gathered that early September morning to see me off and wish me well, I could not help crying. They were all beaming with pride at me—all except my mother, who kept exhorting me, "You can still give this up and go join the army." I don't think she understood that her dreams for me were not the same as my own. The rest of my family could not believe that one of their own had the good fortune to be setting off for graduate studies at an Ivy League university. I still had tears in my eyes when my father and I placed the last bag in the trunk of his car and slammed it shut. I felt homesick and uneasy the entire trip north.

Providence did not, however, turn out to be quite as unwelcoming as I'd imagined. That first year, rather than living in the dormitories, I rented a room in the home of one of the professors in the French department, Dr. Henri Beylance. Although his house differed in many ways from the one I'd grown up in, in other ways it was quite similar. He allowed the students who boarded with him the same kind of freedom and respect my grandmother had showed me, and I found that I fit into his quiet family life fairly easily. Providence turned out to be homelike in another way, too, one that may have been even more important, as this was the first time in my life I'd experienced it: I was surrounded by people who shared my interests and worldview.

During my very first week at Brown I made friends with one woman in my department, Janis Mayes, and one from another of the graduate departments, Yvonne Cormier. I still count both of them among my very closest friends; I am godfather to Yvonne's daughter, and Janis, who is now a professor of African-American and French studies at Syracuse, is still one of the people whose advice I most trust. But sometime that autumn, I managed to find my element and met the friends who so shaped me in the years to come. I met them all through Reed Evins. As part of an exchange program between the two campuses, I had gone over to the Rhode Island School of Design to take an art history class. I noticed Reed in the class, and one day, as we were walking down the street afterward, we fell to talking. And that was that. We were off to the races, becoming lifelong friends. Reed was a dandy, as dandy as Charles Baudelaire, the French poet I so admired and eventually ended up writing my thesis about. Reed was always extravagant, very turned out; he was the kind of person who could eat up all the attention in a room simply by walking in. He was that animated and charming, and always had the most impeccable clothes.

Students at Brown lived either in dorms or, as I did that first year, in rented rooms in people's homes. But Reed and his set—the wealthy set—all lived in their own apartments. Reed shared his flat with Jane Kleinman, who also became one of my close friends. They had the entire top floor of a white clapboard house. Reed had come to school with a whole truckload of antiques, the leftovers from his mother's apartment in the United Nations Plaza. (The same building, I later learned, where Truman Capote lived.) There, in his tidy floor-through apartment that looked out over downtown Providence, he had a complete set of Chippendale dining room furniture, service for twelve of heavy sterling silver cutlery and porcelain plate, a complete tea service, sumptuous rugs, and fancy linen sheets. All of these beautiful things needed careful maintenance, so Reed and Jane had regular maid service in their apartment as well. Everything was of the highest quality, and they took it all for granted. Reed, whose parents were of the now-defunct Evins shoe dynasty, was even more spoiled than my friend Lana had been, but like her he managed not to become a brat. I didn't know anything about the shoe industry or who his family was, only that I liked him and enjoyed eating dinner with him and his friends.

One of his closest friends was Robert Turner, who was originally from Baton Rouge, Louisiana, and whose family had a plantation that he went home to during the holidays. Robert drove an emerald green BMW, which was our preferred mode of transport for our escapes to Boston or Manhattan, where we went shopping. At the time, most of the shopping I did was of the window variety, but Robert would use his allowance to buy things like a YSL Rive Gauche cashmere kimono coat or a wolfskin coat from Revillon, which was the smart fur name at Saks Fifth Avenue. (Robert is now a decorator; under Grace Mirabella he was a fashion editor at *Vogue* and later the editor in chief at Vogue Patterns.) We all loved fashion, so we loved visiting the big cities where it resided. We loved shopping at Bonwit Teller as much as we loved sitting around reading *W.* If for some reason Robert wasn't able to chauffeur us on an expedition in his car, the rest of us might just hop on a bus.

All of these people were rich, and if they were not naturally beautiful, they had the kind of beauty wealth can create—they were polished, groomed, and used to a life of ease. They were intelligent, too, and driven to succeed; and they all had style. But the only person on the RISD campus who could rival Reed sartorially was Madeline Parrish, who had come up from somewhere in Virginia in her own brown two-seater Mercedes-Benz and with every stitch of her clothing from Henri Bendel. She, too, had brought a truckload of incredible furniture with her, and she had a lovely apartment all to herself. Every day, when the rest of us were sitting around the dinner table in the canteen, we would guess what designer Madeline would be wearing and wait for her to come in. She might have been coming from the library or her studio and eating from a cafeteria tray, but she was wearing the latest Paris ready-to-wear: Sonia Rykiel, Missoni, Saint Laurent Rive Gauche. Most of Madeline's things came from Yves Saint Laurent, including her shoes, which were always exquisite. Madeline became an editor at *Vogue* before I did.

And these were students at RISD, studying art! Students today wear denim like it was a state-issued uniform, but back in the day, we knew how to dress. As for the fine furniture, it was strange from my point of view, but probably isn't as unusual as one might think; in England, certainly, people go off to Oxford with whole rooms of antique furniture.

Here I was, away from home for the first time ever, yet I had suddenly found acceptance in a small, tightly woven clique of ambitious and talented people. (Tina Weymouth, Chris Frantz, and David Byrne, who later became the new-wave rock group Talking Heads, were part of the same crowd.) Back home, I had never had so much peer approval, but among all these swank socialites, I was suddenly popular. It was as if I led two lives—my quiet life at Brown, where I hung around with Janis and Yvonne and studied French diligently, and my dream life at RISD. Reed and Jane and I were inseparable. We all fed into each other's hunger for the gilded life as we'd seen it in the pages of *W* and in all those books I'd already committed to memory back in Durham. We loved to get dressed up and go to a local discotheque in downtown Providence. On a Friday or Saturday night, we'd wait around till eleven-thirty or twelve, and then we'd go out dancing. I mean, there Madeline Parrish would be in a real Saint Laurent Rive Gauche dress, on a Friday night in Rhode Island! Or in a Sonia Rykiel skirt she had "picked up" on a recent trip she'd taken to New York to go shopping with her mother. We didn't dress up in glitter, but we certainly did dress *up.* Sometimes after we went dancing, we would retire to Reed and Jane's apartment at four in the morning to make breakfast, and there we'd be, eating eggs, bacon, and English muffins off all their fine china and silver.

My fashion life suddenly sprouted wings. Of course, it had been percolating for a long time. It was back in high school that I had thumbtacked up the big magazine spread of Mrs. Vreeland measuring the exact size, in millimeters, of a pearl. If she once said, "Exaggeration is the only reality," I had lived that creed in my fantasy life from a very young age. In high school and college, with Lana, I had begun to experiment with using it as an outward creed, but now that I was in a place where flamboyance was understood, I could live it to the hilt. For the first time, I was surrounded by fashion-conscious people, and I loved their influence on me. I wrapped myself up in an old black oilcloth rain cape that I found on a trip to New York in a Secondhand Rose sort of store in the East Village; I decorated that cape with black tassels removed from an old curtain. I pulled a big, black marauder hat down on my forehead and sauntered off to class, just the way Mrs. Vreeland had Veruschka (that German countess with feet almost as big as mine) photographed as Garbo in the film *Queen Christina.* The only thing I didn't do was paint my nails or dye my hair; but at Brown, I started wearing Vaseline on my eyelids, as Mrs. Vreeland and the model Naomi Sims did in the pages of *Vogue.* I bought Revlon's deep plum and prune lipsticks and rubbed tons of them across my upper forehead, out along my earlobes and cheekbones. I dared to go off to classes like that! Not every day, but on special days, like when I wore my authentic Army-Navy Surplus bell-bottoms, which I bought extremely short, the way the girls and guys in Paris were wearing them at the time. That's what everyone seemed to be wearing in the photographs of the famous Club Sept, a gay nightclub where all the people in Vreeland's *Vogue* partied: Yves Saint Laurent danced there with Pat Cleveland, and Marisa Berenson with Helmut Berger; Grace Jones lip-synched on a tabletop, wearing a micro-miniskirt the size of a belt and no underwear; and Betty Catroux, Karl Lagerfeld, Antonio Lopez, and Loulou de la Falaise were always smiling in photographs. I had a pea coat, and Cuban dance-heeled shoes, and an incredible rubber mackintosh cape for when it rained. There was still the *Men in Vogue* column, and it was there that I learned about things like velvet pants and French silk shirts, versions of which all eventually made it into my wardrobe.

Most of these clothes I left behind when I went home to visit. At home I would need casual clothes for everyday wear and suits for church, but not a fashion parade. I never had any fear of what my grandmother would think, because I knew that she didn't care what style a person's clothes were as long as they were decent and clean. One time I did buy an incredible navy blue admiral's coat at a flea market; it was a maxi coat, with all this gold braid, and I wore that home. My grandmother didn't think anything of it. (My mother, who thought I looked like the Phantom of the Opera in it, refused to walk up the aisle in church next to me.)

I began writing a small gossip and fashion column for the RISD newspaper. It was a very successful column, chronicling my adventures with Reed, Robert, Madeline, and Jane. I had infinitely more fun writing it than I did working on things for school.

For years on end we ate our dinner together nearly every evening at the RISD cafeteria at five o'clock sharp. Their refectory was about halfway between RISD's campus and Brown's—perfect for us to meet up, right at the halfway point between our lives. But sometimes Reed and Jane might give a dinner party, and that was a fantastic event. Out came the china, the crystal, and that heavy silverware; suddenly vases and vases of flowers appeared on tables and the floor, and elegant food materialized as if out of nowhere. It was nothing like the meager dinners we ate off those durable china plates during the week! They gave the swankiest cocktail parties I have ever attended. And Madeline knew how to throw a party equally well. She would give a dinner party and there she would be in some brown satin Yves Saint Laurent pajamas, right out of a Noël Coward scene. Most of the time, they were content to behave like ordinary college students, but when they put on the dog, they went all out.

During that time I also received my first glimmer of acceptance in the fashion world—a tiny little speck of gold, but one that I recognized as precious nonetheless. I had learned through the pages of *Vogue* that Carrie Donovan, who was at that time an editor there, had been instrumental in shaping the career of Pat Cleveland, the first black supermodel, the Josephine Baker of the international runways. I was wild about Pat Cleveland, for her beauty and her style, and also, of course, because she offered me hope that there might be room for me in the world of fashion, too. I typed Carrie Donovan a polite note, asking her for as many of the whos, whats, wheres, and hows of Pat Cleveland's discovery as she might be willing to share with a young person aspiring to have something to do with fashion. Although she had never heard of me, some grad student at Brown, Carrie Donovan sent me back a handwritten note in kelly green ink. In it, she wrote that it was, in fact, she who had discovered Pat Cleveland when she saw her one morning on the subway on the way to work. Actually, it's not entirely certain that Ms. Donovan's memory was correct—though someone discovered Pat Cleveland on the IRT, it was either Carrie Donovan or her best friend, the director Joel Schumacher. But that small factual detail didn't matter to me in any way. I had received a handwritten note from a *Vogue* editor, and I had it framed.

I earned my master's degree in French literature in the spring of 1972. My topic was the pivotal role played by all the fabulous, exotic North African women in the works of poet Charles Baudelaire and painter Eugène Delacroix. My thesis was based on the whole sense of the importance of Africa to the conception of orientalism as it influenced art and literature in nineteenth-century France, a topic in which I had a keen interest. Delacroix's *Les Femmes d'Algiers* featured prominently, as did Flaubert's *Salammbô.* I truly loved writing my master's thesis, and although I still yearned for the world of fashion, I moved on to pursuing my doctorate without any hesitation.

But the seeds of doubt began to take root anyway. When Reed graduated (which was after I finished my master's and just began work on my Ph.D.), he moved back to New York, into a studio apartment in a high-rise on Fifty-seventh Street, near Sutton Place, with incredible views of the East River. Reed had his apartment decorated by Joe Durso in the minimalist style of the '70s, which aptly suited Reed's urbane sensibility. From time to time he came up to visit those of us who were still in Providence, but most of the time, of course, we went down to visit him in New York. Providence was a lovely place to live, but it could not match the star quality of the big city. It was during those weekend visits to my close friend that I began to question my purported career goal. I knew that I loved learning, but what would it mean to be a professor? In my imagination, I always focused on scenes of heated debate with intelligent students and long days spent writing in a book-lined study. But the further I advanced in my studies, the more I realized that my favorite professors spent a great deal of time copying and filing, creating syllabi, reading for class, grading papers, and sparring in departmental politics. Knowing all of this, I still loved and yearned for the security of the academic life, but I began to see for the first time how clearly a scholarly future in rural New England excluded the possibility of a glamorous future in New York. All my love for Mrs. Vreeland's *Vogue,* for Pat Cleveland and Naomi Sims, for Balenciaga and Chanel, would have no more outlet in academia than it had in Durham. That was a sobering thought.

Reed felt sure I had a future in fashion and set himself the task of convincing me to heed it. Reed is the sort of person who could have argued Commodore Vanderbilt out of his last dime, and it was difficult to resist his sway. I pretty much spent the summer of 1974 discussing my future with him and his favorite professor, the artist Richard Merkin, who commuted from Manhattan to his job at RISD. (Yet another sign, I took it, that the academic life wasn't everything I hoped it might be.) Professor Merkin was a great artist and someone whose values and sense of style I admired. Regardless of what fashions might come or go, he dressed like something out of a Fitzgerald novel. He had a walrus mustache, horn-rimmed spectacles, and natty, bespoke clothes—bespoke shoes, bespoke shirts, bespoke suits, bespoke topcoats, and always a bowler hat. I had never taken a class with Professor Merkin, but he was the cool professor at RISD; everyone loved him. He knew of my interest in fashion, and he encouraged me in it wholeheartedly. As I sat in Providence that summer, teaching in the summer school and sending out letters of application to colleges and prep schools in widely varied locations, I began to see how clearly what I was building was more a house of cards than a life.

When school began again in September, my heart was no longer in it. Robert Turner had made up his mind to start looking for a job in Manhattan, so he engaged a small apartment in Reed's building and began driving down from Providence once every week or so for interviews. Each time he went, I accompanied him and brought along another duffel bag of my possessions, so my move to New York was effected slowly, one bag at a time. One time that autumn I rode down with him and attended the Coty Awards ceremony, which seemed to me the epitome of everything I'd dreamed of—all those fashion luminaries in one place! It was dizzying. I had the opportunity there to introduce myself to Carrie Donovan and to thank her in person for that note that had meant so much to me. She remembered me from my letter and immediately took me under her wing. After the ceremony, she was expected at the after-party for Halston at Joe Eula's house, over on West Fifty-fourth Street. For whatever reason, she decided that I should be the one to escort her. So we went over to Fifty-fourth Street, and she simply ushered me in like it was the most normal thing in the world. Joe Eula, a famous illustrator, was known for his parties; I'd learned that from reading *W* long ago. At the party I saw Halston, Elsa Peretti, Pat Cleveland—everyone from the world of fashion was under one roof, sipping champagne and having a good time. That was it for me. From that moment on, though I went to school during the week, I lived for my weekend life, which I spent entirely in New York.

Sometime that November, I rode down in the BMW with Robert and my very last bag, and that was the end of my career at Brown. I never gave formal notice of my departure to the French department; and I left boxes of my possessions in the basement of the dormitory where I'd been living, which I never went back to Providence to claim. Who knows, there may still be some trunks full of wild '70s clothes in that dormitory cellar. I said good-bye to Janis and Yvonne, but I think they must have believed that I'd change my mind and come back. I never did, and never even looked back.

Instead, I began camping out, spending some time on Reed's pony-skin Knoll recliner or on his floor (which, thank God, was carpeted) and some time on Robert's floor (which was, unfortunately, parquet). I didn't want to wear out my welcome at either place, since both of my friends lived in studio apartments. I slept under a beige horse blanket I'd bought at the Salvation Army, which had the look, to me, of Hermès. I had no idea what I was going to do to get into the world of fashion, but I knew I'd figure out some way to do it. I had no money and no means, no job, but I knew I had to do what was most important to me. In the meanwhile, Reed and Robert were very good friends, and they took good care of me, made sure I got fed if I didn't have any money, that kind of thing. We had so much in common; it was such an important thing that we had in common, that we got excited about fashion. You can get really excited about clothes when you're young. There are still young people today who get excited when they see a picture of a Gucci dress or something Karl Lagerfeld has done for Chanel; in the mid-1970s, we were those people and had moved our lives to a place where we could parlay that excitement into a career.

Reed and Jane and I decided that for starters, I simply had to work at the Costume Institute at the Metropolitan Museum of Art. In 1973, Diana Vreeland had made history there by organizing the exhibition

Balenciaga. To get all the clothes for the show, she had simply used her Rolodexes (all five of them) to call her international jet-set chums, who, of course, owned the designer's most smashing clothes and were glad to lend them to this important exhibit. The show had been a hit. Ironically, it was real-world museum goers who made the *Balenciaga* show such a box office sensation.

The trouble was that the Costume Institute had few paying jobs. They relied on volunteers to do much of their labor, but even to volunteer, a person had to be someone, because everyone wanted to do it. You couldn't just walk in off the street saying you were interested in historical fashion; you had to have an impeccable set of references. Some of the volunteers were ordinary citizens, but many came from the fashion world and offered their services to Mrs. Vreeland on the weekends. Much of what volunteers did was manual labor, such as schlepping the mannequins, which are quite heavy, around. Some volunteers were instructed in how to put the actual clothes on the mannequins, which one did not do with one's bare hands, because the acidity of the skin could damage those delicate fabrics. In any event, Reed, Jane, and I decided among us that the most powerful person we knew was Jane's father, who was then the president of Kayser-Roth Hosiery. He very kindly agreed to write me a letter of introduction. With his letter in hand and my heart in my throat, I went over to speak to Stella Blum, who was then the curator of the Costume Institute. (Mrs. Vreeland was technically their special consultant.) Stella and Liz Lawrence read the letter and agreed that I could come there to work, pending Mrs. Vreeland's approval of me. Stella and Liz, who are sadly both now deceased, were very fine ladies.

So I had entrée to the Costume Institute, which was the place I most wanted to be. But I still had no way to support myself outside my friends' generosity, so I kept going the rounds of interviews for jobs of all descriptions. One day Robert was going for an interview at Andy Warhol's magazine of the same name, and I felt wistful, unable to imagine any job more glamorous. Robert allowed me to accompany him to his interview, and I brought with me my portfolio of snippets from the RISD student paper. Peter Lester, who was the editor at the time, liked my writing enough to say he'd be willing to let me contribute from time to time to *SmallTalk,* a fashion and society column at the back of the magazine. It was a huge, huge break, but it wasn't a job, and I still felt poor as dirt.

In the meantime, my grandmother was becoming increasingly concerned about me. She had, as I'd predicted, been chagrined when I'd given up my studies, and she simply could not figure out what I was doing in New York. Every time I called her, she would say, "Sonny, I'm going to wire you money. You need to come home," or, when she was feeling more adamant, "I'm sending your father up there to come get you." Time and again she would say, "I know what you're doing up there—you're sleeping with a white woman. Now get yourself back home so I can talk some sense into you." I understood that she was casting about desperately to figure what I was doing with myself. I had always been a good child, and good children stayed close to home, unless marriage, a job, or education took them elsewhere. To her, without one of those excuses, I had none at all.

This was the only time in my life that I ever felt I was truly displeasing her, and her disapproval cut me like a knife every time she expressed it. I also spent a good deal of time imagining both her point of view and new ways she might choose to convey it to me, all of which made me even more unhappy. Mama had striven throughout my life to give me everything I could possibly need, including the strength of conviction to try to make a place for myself in a completely new world. The idea that I was using everything she taught me in service of something that upset her seemed practically criminal. What she furthermore could not have known was that her pleas wounded me all the more deeply because much of me wanted nothing more than to come home. Sleeping on a blanket on a friend's floor was fine for a night or two, but it began to wear on me when it dragged on for months. I could not stop thinking about the firm mattress and crisp, white sheets that awaited me should I change my mind and return to Durham. Reed and Robert took turns buying me burgers and fries at Hamburger Heaven, but I yearned for homemade biscuits and sweet potato pie. New York was clearly the place where my future would unfold, but my grandmother's house was home, and I longed to go back there as only a fledgling can.

I had plenty of dark days that November. I was lucky that they were illuminated by one very bright point of light: Diana Vreeland.

CHAPTER NINE

My very first day working at the Metropolitan Museum, I arrived bright and early, wearing a lemon yellow V-neck lambswool sweater, which my grandmother had bought me back in high school, and of which I was quite fond. I hadn't yet learned about six-ply cashmere, which was something I would learn from Halston. I was also wearing navy blue alpaca trousers, the sort of pants my grandmother liked me to wear to church. I was as proper as could be. As soon as I got to the museum, Stella handed me a shoebox, which was strangely heavy, some white cotton gloves to wear while working, and a pair of needle-nose pliers. I took the lid off the box, and inside was an absolute mess of little purplish metal discs. Everything around me grew very still.

"What's this?" I asked.

"It's the chain mail dress worn by Miss Lana Turner in *The Prodigal.*"

There was some solace in knowing that the thing was a dress. "What am I to do with it?"

"Fix it. Put it all back together and arrange it on this mannequin." She pointed me in the direction of a mannequin that was standing there in a corner, naked and faceless, waiting for my handiwork. "Mrs. Vreeland will be here shortly to inspect your work."

"Okay. Thanks," I said, and waited for her to leave the room before I put on the gloves and tried to extricate the dress from its box.

The dress was all tangled up on itself, and it took me a good while to lay it out in something approximating its original shape. It turned out to be a Charleston-type fringe skirt harnessed to a bra and bikini. Once I got it laid out, I realized it would be a lot of work to get it to hang right, because many of the wires connecting the discs were twisted, broken, or missing after years of sitting in storage. I was also not, as you may have gathered, the most gifted user of tools. The pliers seemed an awfully industrial thing to have to use on a dress. So they sat awkwardly in my hand, and I felt as if they might damage the dress if I tried to employ them. But I did not panic. I thought, *I must resolve this problem, because it's been given to me.* And after looking at it a while longer, I realized that it wasn't going to take all that much work to make it look the way I wanted it to. It was the sort of thing that anybody could have figured out. After toying with perhaps a half dozen discs, I found that the task was manageable. After an hour or two, I was both making good progress in my appointed work and pleased with how it was turning out.

Around lunchtime, Mrs. Vreeland sauntered in. This was a woman I had loved for years without even having met her; and in that moment, I was somewhat afraid to make her acquaintance, because I knew she would be judging my work, and I had a premonition somehow that my future hung upon her verdict. I made myself inconspicuous, pretending to do some work behind a column so that I could watch her without being seen. That was the very first time I saw her at work, and she was taking very short, staccato steps, on her toes, as she hated the sound of a woman's heels hitting the floor. You could hear a pin drop as she walked with her ballerina gait across the floor. Even on this routine workday, her entrance was regal. She understood about pomp. She was a solo pageant. The first thing I noticed was her navy blue Saint Laurent pea coat; after that I had time to inspect her Mila Schön double-faced jersey pants and hell-red, Mick Jagger, rock-and-roll boots—her signature Roger Vivier boots, of python skin glazed and treated to shine like patent leather. Her bag was a classic: a Cordovan leather Gucci, polished to a high patina like the boots, with a bamboo toggle clasp and a military-style webbed cord strap.

She was so real. Her legendary pelvis-thrust-forward walk, that was real. Her blotter-thin body, real. Her makeup (which definitely was "Kabuki enough"), real real real. She was wearing red rouge that glowed under a layer of Vaseline at her temples, and it was smeared to a degree of outlandish exaggeration. Real. Her raven's-wing blue-black hair was tinted of course, but it was entirely real. Her red eagle-talon nails—it was all there.

My dream walked by as I hid behind that column. She didn't have a greeting or a word for anybody. But as she glided by the mannequin wearing my attempt to pull together the purple, silver, and faux stone bra, bikini, and fringe, she paused and foghorned out, "Who did this?" I couldn't tell if her tone expressed joy or horror.

Liz Lawrence said, "The new volunteer, Mrs. Vreeland."

She continued gliding through the gallery. My radar couldn't get a very good reading on her, but I thought, *She hates it.* Three minutes later, when the Empress must have arrived in her office and taken off her coat, Liz came to tell me that Mrs. Vreeland would see me then, in her office. I knew that the summons could mean a host of things, and I hoped it was a favorable one. Something had happened in that Ziegfeld dancer pass-by, and to this day I'm not certain exactly what it was.

When I walked into her office, Mrs. Vreeland was eating her

sparrowlike daily lunch: one small shot of Dewar's White Label Scotch and a tiny, tiny finger sandwich sent over from Poll's on Lexington Avenue. "Please be seated," she said crisply to me. Although we had not been formally introduced, I could tell from the look in her eye that she had approved of my messing around with Lana Turner's shake-and-shimmy fringe thing.

Perpendicular to her formal desk Mrs. Vreeland had a workstation covered in red oilcloth, which was another Vreeland signature. There she took her lunch and telephone calls. That afternoon, I noticed a little Oriental pleated fan card, which remained on that desk as long as she worked at the museum; I later learned that Veruschka had sent it to her on a trip to Tokyo. As I sat there, Mrs. Vreeland took out a yellow legal pad and a sharpened pencil and hunched slightly over them. She was wearing a turtleneck polo and the two Grès jersey apache scarves she always wore, one looped around her neck, the other slung at the waist. She also had on a tiger's tooth on a gold chain. "Now what is your name, young chap?" she bellowed out foghorn style, while elongating her concave chest beneath all that decoration. The strength of her voice issuing from her small, thin body reminded me of my grandmother when she used to call me home to dinner.

"André," I replied.

She began to write that out in her large, grandiose longhand. Next to my name—I could read what she was writing upside down, her script was so enormous—she wrote, "The Helper."

"Now," she said, putting the pencil down, "you will stay next to my side night and day, until the show is finished! Let's go, kiddo. Let's go out into the gallery. Get crackin'!" All she could have known about me was that I had come from Brown and been recommended by Jane Kleinman's father; her intuition came from some other place.

And that was that. I left feeling encouraged and excited. And that brief conversation changed my life.

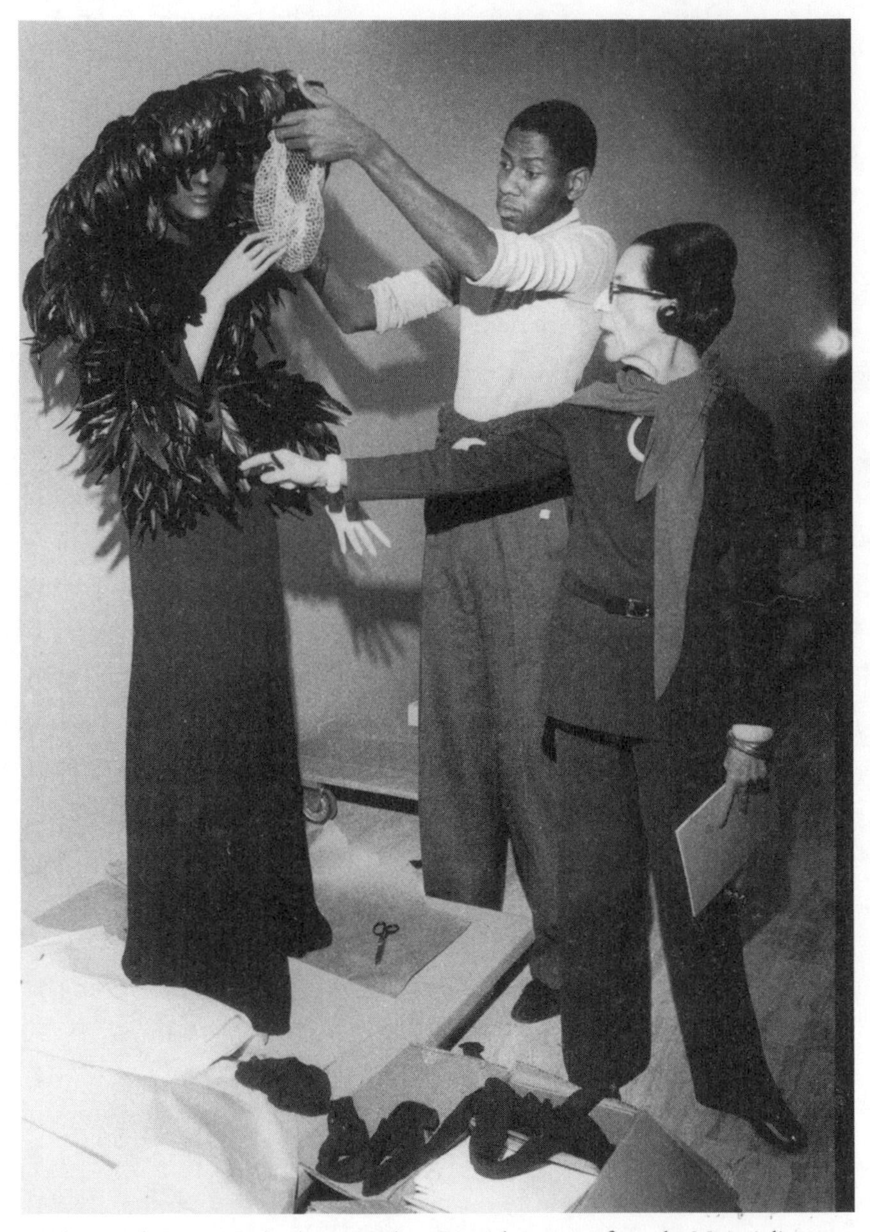

Working with Diana Vreeland on a Marlene Dietrich costume from the Metropolitan Museum of Art Costume Institute exhibit *Romantic and Glamorous Hollywood Design,* in November 1974. *(Copyright © 1974 by Bill Cunningham)*

Over the following six weeks of great work, I had very few one-on-one conversations with her. She was a busy woman with mountains of work to attend to in her office. Those few words she did speak to me, however, seemed imbued with support and encouragement. She was even then feeding me romantic reverie and taking me along with her on her wild ride. As Lee Radziwill once later said to me, "André, you can be elevated off a Diana Vreeland conversation for weeks on end." And it was true that when you left the museum after working with her all day, every pronouncement, every Martha Graham stroll down the galleries echoed in the mind and replayed in the mind's ear. I was simply thrilled to be working there, thrilled to be able to see her and observe her.

She was perhaps more given to far-flung pronouncements than anyone I have ever known. As we were preparing *Romantic and Glamorous Hollywood Design,* I ended up working on Claudette Colbert's gold lamé dress from *Cleopatra.* It had been designed by Adrian with all that '30s bias cool and was really more of a swimsuit with a dramatic train than a dress. Before I began work on the dress, Mrs. Vreeland called me into her office, because she wanted to talk to me about how the dress should be presented and portrayed. But rather than tell me outright, she sat behind her desk and said, "Now, you must remember, André, that she is a queen, the queen of Egypt! She is a queen, but also a girl of fourteen, who lives all day, every day, in the sun. And she walks in a beautiful garden in the sun. This is a child of fourteen and a queen! And in her garden, she walks in the sun, with her white peacocks flapping at her hem. White peacocks, the sun, and this is a girl of fourteen, who is a queen."

Then she leaned back in her chair and said, "Uhhmmmmmm," that delicious utterance she always made, as if she had eaten a chocolate soufflé or Sevruga caviar, or drunk the cool water from a well.

That was all she had to say to me about the Cleopatra dress. After a pause of a moment or so, she said, "That's all, now get crackin'! Right-o." And I was dismissed.

I mused on her oracular speech as I walked back to the gallery—even then, I was used enough to her style not to be daunted by it. But in this way she was exactly like my grandmother: She never once instructed me but instead fed me a dream. *Queen in the sun,* I thought. *What to do?* The dress was waiting for me back in the gallery, as delicate as moth's wings. Suddenly, as I looked at it, I understood the answer to the sphinx question Mrs. Vreeland had posed. I quickly covered a clean platform with acid-free tissue paper, then carefully laid the restored golden dress of silk tissue on top of it. Then I ran off to the paint department, grabbed two cans of gold spray paint, ran back to the gallery, and went to town, spraying the mannequin's whole body the same gold as the dress. And I had never even seen *Goldfinger*! I just wanted to express the idea that the sun was so bright and so golden that its rays were one golden blur. It was the rule that we didn't place any costumes on dummies until they'd dried for twenty-four hours, so I waited until the next day and arrayed the dress in all its splendor.

That afternoon, when Mrs. Vreeland came in at her usual hour—12:30 or 1:00—she saw my Cleopatra, and she smiled from rouge-laden ear to ear. "Right-o, right-*o,* André! I say!" she barked out and then moved on. Her words of encouragement seemed to echo from the rafters, like everything she did.

Another moment of triumph occurred when Mrs. Vreeland called me into her office to explain, in her typically Delphic fashion, about the look she wanted for the hair on the mannequins in a certain room. "Jane Austen macaroons," she instructed me. I chewed on that one for a couple of days. In the meanwhile, Betty Catroux came to town. Betty was another of those "it" people I'd always read about in *W* up at Brown, well known to be Yves Saint Laurent's *high muse.* We had met on the social circuit and had soon discovered that we had a lot to talk about. A day or two after Mrs. Vreeland spoke to me about the mannequins, Betty and I went for lunch at La Grenouille, and when we had placed our napkins beside our plates and were preparing to leave, she told me that she wanted to make a quick run down to Woolworth's on Fifth Avenue.

"What in the world for?" I asked her. I couldn't imagine she wanted a milkshake.

"Fruit of the Loom boys' T-shirts," she answered.

It turned out that she liked to wear these cheap, three-to-a-pack undershirts underneath her very best Saint Laurent couture pantsuits. Everyone else in the world, including Yves's other friends, wore the suits in a uniform fashion—with a silk charmeuse blouse with a bow—but Betty was an original.

So the two of us walked down to Woolworth's. I felt like going there with her was a bit of an adventure. She was a glamorous woman, not at all the kind one would expect to see standing next to a wire basket of shower thongs. As we were passing down an aisle, what did I see but packets of hair nets, the same kind my grandmother had always bought from the five-and-dime down home in Durham. There had always been a few on her dressing table. They took me back home, straight to my grandmother's dressing table in North Carolina, there in the middle of New York City.

I picked up a few packets of silver, the color she always wore. They were cheap, still twenty-five cents for a packet of three. Betty got her T-shirts, and I headed back uptown to the museum. I had a feeling that those silver hair nets—sent to me by my grandmother, I felt certain—might help me to solve the problem Mrs. Vreeland had posed.

She herself had invented the style of covering the mannequins' ghastly faces with pantyhose, which made them seem more mysterious, enchanting. The pantyhose made them look like chic little aliens. I began making macaroons by stuffing the silver hair nets with pantyhose, the same tone as those used to cover the faces, and attaching them to the heads like cocker spaniel ears. I even placed the glittering hair nets right over the faces of some of the mannequins. Mrs. Vreeland was ecstatic. She sent me running back to Woolworth's to buy up their entire stock of my grandmother's plain old everyday silver hair nets.

There were marvelous things in that exhibit. Mrs. Vreeland had gone to Hollywood to look at all the costumes in MGM's storage rooms and had unearthed treasures. She had found and eventually borrowed some of Vivien Leigh's remarkable clothes from *Gone With the Wind,* including that stunning green velvet dress. What Mrs. Vreeland appreciated most were Greta Garbo's clothes from the movie *Camille,* which were as beautiful as couture. All of those dresses had been incredibly, painstakingly handmade by people who were trained in the most elegant and refined dressmaking skills. There was delicate embroidery; there was an opera coat bordered in sable and lined in the finest French silk chiffon. And the most wonderful thing about all of these clothes was that, although they had been made for a black-and-white movie, they were in the loveliest and most carefully chosen colors. I found it fascinating that the designers had gone to all that trouble for something that, except for Mrs. Vreeland's show, only a handful of people would ever have seen, hanging in a dressing room.

I worked fervently, as a volunteer, to help, and when it opened in December, I was proud to be at the dinner celebrating it. All around me were the luminaries I had read about in *Vogue* and *W,* and though practically no one knew who I was, they were all admiring the work I had been part of. Mrs. Vreeland was wearing a fabulous black Madame Grès dress and fabulous black shoes. Toward the end of the party, she subtly beckoned me aside, into her office, with her friend Bill Blass. "Follow me," she said. "Just follow me, and go left." I would never have approached Mrs. Vreeland for a tête-à-tête, let alone for a casual conversation, would never have asked about the weather or her health. She did not invite small talk; one waited to be summoned by such a creature as she, and otherwise one kept one's peace. Even when people at the museum were working, they figured out subtle ways to make themselves not be noticed when she was on a tour of inspection; one didn't stop and say good morning to her. That evening at the party, I wondered what she and Bill Blass could be inviting me in to discuss.

"André, you know," she began, pouring herself just a thimbleful of Scotch, "I'm going away on vacation in Santo Domingo, with Françoise and Oscar de la Renta. But before I go—before Christmas—I want you to come in and see me here, in my office."

"Did I do something wrong?" I asked.

"Certainly not. I want to have a word with you, but not at this party."

When I arrived for my appointment with her three days later, she was sitting behind her desk, dressed in her everyday work clothes, her hair and makeup perfect, her well-manicured nails tapping on her blotter. "Right-o, André, come in," she said. I sat down in my usual place, across the desk from her. "Now I would like very much to hire you at the museum, but there's no budget. That's why we have volunteers, because there's no employment here; there's no job for you. I am telling you this because I don't want you to go home for Christmas," she said.

"I'm sorry?" I said.

"Don't go home for Christmas. Just don't go home!"

"Why not?" I asked. She was looking right at me with her frank brown eyes, but I couldn't imagine what she was thinking.

"Because if you go home right now, you'll never come back to New York. Can you stay here over the holidays?"

The thought had never occurred to me; I couldn't imagine not spending Christmas with my grandmother. "I guess I could stay here," I answered. Reed, after all, was Jewish, and he wouldn't mind having a guest over the holiday, and Robert was going home to Baton Rouge. "Why, though?"

"Because if you return to the South, you may never get out of there again. Let me tell you a story."

Now, Mrs. Vreeland was not a chatty woman. As a volunteer in the museum, I was more accustomed to hearing her give her no-nonsense, upbeat orders than this kind of talk. But my years of experience reading *Vogue* had led me both to trust her opinions and to be deeply interested in her views, so at that moment, as always, I listened to her every word.

"This is a story about an ordinary man who walked into a funeral home one very cold night to warm up and left the funeral home a millionaire. You see, uhhmmmmmm"—her characteristic filler sound—"this fellow had been walking a long time in the cold, and when he saw a light on at Frank Campbell's funeral home, he decided to go inside and get warm. There was no one else in the funeral parlor. It was this ordinary man's good fortune that the embalmed corpse who was lying there in state had been a friendless man and had stipulated that when he died, the first person to come into the funeral parlor and view his remains would inherit his fortune. You see, this hadn't been just any man, but a very, very *rich* man, my friend."

And that seemed to be the end of her story. She scribbled something down on a legal pad.

"Mrs. Vreeland," I asked, "what does this story have to do with me and my predicament? My grandmother would be incredibly sad if I told her I wasn't coming home for the holidays."

"It has everything to do with you. If you stay here and don't give up, everything you want will come to pass. Now get on to work and get crackin'."

"Thank you very much," I said as I let myself out. I didn't quite understand her advice, but I loved the fact that she thought this story connected to my situation. As much as I thought, *This is strange,* I also thought, *Well, this is the way she thinks, and I've always admired her, and I have to trust her.*

I didn't go home for the holidays. It was not that Mrs. Vreeland was right and my grandmother wrong. But I realized at that moment that it was my grandmother's enduring love and the safety of home that allowed me to pursue my dreams.

On that Christmas Eve of 1974, I walked from Robert's apartment over to Saint Thomas Episcopal Church on Fifth Avenue, a grand and beautiful church where I often went to meditate and collect my thoughts. It was a wonderful church to be in, if I couldn't be at home at Mt. Sinai. Although the church was quite elegant, I also found it inviting, the sort of place that encouraged me to search my soul and to pray. (I later learned that it was the very church in which Mrs. Vreeland had been married; fifteen years later it would be the church from which she began her journey home.) In my coat pocket, I had stashed the Christmas present my mother had sent me, a functional man's wallet. Because I was already in a dark state of mind, that gift struck me as hopelessly depressing; it seemed like the sort of gift one might give to a business colleague or a trusted accountant, not to a son who was trying to break into fashion. I thought I would much have preferred a home-made fruitcake. Her gift, however good her intentions had been, seemed unutterably sad. After I finished praying, I left that wallet in its neat brown box on the pew. Someone would find it there and think they had discovered a wonderful thing, just in time for Christmas. I couldn't bear to carry the thing around with me anymore.

My grandmother kept calling me that evening, still deeply upset about my decision not to come home on that most important holiday. "I'll wire you money, sonny boy," she said. "I know you must be living with a white woman. Please just come home." She didn't believe my explanations—that I wasn't sleeping with white women, that I simply didn't want to go home for Christmas, that Mrs. Vreeland had instructed me not to go home. I did tell her I'd been sleeping on the floor, and that made her even more upset. All she could say was, "You should just come home." I told her I was certain things would work out for me in the new year, because Mrs. Vreeland had told me so. Eventually she hung up the phone—and I stayed put in New York City—but she had my father call me, too, threatening to drive up and get me, once and for all. Meanwhile, I had never been away from home for Christmas, and hearing my father's and grandmother's voices flooded me with sadness.

I was camped out on Robert's floor, starving in my soul for a brighter time. He had already left for Louisiana, and Reed had gone out to visit his mother, who lived down the street at United Nations Plaza; it wasn't a Christmas dinner, but it was still a family affair, and I didn't feel comfortable inviting myself. Reed had taken me out for lunch—at one of those places such as Soup Burger that we frequented—but that had been hours ago. I had all of two dollars in my pocket and couldn't have bought myself much of a dinner even if I'd wanted to. But I didn't want to. I wanted to stay home, alone, indoors. Robert lived a typical bachelor existence with regard to grocery shopping, and both the refrigerator and his one-cabinet collection of staple foods were bare. In the back of that cupboard I found an unopened tin of Hershey's chocolate syrup. I unearthed the can opener in the back of the cutlery drawer, took the can of chocolate and a spoon, and went to curl up under my horse blanket. That was my dinner that night—Hershey's syrup, with no milk or ice cream, right out of the can. I ate the entire can. It was a far cry from the holiday meal I would have been eating at my grandmother's house if I'd gone home, and its sweetness could not overpower the bitterness I felt rising in my heart. That was the first time I became aware that I was very alone in life, the first time I had a really agonizing realization of loneliness.

But even to this day, when I speak to Mrs. Vreeland in my mind and memories, I thank her for telling me not to go home that Christmas. Because I truly believe that she was correct; that had I gone home then, I would never have become who I am today. My spirits—worn down by camping out like a vagrant on people's floors, by greasy diner food, and by glimmers of doubt about my choice to abandon my education in pursuit of a dubious dream—were at an all-time low ebb. If I had gone home to my grandmother's cheerful, welcoming home, I would have found it hard to leave that safe refuge. Perhaps I would have gone back up to Brown and continued with my studies, only to accept a junior professorship someplace in the South a few years later. Perhaps I would have given up my studies and taken a steady job with a good salary at North Carolina Mutual Life. But I would never have come back to stake out my place in the fashion trenches.

When Mrs. Vreeland returned from her rest in Santo Domingo, she went the full mile to make her prophecy for my life come true. She wrote to Carrie Donovan at *Harper's Bazaar,* to Mary Campbell at *Vogue,* and to her best friend, Fred Hughes, at Andy Warhol's Factory, on my behalf. It was clear that Mrs. Vreeland was in my corner. Carrie Donovan wrote to tell me that she had never in all her days received such a letter of recommendation from Diana Vreeland and that she simply had to see me. And she did.

Condé Nast Publications did not hire me at that time, in January 1975, but I realized that for good or ill, it was time for me to set out on my own. On a cold, rainy January day, I took a temporary job at the ASPCA animal shelter on the Upper East Side. My job was simply to be the receptionist, but it was agony. As I stared at the telephone console, I heard those dogs and cats cry out all day. It seemed as if they knew how likely they were to face an untimely end. I logged in found dogs and cats, and occasionally had the pleasure of reuniting someone with a lost pet or seeing someone choose a new one, but mostly, the job was a miserable constant reminder of death. In the meantime, I needed money to eat, so I kept going to work, going home to Reed's or Robert's at night, saving up my money to move out on my own.

Finally, at the end of January, some good news came, in the way it always seemed to in those days—at a party. I had a good friend at the time named Gail Lopez Smith, a wonderful married woman who lived in Mrs. Vreeland's building and who was very much a part of the fashion world. She had lived in Paris and was friends with Marisa Berenson, and had been photographed in *Vogue* and, it seemed, in all the magazines. Gail liked to take me out to parties, which she always attended in the most fabulous clothes. One cold, cold night she brought me to a party at Halston's, and when Fred Hughes walked in and saw me, he said, "Would you please come in and see me tomorrow? At the Factory?"

There was a job available at Warhol's *Interview* magazine, where I was already contributing my squibs to the *SmallTalk* section, and thanks to Mrs. Vreeland's laudatory letter of recommendation, I was being offered the position. Although I had no professional credentials, Mrs. Vreeland's recommendation carried a lot of weight, and the *Interview* staff was already pleased with my writing. When I arrived the next day, Fred Hughes told me that "Mrs. Vreeland said we just *had* to have you," so I was hired, for fifty dollars a week, as a typist, runner, and receptionist for the magazine, and allowed to continue moonlighting as a contributor. This was my first big break, my first foot in the door. I was to arrive every day at noon to answer the phones, and would leave at eight to go to all the parties. The job may not have been the world's most lucrative, but it certainly was up my alley. The Factory and its denizens were well known for their parties (Warhol himself, who was the ultimate party hopper, and his coterie of beautiful people—Baby Jane Holzer, Ultra Violet), and it was wonderful to be expected not only to attend them but to report on them.

Mrs. Vreeland had gone out of her way to help me, but that was exactly the sort of thing she was famous for—truly, truly caring about the futures of younger people. Ali McGraw was once her assistant, and strong fashion icons such as Lee Radziwill and Nan Kempner had also worked as her junior editors. They all chose to go through the Vreeland school, which was the only school. She loved young people and loved to be surrounded by them; I think she felt that they were the only people who had any vitality or zip.

The one place I could afford to get a place of my own was at the Downtown YMCA on Twenty-third Street, but that seemed better than nothing, so I moved in with all the cockroaches (the insect kind and the human kind). It wasn't as bad as you might think. For one thing, it was better than sleeping on the floor. And for another, it was such a short walk to the Factory, in Union Square, that I could roll out of bed at eleven and get to my job at noon.

Besides, things no longer seemed so grim to me, because people in the fashion world were starting to take notice of me. Halston, for example, sent over a wonderful Chinese chest, along with some other old furniture that had been gathering dust out in his garage, and some Ultrasuede jackets and zip-front, hooded cashmere cardigans of his own design that he no longer needed. (It was a boon that Halston and I were almost exactly the same size; it meant that I got some fabulous hand-me-downs.) This helped my wardrobe tremendously. Until Halston's gift, I had only one truly great piece of clothing, an Yves Saint Laurent navy blue balmacaan coat, something I had acquired at a Madison Avenue shop by cashing a badly needed stipend check during my graduate school days, which now seemed to have taken place a thousand years before.

As a gift to congratulate me on my success, Reed made me my first pair of bespoke shoes—black silk faille or peau de soie evening slippers, all sleek, with a box toe and no decoration. My first made-to-order shoes! They were so elegant, and I adored them. Until then I had had shoes that served me well and shoes that I liked; but those shoes that he'd made me were my first favorite pair of shoes. I kept them for years and wore them dancing so much that they literally fell to shreds. He gave me those shoes in 1975, and despite literally hundreds of nights on the dance floor, they were still with me when I left for Paris a few years later.

Within a month, everyone at *Interview* was so happy with my work that they decided to promote me to fashion editor. And in August of that year, Mrs. Vreeland's recommendation helped me to move on to the job that became my real stepping-stone into fashion editorial—accessories marketing editor of *WWD.* (Within only two years, I would become this magazine's Paris fashion editor, and shortly thereafter the Paris bureau chief.) At long last I could truly think and write about fashion in the public sphere. My childhood idol John Fairchild was then still king at the magazine, and while I sat at the typewriter funneling my stream-of-consciousness impressions onto paper, he sometimes stood behind me, helping me refine my style. The impressionistic, staccato, Teletype style in which I still write my *StyleFax* column for *Vogue* is largely a result of his wonderful teaching. Mr. Fairchild also helped me learn how to say what I wanted to say quickly and concisely, for it was at *WWD* that I had to learn how to file a story at breakneck speed.

I loved working at *WWD*, and it was under this venerable publication's auspices that I had the pleasure to meet one of my great idols: Truman Capote. I was asked to interview Truman for a large feature article in the summer of 1976, and I relished the opportunity to meet him. I felt that I owed him a debt both for writing *A Christmas Memory*, which was all the more precious to me now that my quiet life with my grandmother was a thing of the past, and for throwing the Black and White Ball that had so fired my imagination.

On the appointed day, I went up to his apartment in the United Nations Plaza, and we sat talking for hours, as if we were old friends. He told me that day that Gustave Flaubert was his favorite author, because Flaubert had such a thorough understanding of style. I nearly fell off my chair when he told me that; and when I told him that Flaubert was also my favorite author, I think we both knew that we would become friends. During the years that I was fortunate enough to know Truman, I often went to his home, along with other of his friends such as C. Z. Guest and Diana Vreeland; whether we were *à deux* or in a group, the conversations at his home were long and sparkling.

Truman had style in everything he wrote, everything he said and did, and everything he wore. There was grace in him—the kind of grace that angels have. His grace made him noble. We never became close, but I always felt blessed to know that fallen angel, to be able to visit him in his apartment or call him up on the telephone. He was troubled, gifted, mercurial, addicted, charming, witty, and always generous. He once called me at work from Silver Hill, the substance abuse rehab clinic he spent time in; and I noted even in his lowest times, he was someone whose every word filled you with a sense of goodness. Getting a note from him was like walking by a park fountain and feeling the cool mist from the water kissing your face.

That same year, Mrs. Vreeland mounted another spectacular exhibition at the Costume Institute, *American Women of Style*. Although I was busy as sin at the time, I volunteered huge amounts of time helping her put the exhibition together. In the section of the show devoted to Millicent Rogers, Mrs. Vreeland once again made use of my silver hair nets, because she wanted Ms. Rogers's incredible clothes to look fresh. Mrs. Vreeland had some of Mrs. Rogers's spectacular clothes; some Mainbocher evening skirts with billowing blouses; and some extraordinary, wacky jewelry that Rogers had made while she was propped up ill in bed in Taos, New Mexico. Those baubles were made of twenty-four-carat gold and diamonds, and she had made them with a nail file. The cheap, cheap hair nets set them off perfectly and became a signature look.

That show was Mrs. Vreeland's masterwork, a true expression of her own personal history and tastes, every bit as much as her book *Allure* would be five years later. The show was especially dear to my heart because it featured the first African-American style icon, the legendary Josephine Baker. As we were putting the show together, Mrs. Vreeland knew that she would simply not have enough money to complete it, so she began writing letters to prominent people, soliciting funds. She wrote to the Johnsons of the *Ebony* magazine company, and they sent a check large enough to install Josephine Baker's clothes in her own whole segment of that show. This was an important moment; no African-American woman had ever, until then, been placed in the same stylistic league as, say, Isadora Duncan.

Nineteen seventy-six marked only my second Christmas away from home, but it was light-years different from the year before. I still missed my grandmother terribly and spoke to her nearly as often as I thought of her; but in that year, I had begun to create a new home for myself in New York. My life seemed to have been playing on fast-forward for nearly a year. During that time, I met many of the people who would become my lifelong friends—people like Paloma Picasso, Manolo Blahnik, and Loulou de la Falaise. These three very stylish European personalities were truly the "it" people of that time; when they came to Manhattan, everyone wanted to invite them to dinner, drinks, or screenings. At that time Paloma wasn't yet a millionaire, because she had not yet inherited her share of her father's fortune, but she lived in the Waldorf-Astoria, went around town in a big limousine, wore Saint Laurent couture clothes, and always picked up everybody's dinner tab. If anyone had told me, during that dark November of 1974, that only a year later, I would regularly be eating dinner with such a marvelous person, I wouldn't have had the imagination to envision it. In 1976, the world I had read about in magazines just a few years before had become my own world; and it was all, every bit of it, thanks to Mrs. Vreeland's grace.

CHAPTER TEN

It seemed like when I was hired at *WWD,* my clothes were upgraded overnight. From a few Halston castoffs, suddenly I had a wardrobe of incredible things. I was wearing those Halston cashmere sweaters with Saint Laurent Rive Gauche velvet evening trousers; and as for Halston's Ultrasuede safari jackets, they were some of the best fashions ever invented, in my opinion. Ultrasuede was so economical for cleaning; you really could throw those jackets right into the washer, and they came out of the dryer like new.

I met Karl Lagerfeld one Sunday afternoon in May 1975, at the Plaza Hotel, with Andy Warhol, Antonio Lopez, and Juan Ramos. Karl and I hit it off instantly, and we are still the best of friends. That spring, when Karl was in town to launch his fragrance Chloé, his suite at the Plaza was the place to be. He had thirty-five matched pieces of luggage piled up there! At the end of his trip, he gave me two shirts. They turned out to be my first three-ply silk crepe de chine shirts, originally made for him by Hilditch & Key, in Paris. I wore them until they fell apart. Since those early days of our friendship, Karl and I have only grown closer. He is one of the few people I have ever met, besides Mrs. Vreeland, with whom I routinely have four- or five-hour conversations. It's a rare thing to connect with someone on so many levels that you can discuss a multitude of topics in that way. Like him, I am someone who has cultivated himself through reading and learning, and it is always a joy to talk with him, not only about fashion but about history, art, or any other topic. At his home I have experienced some of the most restful and happy vacations of my life—a wonderful gift. Karl concentrates on the finer details of life. He has different, beautiful stationery made specially for each of his houses, and always has the most beautiful rugs, candles, flowers, and furniture. Everything is always perfection. His interest in polish, both in its literal and metaphorical senses, reminds me even now of both my grandmother and Mrs. Vreeland, and I am grateful to him for that.

(I will also never forget his generosity in the most terrible year of my life. After my grandmother and Mrs. Vreeland died in quick succession, I was utterly depressed, and at Christmas, I went to spend the holiday with him in France. He sent a ticket for me. I arrived on Christmas Eve on the Concorde, and at midnight we opened presents. Mine was a small, cone-shaped container that looked like it might hold candy. Inside was a Fabergé pin with my initials, ALT, in diamonds. This struck me as one of the most thoughtful—never mind lavish—gestures that anyone could make to someone in my fragile position, and I was deeply touched.)

But back to New York in the 1970s. I advanced fast on a combination of talent, passion, curiosity, good fortune, and a little dose of Southern charm. (I never slept with anyone to get ahead.) I had been raised to be polite and courteous, which, as it turns out, is rare enough to take a person far. I was also truly having fun. One time, when I went to Calvin Klein's penthouse with Carrie Donovan for a huge bash, I was wearing khaki Bermuda shorts and a striped, custom-made Karl Lagerfeld shirt (which he had sent me from Paris, after I wrote to tell him how delighted I was with the shirts he'd already given me) with a starched stovepipe collar that nearly choked me to death. To top it all off, I wore a dandified boater.

I did, after a time, manage to move out of the Y—first to a summer sublet, a walkup on the East Side, and then to my own studio apartment on Fourteenth Street. That apartment was basically a changing room, but even then I had my Saint Laurent sheets and my Saint Laurent yellow monogrammed towels, both of which I had bought at Bloomingdale's. (Someone once stole one of those towels, along with a Chinese kimono, from the laundry room of that apartment building. I was very upset.)

During those years, I went home infrequently—usually for a short visit at Christmas, and sometimes for another in August. If I was lucky, I could also manage to go home for Easter. I yearned for home all the time and spoke to my grandmother constantly, but my life in New York and later in Paris was such a whirlwind of activity that I simply couldn't afford more time away. I did always manage, though, to take those trips home, to ground myself and to remind myself of what was most important to me. Home was always the one place that I really wanted to be. I never truly felt "at home" anywhere else. I always looked forward to being in my grandmother's company and sleeping in my own bed. And I loved the opportunity to sit at my grandmother's table with my many relatives. I have never found anything to replace that sense of peace and comfort I had at home, and I do my best to keep it alive in memory, so that I can still take solace in it.

This was especially important when I moved to Paris for *WWD*. I had never imagined myself quite so far away from home, and it required a certain amount of adjustment. But I loved Paris—loved the air, the colors, the pace of life, loved everything about it. And, of course, I had some of the most important fashion experiences of my life while

I lived there. My first big job in Paris was to file a report about the Yves Saint Laurent couture collection, in January 1978—a collection he called the Porgy and Bess collection. These were strong, masterfully designed clothes, which I thought captured perfectly the way black Southern women dressed—suits with strong shoulder pads, worn with ankle-strapped shoes; bold color combinations such as black, red, and yellow; big chiffon scarves and hats placed just so. When I interviewed Yves about the collection, I was shocked to learn that he had never even *been* to the American South. Remarkably, he had heard that wonderful Gershwin opera one morning on his car radio and had based the entire collection on the impressions the music had made upon him. I was bowled over; those clothes spoke to me on such an emotional level that even then I recognized it was a watershed moment. I had to file my first big report, at 11:30 at night, about that collection—and when Mr. Fairchild received it in New York, he was impressed by the immediacy and emotional truth of the piece and wrote to congratulate me about it. Later, Mrs. Vreeland herself sent me a letter of wholehearted praise for the article. That was when I knew I had succeeded. (She even said that she had spoken to Yves about my piece, and that he had loved it, too.) I have treasured that letter ever since and still keep it by me to buoy me up when times are tough.

Whenever I found myself back in New York—in 1980 for good, but before then, for stretches of time—I felt lucky to have found a place where I fit in. Halston was one of the people who made the city feel most like home—he was that good a friend, even though it was hard to see him apart from a huge group of people. In 1975 I coined the term Ultraettes to describe the posse that always went everywhere with him. Many of these people were notable in themselves—Elsa Peretti, the Italian heiress and gifted jewelry designer; all the models, including my favorite, Pat Cleveland; and Victor Hugo, Halston's Venezuelan lover, who had formerly been a rent boy. Victor saw himself as a self-invented Dada artist, but he was really more of an imitator of anyone or anything he could ape from the studio of Andy Warhol, who genuinely liked him. Victor once decided to make art in Halston's town house. He bought some live chickens, dipped their feet in red paint, and let them walk all over the pale, lush carpets that covered the upper floors. Years later, when Andy Warhol did his infamous series of portraits of male anatomy, Hugo's Rubirosa-scale member was the star of the season.

Back then, people did a lot of drugs at clubs, and you knew who was doing them. They were the ones who went two at a time into the men's room and locked the door, forcing people who simply had to use the facilities to endure a long wait. People did their drugs like that, in bathrooms and in back rooms, in the dark. Of course, there were other kinds of hedonism going on in those locked stalls at that time. I remember that once, one summer when I came back from Paris and stayed with my very close friend Diane von Furstenberg, when she lived in the old Rockefeller apartment on Fifth Avenue (I simply took up residence in one of her seemingly endless guest rooms), a friend came up to me at 54 and said, "I have to show you something." He led me off to a remote corner of the terrace, and there were couples of every description having sex! Gay couples and straight couples, having sex in public, and people were just standing around watching. In the mid '80s, there was a place called the Saint, where you heard of all kinds of crazy things, like people having sex with snakes. But I will get back to sex clubs.

In those days, you didn't go every night to a dance party or a huge fête at someone's house, but the Factory crowd went out absolutely every night to do *something*. We went to gallery openings, movie premieres, and Off-Broadway plays, then went out to dinner in small groups of friends. After work there was always an extension of the office through its social calendar, which was full up with interesting events. Even if it hadn't been "mandatory" to go out every night, I had to find things to write about in *SmallTalk*. I went to tons of movies and movie openings; I recall one opening that took place in a subway station right on Fifty-seventh Street. (The location may have been too memorable for the filmmakers' own good, because as well as I remember the venue,

I no longer recall what film it was.) We were always going around, and it was very, very exciting. I felt like I had a grand tour right here in Manhattan.

I was there the night Studio 54 opened, and also there the night it closed. Before I went, I didn't expect much of it; to me it was just an event where everyone was going to be, something I looked forward to, but not with wild anticipation. Once we got there, I saw immediately what a great, great place it was and knew that this would from now on be the place to go to see anything or anybody new. It was quite extraordinary to watch the moon come out of the ceiling! There were, of course, many other places that we liked to go in order to dance. There was a place called the Loft, a private dance club someplace downtown that we all frequented; we'd show up around midnight and dance till seven in the morning. The Infinity and the Limelight were also popular places of approximately that same vintage; Regine's on Park Avenue was a favorite; but 54 was truly the epitome of a great discotheque. It was fabulous, glamorous, and very decadent. I can't say that it changed my life, but I can certainly say that it was unique. The world passed through 54—everyone from artists to actors to movie stars to socialites and politicians. Every famous person in America, it seemed, was there. You'd see Sylvester Stallone, Arnold Schwarzenegger, Maria Shriver, all manner of famous people. It was a meeting of minds, a meeting of all the various levels of culture, of a kind that I just don't think happens anymore.

The night culture then was not so much about music as it was in the '80s, when people went to Danceteria. It was about fashion and disco, the glamour of dressing up for the disco moment. Before 54, there was a club called Le Jardin on Times Square, which I thought was absolutely extraordinary. It was up on a rooftop and decorated with silver palm trees. The music and the people there were great. You might go and see Yves Saint Laurent or Bianca Jagger. It was a fabulous nighttime world. And everybody danced disco in the outlandish clothes of that era: the women were wearing Goody Two Shoes platform shoes, and the men were wearing enormous platforms—horrific Carmen Miranda shoes. And everyone had them on, those wedgies! Naomi Sims and the Halston girls used to wear them with shorts and knee socks and actually dance in those things. And everybody looked great. You could go in something as simple as a pair of jeans, but the attitude you wore it with was very important. Despite which, the atmosphere there—and all over New York in the '70s—was very democratic. It wasn't xenophobic, homophobic, right wing, or left wing—it was all just people getting together and having fun and creating a lot of positive energy. Calvin Klein gave his first big show in a disco, with hundreds of models—it was quite an event.

As strange as it may sound, the friends I made during those years of party hopping have become some of my most lasting friends—in addition to Mrs. Vreeland, people like Carrie Donovan, Karl Lagerfeld, Fran Lebowitz, Oscar de la Renta, Diane von Furstenberg, and Calvin Klein. We may have found ourselves in a climate that lent itself to artificiality and posturing, but when people had good hearts, those still managed to shine through. Bianca Jagger was absolutely my kind of person. Now she's no longer the fashion plate—she's busy fighting for causes such as Amnesty International—but at the time, she was very stylish and a true role model to anyone who aspired to high chic. The first time I met her, it was to pick her up by limo for an *Interview* cover shoot. I went to her room at the Hotel Pierre, and when I got there, Mick was sleeping. She said, "Don't disturb him. Come into the closet." It was an enormous walk-in closet, full of beautiful clothes and the Vuitton rifle cases she had made expressly to store her evening dresses, so that they wouldn't have to fold. Even to go to a photo shoot, she packed her shoes and clothes as carefully as anyone else would to go on a week's journey.

At one point, Bianca rented a house on the Upper East Side. One December, we were all hanging out there every night before going to 54. Halston would always be there, because they were very close friends. And she would receive us all on the sofa in the most extraordinary tea gown. I have no idea where it had come from, but it was absolutely divine—a confection of miles and miles of silk and ruffles and bows that made her look like some nineteenth-century painting. Later on, she'd change into something more au courant, and we'd all head out to the clubs. But whatever she was wearing, Bianca had the style of a 1930s film star; she called to mind Greta Garbo or Carole Lombard. The care and attention to her hair, makeup, attitude, and beauty gave her a phenomenally powerful presence. And Bianca did not spend all her time putting together outfits; it was a natural talent she had, something she could do effortlessly and quickly, which impressed us all in those days of dressing up and going out.

That one summer when I stayed with Diane von Furstenberg, we would both come home from work and sit around until eight-thirty or so figuring out what to wear to dinner and to Studio 54. Her chauffeur would whisk us over, and we'd sit around the banquettes and dance. That's what we did almost all of the time.

Disco diving till dawn was *the thing* in those days. Hurrah was uptown, on the West Side; there were too many clubs to count, downtown; and after hours we might all go to Miss 220, which didn't open until around four in the morning. Everyone was frisked before going up the rickety stairs to this second-story bar—the bouncers were looking for weapons. Inside, middle-class straight men groped up various she-man Diana Rosses, Chers, and Donna Summerses.

I don't miss 54, exactly, but I do sometimes think it would be great if New York could have a place like that again. Or a place like Regine's, where it was always so wonderful to go after a big party. Everyone was always saying, "Let's go to Regine's!" And you'd go and sit—sometimes for less than an hour, but it was just so wonderful to go to a place where you knew you might run into friends from all over the globe. There would be people there from Paris and people there from Queens. And people then did not seem to be as cliquish or snobbish as they do today; there was lots of mixing of people of different professions, classes, genders, and races. It would be nice to have that feeling again, though in truth I no longer feel like going out dancing every night.

There were other kinds of decadence in the Warhol and Halston crowds. It was a very attractive and glamorous group of people, sort of like Hollywood is today, only more interesting. It was modern, dressy, witty, and snappy. At one party you might have Liza Minnelli, Martha Graham, Diana Vreeland, Mikhail Baryshnikov, and Sao Schlumberger. (Sao is a wonderful European art patroness, a grand lady and a great supporter of Andy's.) And even if you went to Halston's house in a turtleneck sweater—which people certainly did—it was a very carefully *chosen* turtleneck sweater, one that conveyed an impression.

As all of this decadence transpired around me, I had my Vreeland life, which was a quiet, thoughtful life, but equally entertaining. My friendship with Mrs. Vreeland didn't evolve. It just happened! Things didn't "evolve" with her—they were what they were, and then one day, almost out of the blue, she said, "Come up to dinner." Until then, we had been in the same world, running into each other at various dinners. I would be invited to the de la Rentas', or to Halston's, and she would turn out also to be a guest; Andy Warhol, who always included me in his social life, would invite me to a restaurant, and there she would be. When I became fashion editor at *Interview,* and later when I moved to *WWD,* I started receiving invitations to all the designers' openings and to other events at which I needed to represent the magazine, and Mrs. Vreeland was always at these events. When I went to Rome to cover the couture, I spent time with her there. I remember once being at a Patti LaBelle concert, in some theater on the Upper West Side, and seeing Mrs. V. come in with Lee Radziwill, Fred Hughes, and Andy Warhol. That was how things were in those days—people connected to the Factory could get free tickets to anything, and we all went to everything, whatever it was. Mrs. Vreeland always tactfully bowed out of anything that seemed remotely likely to become wild. If she did show at Halston's, she would go home early, on the arm of Fred Hughes. She was, however, frequently out and about with the Warhol crowd. I always treated her formally. In all our years of friendship, I never once called her "Diana"; she was Mrs. Vreeland to André.

I think that early on she recognized the way her own iconoclasm—

that quality that had both made her such a visionary editor at *Vogue* and gotten her fired—was reflected in me. She could tell that I did not like things or do things because someone else told me to, but rather, because I had my own understanding of taste and style; that although it was constantly evolving, it was always done by my own hand.

By the time I moved to Paris, she was my friend as well as my supporter. I don't know exactly how it happened, except, as I said, that one night she invited me over for dinner. Fashion may be full of people who smile to your face and snipe at your back, but she was always unequivocal in her opinions. When I first moved to Paris, I felt like a salmon swimming upstream, so little did I know about what I would do. But she offered me her unwavering, wholehearted support. And it was when I returned from Paris, in the 1980s, that we began spending such huge amounts of our time together.

Now, Mrs. Vreeland was no druggie. I never saw her stoned on coke or pot. But when we began having dinner alone, just the two of us, dinner was always followed by us going into her drawing room, where we sat and drank vodka. She drank her vodka straight, Russian style—at room temperature. In fact she liked all things Russian, so vodka in a straight little shot glass was the rule. And although during those long evening talks, I frequently got up to go to the wet bar to replenish our drinks, she never drank to the point of drunkenness. Rather, liquor was part of the atmosphere of an evening, part of what made conversation so entrancing; never something to be abused.

Mrs. Vreeland loved just about anything from Russia (which she pronounced "*rush*-hour") and obsessed on that country's extravagance. She had a taste for anything that smacked of the courtly; she loved Marie Antoinette, and *adored* England's Queen Elizabeth I ("Took her *four hours* to get dressed!" she once foghorned to me) for that reason. She was interested in all matters that related to food, dress, flowers, manners, courtesy, or the science of wearing jewels. She was big on ballroom dancing. I think her entire interest in Russia stemmed from a tale she once heard that Empress Catherine the Great had five thousand dresses. Mrs. Vreeland had the chance to inspect a trove of them in person when she went to the Russian Museum's archives in Moscow to research the show *Russian Style* for the Costume Institute.

She loved the dress Catherine had worn to her wedding: It was as wide across as a little sofa and made entirely of spun silver cloth. And I know she loved the myth of Catherine riding up the stairs into one of her palaces on her white stallion. Mrs. Vreeland was constantly talking about Marlene Dietrich performing that very stunt in the film *The Scarlet Empress*—she loved to relate how Catherine had completed her coup by killing off her degenerate, deranged, syphilis-ridden husband, and then ridden up the steps of her palace, triumphant, on a white mount. (She also frequently told the story of the Electors of the Palatine in Brühl, Germany, who also rode their horses up the stairs of their magnificent palace. After her death, I once took a plane there from Paris, just to see this place she so adored, just to see that grand staircase. She was all about the grand, dramatic, theatrical gesture. It seemed a fitting tribute to go there in her honor.) She loved caviar and blini, in addition to her vodka. She loved the Ballets Russes. She was mad for Nureyev, for Saint Laurent's Russian peasant look, and for his grand, operatic Russian couture of 1977. She loved brocade, lamé, the onion domes and the wood of Russian churches, and the legends of all the great tsars and tsarinas. I think she identified with Russia because it is an exaggerated country, full of contradictions, juxtapositions, strength, and flamboyance. When she put the show together, she could have done much of the planning over the telephone or by mail, but she chose instead to go to Russia herself, accompanied by Fred Hughes. It was important to her not only to have knowledge of her subject, but to have acquired it herself. That was the kind of inquisitive mind she possessed. If she spoke about a subject, you knew she was well read in it. She invented her own world, through her reading and her knowledge.

Her flat was grand, but she did not live like a tsarina. Her red seraglio, done by Billy Baldwin, never changed. It was all done up in a typically cozy yet grand English style. Her living room was small and had an L-shaped dining area in which wooden storage bins had been made into banquettes. Red was the predominant color in that apartment, and everything had been finished in impeccable good taste, every detail carefully orchestrated. In ceramic bowls filled with earth, she would light lemon verbena joss sticks that she had specially shipped to her from a source in California. Parrot tulips by the dozens were thrust into cylindrical vases in a dense, informal style. Going to dinner at Mrs. Vreeland's was an occasion full of pomp and pageantry, every bit as much as at her public sorties. Her apartment was my Parnassus.

When I first began going to her apartment, I marveled at the riches she had in that modest-sized space—under the tables she kept loaded with potted gloxinia she had "tortoises," made from real carapaces, but with solid silver heads and legs. I asked her once how and where she had acquired such riches.

Sitting in her pint-sized Georgian easy chair, she smiled and said, "I did not buy a single thing in this room. Everything you see was a gift from some generous friend, whom I have loved, and whom I have worked hard to support."

I remember thinking that she must have had extravagant friends who loved her dearly, because they lavished her with Scottish horn snuffboxes, Himalayan snow leopard throw pillows, *bibelots* of every description, and Venetian blackamoor wall sconces, among other things.

Mrs. Vreeland went on record making all sorts of outlandish pronouncements, such as how she learned everything she knew, including her attenuated gait, from the Ziegfeld Follies showgirls. I believed her when she said such things. One has only to look at the photographs of the dancers she selected for her book *Allure* to see how absolutely magical they are, even today. (And it's easy to imagine how much more so they would have been in an earlier, simpler time.) Their bodies and costumes describe the most elegant, eloquent lines—of course, she loved them and modeled herself after them. If people did such things more often, imagine what a wonderful spectacle the streets of Des Moines or Allentown would be.

Whenever she said anything outlandish, I believed it to be so. What she said didn't have to be true to the letter of the law to be true to her spirit, her memory, or what she was trying to convey. Mrs. Vreeland was childlike in her fascination with detail and capable of the sort of visual excitement that only a painter or photographer could rival. There was never any reason to disbelieve her. Her unfeeling and ungenerous detractors—mostly jealous social types and envious competitors—said, after her death, that everything about her had been an elaborate hoax, that she wasn't from the U.K. at all but from one of the outer boroughs. Nothing could be further from the truth. Right after she died, I spent six long, emotionally difficult weeks in England, researching her roots, and just about everything she'd told me turned out to be a documented fact. During that time I went to her niece's home in the English countryside (this was the niece, some might remember from *D. V.,* whom she dressed from Hattie Carnegie in New York during the Second World War), to learn about Mrs. Vreeland's family history. All along the corridors of her stately manor house were photographs of Vreeland's kin and ancestors—prosaic documentation of the mythology and the legend. (Si Newhouse had first seen these photographs of Vreeland's family on a visit to the famous Gertrude Jekyll gardens that belonged to this home.) There was evidence of everything she'd spoken to me of—the nanny, Pink; growing up in the Bois; the beautiful dress she'd worn to be presented to the King and Queen at Buckingham Palace in May of 1933; even learning to ride with Buffalo Bill Cody in Wyoming. (I wasn't able to track down evidence that Mr. Bojangles had taught her to tap-dance, but since the Buffalo Bill story was true, I suspect that one was as well.) I had always believed every word Mrs. Vreeland spoke to me, yet it was thrilling to see her stories documented in all those precious sepia-toned photographs. Her niece generously allowed me to travel to New York with her family albums, which remained safely locked in Anna Wintour's office until it was time to do the layouts in the magazine in honor of Mrs. Vreeland's life and legacy.

Truman Capote once said that she was "like some exotic parrot flung out of a tropical jungle. You either get her or you don't."

I got all of her. Her public self and her private self, her ideas and their execution; there was no part of her that I disliked or didn't understand. Even the ways we were different were dear to me.

For example, Mrs. Vreeland hated any kind of talk about money. Because of her horror of discussing it, I never discovered exactly what this was about, but I suspect that she must have considered it sordid. She couldn't bear to hear people talking about their finances being in good shape or bad. Once when I was flat broke I tried to ask her for advice, and she simply went blank and changed the subject, resolutely having nothing to do with it. She cared deeply about me and any hardship I might be going through but had no notion of how to cope with the issue I was raising. Perhaps the only time I heard her raise the topic of money was once when she interrupted my reading to ask, "Do you think you could get Gianni Versace to buy this bed?" It was a famous Syrie Maugham bed, a sleigh bed with an elaborate, upholstered headboard, and she felt that Versace could afford to pay the outrageous sum she was hoping the bed could command; I can't remember the exact figure, but she was throwing around numbers of the magnitude of twenty-five thousand dollars. I didn't respond to the question about Versace, and she didn't ask again.

Although she must have worried about money—at times she had up to five staffers working for her in that small five-room apartment, and she saw her kitchen perhaps twice in her life—I never once heard her complain about it. Toward the end of her life, she was frequently harder up than I think anybody realized. That was the time when I used to go up in the evenings to read to her; I would sit in an old Indian wicker chair in her bedroom, and she would be propped up in a bed she hardly left any longer, but always still beautifully groomed. She would lie outside the bedcovers, wrapped up in a terrycloth robe, with her beautiful pedicured feet propped up on a small cushion.

People always thought of Mrs. Vreeland as wealthy because of her extravagant and elegant taste, but that really wasn't so. This was a woman who worked all her life. She had been fired from her job at *Vogue* at the age of sixty-nine yet had managed not only to land on her feet but also to invent a whole new way of seeing clothes: in a museum setting. Her shows at the Metropolitan were always, always sold-out hits on the scale of a Broadway show like *The Producers*. And, to her credit, she came in under budget every time and always met her deadlines.

She had other sources of income—her friend Bill Blass, concerned about her finances, got her a scented-room contract and a bedsheet license. For a brief while, the world had D.V. sheets. Blass, one of her most loyal friends in New York, never let her down. Neither did Oscar de la Renta and his late wife, Françoise. All the people Mrs. Vreeland had helped while she was at *Vogue* took care of her in her time of need, as well they should have. She had made so many careers.

I began to read to Mrs. Vreeland after dinner on weekend evenings long before she lost her sight. We began around the time of her Russian show. These reading sessions seemed to me like natural outgrowths of our marathon telephone conversations. (I distinctly recall talking to her once about espadrilles for more than three hours. If I were to tell you that about any other person on earth, I would give you leave to think that person lacked inner resources; but with Mrs. Vreeland, such a conversation was lively, intelligent, and full of relevance beyond the topic of mere shoes.) These long phone calls metamorphosed into long evenings talking, and then became evenings reading at her apartment. She liked my voice, because it reminded her of the deep, rich voice of her late husband, T. Reed Vreeland. He had read to her during the early days of their long marriage, so when I began to read to her it seemed utterly natural and familiar to her. It was wonderful. We were both entertained by whatever I read, and we bonded over the experience of sharing books. I have a strong voice that could easily endure four or five straight hours of reading aloud. And she loved having me read to her, because she knew that I loved the joy of discovery in exactly the same way she did.

The first book I read her was *The Last Romantic: A Biography of Queen Marie of Roumania* by Hannah Pakula. I read her the entire book over a series of weekends—Fridays, Saturdays, and Sundays. The first weekend that we spent that way, I thought, *This is so much better than going to Connecticut or upstate for some house party!* When I returned to work that Monday morning, I felt refreshed and revivified, instead of tired. After that first book, I read Queen Marie's own memoirs. Mrs. Vreeland simply adored her descriptions of luxury, as well as her accounts of the tactics a queen took to ensure her own survival. Mrs. Vreeland was, after all, a sort of empress herself, and this was useful, necessary information. I also read to her from Guy de Rothschild's memoir, *Whims of Fortune.* We both loved drinking in the luxurious details of Guy's life as a child in his family's elaborate country estate at Ferrières, outside of Paris. We went wild for the way food was prepared there: in an entirely separate building behind the house. It was transported to the main house via a subterranean railroad, then brought to table by a servant. We loved hearing about the elaborate system for keeping the fires burning equally in all of the upper rooms, and loved, in general, his evocation of what life was like before the First World War. Mrs. Vreeland particularly loved it, because she remembered those days, and her life of smaller-scale yet still marvelous luxury, so vividly. Her friend Jackie Kennedy sometimes sent us suggestions for our reading, too, which struck me as an honor.

We never read newspaper articles, but we often read magazines together, and, as I'm sure you've gathered, we never watched television. You might be surprised to learn that Mrs. Vreeland had a television in her bedroom, but she never seemed to switch it on, in my presence.

After dinner, we would retire to the living room, where demitasse was served. She liked to sit in her little Charles I chair—for all the world like a queen on a Mini-Me-sized throne—and saw to it that there was a shot of vodka waiting for each of us, for after the coffee. As we sipped our coffee, we talked over the most ordinary, entertaining things—the events of the week, the latest gossip, the kinds of things that in themselves may be inconsequential, but the sharing of which makes up so much of being best friends. Once that prelude conversation had drawn to its natural close, Mrs. Vreeland would chime in with her "Let's get crackin'!" just as she had when we worked together at the museum. She'd say, "I want to hear every word." And off I'd go.

Some books, as I mentioned, we read straight through, both of us hanging on every word, but much of the time, I read chapters to her by subject interest. Almost never could I read an entire book in one sitting. And though we frequently stayed up reading and talking to four or five in the morning, sooner or later I went home and she went to bed. Magazine articles were always very much in demand with Mrs. Vreeland—she loved keeping abreast of what was current, and we both loved the energetic style the best articles could convey.

Reading those magazine articles sometimes did, however, point out to me what different worlds we came up in, though we shared so many interests and affinities. One such article was in the magazine *Musician,* about the artist Prince, and we both found it quite interesting. After I had finished it and replenished our tiny glasses, she said, "Now, when are you bringing him around for a meal?"

I said, "Mrs. Vreeland, I don't know him at all."

"Well, ring him up," she said, incredulous. "Get him over! I want to meet him, as he sounds most fascinating."

She thought it would just be normal for me to call up Prince, wherever he lived, in Minneapolis, and say, "Come over here, meet Mrs. Vreeland for dinner." Because the people who came to dinner in her prime were extraordinary—Mick and Bianca Jagger, Cecil Beaton, Truman Capote, Jack Nicholson, Jacqueline Kennedy, Sister Parrish, Isak Dinesen, Greta Garbo, and Maria Callas, who once went to Mrs. Vreeland's house for Thanksgiving. In the 1930s, she was friends with Schiaparelli, with Jean Cocteau, with the painter Christian Bérard. (She once told me a story I cherish, about Bérard's little poodle, which was called Jacinthe. Bérard really loved the dog and always had him around while he was working; as often as not, he ended up wiping his paintbrushes on Jacinthe's coat. The dog was extremely well cared for but multicolored.) It was a badge of honor to be invited to Mrs. Vreeland's apartment.

Today, she would probably say to me, "Bring your friend Macy Gray." (That would be an easier request to fulfill, because I know her.) You see, Mrs. Vreeland loved black culture. She loved the Saturday morning dance show *Soul Train;* my grandmother cared nothing for it. Mrs. Vreeland had a fantasy that all the races of color would take over the world in every sphere one day—she would have beamed with joy if she had lived to see the 2002 Academy Awards, in which Halle Berry, Denzel Washington, and Sidney Poitier were all honored. She went hog wild over every manifestation of black style. It all began, I think, with Josephine Baker, who truly was one of the most stylish women ever to have walked this planet. Mrs. Vreeland loved to tell a story of watching a movie one night in the balcony of a Paris cinema, back in the 1930s. She had her elbows on the armrests and was intently watching the film, when all of a sudden, one of the armrests *moved.* She turned to see what could be going on and found that she had been resting her elbow not on the arm of the seat, but on the head of Josephine Baker's pet cheetah and that both the magnificent cat and its magnificent owner were now getting up to leave. Mrs. Vreeland watched speechlessly as the cheetah padded in a stately fashion up the aisle of the theater, Josephine Baker walking regally behind, wearing a daring, bias-cut Vionnet dress, with no underwear on beneath it.

That must have been the beginning of an obsession for Mrs. Vreeland every bit as intense as her love affair with Russia. She remembered Harlem from its golden cultural heyday and fondly remembered going up there to take those dancing lessons with Bill "Bojangles" Robinson. She loved the fashions modern black women wore, and the care and creativity with which they styled their hair. She loved the way they walked and the way they did their nails in the most extreme, outlandish shapes, colors, and patterns, especially when they had those fake or real diamond implants. Had she ever had the opportunity to attend a service at Abyssinian Baptist Church with me (and I wish she had; though I am at least glad that the plaques I donated in her memory and my grandmother's adorn its walls today), she would surely have agreed with me that the women there are the *ne plus ultra* of New York style. She used to call us "The New Blacks," with that incredible smile upon her face.

Diana Vreeland *loved* Diana Ross. Once, when the singer came to dinner, she sent over the most extravagant present the next morning—an exquisite Fabergé egg cup, from that posh Fifth Avenue purveyor of the beauties of Tsarist Russia, A La Vieille Russie. Mrs. Vreeland promptly brought the cup into her bathroom, where she proudly used it as a Q-Tip holder.

The truth was, Mrs. Vreeland's interest in black artists and cultural figures was much like her interest in Russia or India—she believed that beauty came from all places. She could appreciate the exoticism of other cultures or people without thinking them somehow less important because they were different.

After our reading was completed, Mrs. Vreeland and I would stop and talk again. There would be more vodka for both of us, and a few more cigarettes for her. She smoked cigarettes in the same way my grandmother dipped snuff. She partook of this vice daily, and clearly always relished it as a particular treat. There were many, many Friday, Saturday, and Sunday evenings when I would leave her apartment at dawn. And as the years went on, I would even be there to read to her on Christmas Eve—flying out early the next morning to spend that important holiday with my grandmother—because we loved each other's company so much.

Mrs. Vreeland was a woman of strong tastes, strong affections, and equally strong whims. One afternoon during her long illness, she confessed to me that she was experiencing a yen for red sheets. Why? Who knows? But such things were as serious to her as another person's craving for a favorite food might be. I relayed her hankering for the sheets to Paloma Picasso, who asked me to meet her later at Pratesi. Together we picked out an entire set of red damask sheets and pillow slips, which Paloma gladly paid for and sent over. Though Mrs. Vreeland exclaimed passionately over the sheets' beauty—they definitely satisfied the craving—I never once saw them on her bed; they went straight to her well-organized linen closet, only to be removed after her death.

She knew a lot about luxury, and it was always beautifully expressed in the decoration of her bed. She liked wild Porthault patterns in bright colors, a holdover from her '60s Youthquake fever. Some of her patterns dazzled, others clashed madly, with jarring colors. She really used those exquisite linens, except for the mysterious red set. In all the time I read to her, I never saw one pillow or bedsheet wrinkled.

The way everything had been done when she was healthy—as if she lived in a grand house with a *Gosford Park* staff—continued unchanged when she was ill. I mean, if you could have seen the nursing students employed to help her! They were drilled in every last detail, taught to organize and to arrange as if Mrs. Vreeland remembered a life as a duchess from the days before she'd had to go to work. I remember one Saturday afternoon, a rare midday visit, when I was there to photograph her shoes for a spread for *W.* Mrs. Vreeland was packing for a trip abroad, going about her house barking orders exactly as she had done at the museum, wearing a sort of red Austrian hausfrau dress and espadrilles. She had a hired girl down on her knees, packing her Vuittons, and she micromanaged the pleating of the tissue paper between the layers of clothes. (The suitcase she was packing when I arrived contained nothing but trousers and polo sweaters. An entire suitcase full of trousers and polo sweaters!) How she reminded me of my grandmother then, wrapping and packing as if the fate of the world depended on it. To a small extent, of course, it did. Without that commitment to rigorous care, to the importance of luxury, appearances, and doing things right, the world would be a less beautiful place.

She loved the idea of regimental, almost military discipline, exactly as my grandmother did. Her gloves were always properly stretched, her Roger Vivier boots and pilgrim-buckle ring lizard shoes well cared for. That is what she was all about, keeping up appearances and brilliant upkeep. She kept her style up until the end, never failing. I never saw her cry—she was too disciplined for that—but I often saw tears well up in her eyes because of happiness.

After Mrs. Vreeland's sight became weak, she took to her bed. That was 1986, the same year that she did not show up for an opening night gala at the Met. The show in question was about Indian costume, whose manner and excess pleased her almost as much as Empress Catherine's dresses had.

That Sunday evening I escorted Carrie Donovan, and we both went to the party. It was a wonderful night—another manifestation of Mrs. Vreeland's genius. But as the evening wore on, I began to worry about her. It was unlike Diana Vreeland ever to be late, let alone not to appear at a party whose primary aim was to celebrate her. Her absence cast a pall over the entire affair.

The next morning, as soon as I awoke, I rang up ELdorado 5-2288. The phone was immediately passed over to Mrs. Vreeland by Dolores, her secretary.

"Come up for dinner this evening, André," Mrs. Vreeland said without even saying hello. Her tone was as bright and energetic as ever. "I want to know all about last night at the museum."

I didn't dare ask on the phone what had happened, why she had not shown up at her table in her new pink Yves Saint Laurent tunic and skirt. I agreed to dinner and signed off, still wondering. That December evening, a dreary Tuesday, as I recall, was the first time I was received by Mrs. Vreeland in bed.

Her explanation was simple. "André, I've had such a wonderful life, and now I've decided to take it easy. Look, I've done so much for so many people. Look at all the boys I helped down on Seventh Avenue. I have done so much for friends like Oscar, Bill, and Halston. Now I am going to sit back and relax. It's time now to just lie here and enjoy life, from this room. Quite simply, I've had it!"

How did Mrs. Vreeland go blind? Simply, it seemed, as a result of her advanced age. When her sight was nearly gone, I asked her once what exactly had happened to her. She said, "One morning, I simply woke up, André, and when I began to read the *Times,* I simply could not see the words. Everything was a blur. And since then, I haven't been able to see well enough to read. I'm sorry not to be able to, for reading is our passport to life and all its *splendor.*" She savored that last word; it was always one of her favorites.

Like Miss Havisham, but without the dust and relics of a lost happiness, she took to her room and no longer went out to receive guests. They came to her in bed. Once I went up to visit her there with Paloma Picasso. Her grandson Alexander and I often sat there talking to her, with a nurse in the corner. She may never have left that bedroom again, but that apartment was still run by her iron hand in its velvet glove, as smoothly and precisely as a Porsche shifts gears.

When Mrs. Vreeland told me that evening of her desire to take it easy after a life of service, I thought at once of my grandmother and me, watching the funeral of Dr. Martin Luther King, Jr., on our black-and-white television set. When a soloist in that choir began to sing, "If I can help somebody, then my living will not be in vain," my grandmother turned to me and said, "That is the motto we have to live by."

Mrs. Vreeland and my grandmother lived their lives a world apart, but with a common purpose: They lived to help others. By helping others, they did not live in vain. Mrs. Vreeland helped many careers to flourish and did a great deal for her chosen field. My grandmother was a tower of strength, doing all she could to help everyone whose life she touched in her various roles, as mother, grandmother, surrogate mother, cousin, aunt, sister, and good friend. Everyone looked up to her.

They both walked with abundant dignity, even when they were old. Mrs. Vreeland was as well manicured in her bed as she had ever been at *Vogue,* and by the time my grandmother retired, I had given her as many Chanel suits, dresses, and shoes, as many Gucci bags as she could ever use. She had never been in the presence of such an icon of style as Mrs. Vreeland, but her best crepe de chine print dresses were made from fabric sent to her by Karl Lagerfeld himself. If she and Mrs. Vreeland had gone walking down Fifth Avenue together, or walking down the aisle of Mt. Sinai Baptist Church, everyone's heads would have turned to see those two most elegant, most spectacular women.

After my grandmother died, I inherited her house and most of the things I had associated with her. Whenever I return there, I see those pictures, that furniture, and I think about her and feel close to her. When Mrs. Vreeland died, she of course had a family of her own, and it was their decision to dismantle her apartment and to sell off many of her possessions at auction. She had, however, once given me a beautiful jade belt buckle, which I keep on the table in my living room; that reminds me of her. And when they held the auction in 1990, I was in Paris, so I bid on one thing over the phone—a Napoleonic-era scarf that she had framed and hung in her husband's bedroom. I bought that scarf for seven hundred dollars and now have it hanging in my house. I think if I had been in New York, I would have bid on other things as well, but it was too difficult from far away; so I have few material reminders of her incredibly strong presence in my life. But that isn't the worst thing. After all, my memories of her are not memories of physical things, but memories of something much deeper and less tangible—the profound, soulful bond we shared. As with my grandmother, the things she truly left me are things of the spirit: the strength and conviction to move through a sometimes ugly world with a sense of beauty and a modicum of grace; the rare and wonderful sense of having been loved completely for the person I am; and the enduring image of her rapturous and infectious smile.

CHAPTER ELEVEN

Just recently, when I traveled to North Carolina for my annual August pilgrimage home, I received one of the most beautiful, meaningful, and unusual gifts I have ever received: a gallon of well water from deep within the woods of my aunt Jennie's tobacco farm. My cousin Alice Crowder brought me the water. She hefted it out of the backseat of her champagne-colored Toyota sedan, an immaculately kept car that has seen its thirteenth birthday and done its duty on thousands of miles of I-85 and I-95, as Alice traveled back and forth between Aunt Jennie's home in Roxboro, North Carolina, and Washington, D.C. This unexceptional-looking Toyota has ferried countless such plastic gallon jugs of well water. Until she recently decided to move home to North Carolina, Alice made frequent trips down to visit our elderly aunt, and each time she brought some of the water back to the city with her. The place the water comes from has not changed significantly since I was a child. The house—what Alice calls Aunt Jennie's "shack of a house," perched on top of a hill—is still more or less the same, but it used to sit in the midst of a hundred-acre tobacco farm owned by my father's Bradshaw relations, who had lived in Roxboro longer than anyone can remember. I didn't know my father's family well until later in life, though one treasured childhood memory was going with him to visit Aunt Jennie's farm. The hill her house was at the top of was so steep, and at the end of a dirt road so winding, that in any kind of foul weather, my father had to park his car at the bottom so we could walk up. I remember once getting out of the car and seeing a buckboard wagon heading out to the tobacco barns. Today, after an acre here and an acre there have been parceled off, the low woods down the hill now all belong to white families, soccer moms and dads, who, tired of the rat race in the big cities, have returned to the country, purchased land at an average cost of seventy thousand dollars an acre, and built themselves log cabins on a lavish scale and with all the modern amenities.

Alice has, in my post-1989 life, become one of my heroines.

Always one of my father's favorite kinswomen, she is now a woman of forty-six, with a close-cropped natural Afro, rare in these days of weave-o-rama processed hair. After working diligently at the Library of Congress for twenty years, she recently decided to move home to Durham and start over. She never married or bore children and is currently between boyfriends, so she has time to devote to what is, at present, her favorite and most important task—her weekly drive to Roxboro, to look after her mother's only sister, Aunt Jennie. Alice is an intuitive and smart person.

On this particular visit, Alice and I met for dinner at Fishmonger's, a local seafood eatery, where Alice spent over an hour peeling the crackling skins from a pound of tiny pink steamed shrimp swimming in enough spicy pepper sauce to wake the dead. After dinner, however, as we met up in the parking lot, Alice came over to my car and swung the gallon of water up onto its hood.

It took me a moment to realize what she'd brought me, but as soon as I understood, I was overwhelmed with gratitude. For that water, in a plastic Food Lion jug, had come to me from the hands of a much-beloved cousin who links me as strongly as the steel beams of a bridge to a wonderful part of my family's history—Aunt Jennie's tobacco farm, which is still tended by sharecroppers. The gift of place, the rootedness I felt in contemplating that clear gallon of water, is beyond price.

"I used to come here from D.C. and load this car up with nothing but jugs of this water," Alice told me after dinner, in a voice that struck me as remarkably un-Southern. Having lived nearly all her adult life in Washington, D.C., she speaks with the succinct clarity of a person who has frequented the marble halls of our nation's capital. "The world is changing so quickly. I regret not having married or having had six beautiful boys to bring up. After my best friend, Carol, died of pancreatic cancer, I realized that life is just too short not to be where you want to be. Everyone thinks I'm crazy to have given up my pension at the Library of Congress, but I'm so much happier."

By "everyone," Alice meant her sometimes bossy older sisters, Rothane and Chainie, and her brother-in-law, Roger. Alice was a young woman of twenty-nine when she lost her mother, Reversia, who had also been one of my father's favorite kinfolk. She still misses her mother, much as I miss my grandmother, and visits her frequently in the graveyard of Red Mill Creek Church in Roxboro, where my father is buried, and where Reversia's sister Jennie will also, one day, come to rest.

The Sunday afternoon before we met up for dinner, Alice had conditioned Aunt Jennie's delicate hair, the two of them seated out in the yard, under a shade tree. Then she took Jennie inside and rinsed out the conditioner with water from that well.

"Everything is different with that well water," Alice explained to me. "You wash your face with it, it feels different. Your hair feels different. Cooking with it makes the food taste different. Aunt Jennie has never paid a water utility bill—that well has always been there for our family. When Rothane and Chainie were children, they had to go down into the woods and collect water in buckets for the entire household. I prefer not to drink any water but the water from that well."

When I brought the water home that night I felt I had to pour it out sparingly. When I drank the first half a glass, I thought, *It truly does taste sweeter and look denser than ordinary water, if such a thing is possible.* I sat in my house, with the plastic jug before me like a window back in time. I felt as if Alice had opened some long-closed shutters and allowed a marvelous, golden light to pour through those rooms of memory that I air every August, when I make my journey home. With a gallon of water, Alice had managed to transport me away from the modern world and back to the world of my childhood. She had opened the door for me to think about Aunt Jennie's rich, full, difficult life and to pay homage to another extraordinary woman who gives me faith in the rightness of this world. And I realized that with all the treasures of the world before me, with all its grandeur and glamour, one of the things I most value is to go home.

Aunt Jennie Brand, now eighty-six years old, is a reed-thin woman. She is childless, and in many respects she might as well be husbandless, though her trying husband, John Albert, can still manage to get up and walk from one chair to the other despite glaucoma and two hip replacements. They live in that dilapidated old farmhouse, where woodstoves provide the heat but where Aunt Jennie, in her one concession to modernity, cooks electric.

At dinner, Alice had told me, "Every morning, Aunt Jennie gets up and bakes biscuits, Ray," opening the floodgates of memory when she called me by that nickname my grandmother, my father, and so many of my long-dead kinfolk used. "I don't see how she can take another winter of toting wood into the house for the heating stoves. It'll surely kill her."

Aunt Jennie has silvery hair, and her skin is as dark as ebony—so dark there is a purple, almost amethyst hue to her slender arms and hands. When you hug Aunt Jennie, and your face brushes against hers, her skin has the papery velvet texture of a fresh, green gloxinia leaf.

She has never lived in a house with modern heating or air-conditioning. There's hardly an electric fan. During the cold winter months, Aunt Jennie gets up every morning, stokes the stoves to heat the house, and goes to her kitchen to bake those fresh biscuits, using the remarkable, unpolluted water from the source deep under her land. Her laundry, her bathing, her food: All of these rely upon her land, upon that wellspring down in the woods.

Uncle John Albert is a deacon and still gets to church nearly every Sunday, while Aunt Jennie is fading fast—those decades of carrying kindling and wood, making fires, baking biscuits, and keeping house have taken their toll. Her only outings at present are visits to neighbors, weekly grocery shopping trips with Alice, or checkups at the doctor's. Jennie suffers from Alzheimer's, but her medication, prescribed to her by a white female doctor, has slowed the disease's progress. So, according to Alice, "It's not as if pots are left on the eyes of the stove to burn, while Aunt Jennie is all over the house, doing some other thing. Thought I don't know what will happen when that comes to pass." In the meanwhile, there is no lack of rich food on Jennie's kitchen table, the same food that my father always looked forward to when he went down for a visit and slept on their couch. Alice now sleeps on that couch every weekend.

Thanks to Alice's ministrations, Aunt Jennie and Uncle John Albert will, no doubt, never end up in an old folks' home or an "assisted living residence," as the signs somewhat depressingly say.

If the next winter proves too much for Aunt Jennie—if she can no longer tote the wood cut for her by men paid to stack it neatly in the woodshed, if she can no longer get up at the crack of each dawn, thanking her Lord for a new day, if she can no longer provide fresh biscuits for her spoiled husband, she will begin to decline. But she has provided well for her victory services; she has saved up, in a lifetime in which she never had any job besides devoted housewife, more than twenty thousand dollars. Her bank account owes its heft to years of hard work, of selling tobacco crops, and of scrimping where she could.

"If she dies before I do," Alice told me, "I am determined to put it all in the ground with her. That's what she saved up, and it's hers."

Aunt Jennie has never traveled farther north than her sister's home in Northeast Washington, D.C., or farther south than Durham, which is half an hour by car from Roxboro. And she is still faithful to her husband, despite his wanderlust, which is now mostly (thankfully) in his head.

The same sense of duty that shines in Aunt Jennie beams from Alice. She literally lights up when she talks of her favorite aunt, the minutiae of her daily life or the hardships of having a husband who still thinks he has some Lothario left in his brittle, artificial hips. Like all the women I have loved and admired, Alice has extraordinary wisdom. She has found that for her, the secret to living well is as simple as a journey home on the weekends, as simple as spending time in a house with no air-conditioning, where the nights are so hot that she sweats right through her nightgown and often finds herself praying silently, "Lord, give me the strength to survive this heat."

The love and devotion she shows for her mother's only sister are an enduring strength, part of the concrete foundation of Alice's own sense of self-worth. I have no doubt that this woman, the youngest and most dutiful of three sisters ("Your father brought me home from the hospital, Ray," she recalls, "because my father wouldn't come and get me; he was that disappointed I wasn't a boy"), has achieved something nearly impossible in this world we live in: She has earned herself the noble crown of one who loves family, history, and the land better than she loves anything else in the world.

That evening we spent talking at Fishmonger's, Alice and I found that, despite the few years that had passed since our last meeting, we got along like two sparks flying along parallel paths together in the same fireworks display. We have sought the same thing, though in widely different ways—the sense of well-being that comes with returning, either in memory or in reality, to the places and people who gave us our understanding of our place in the world. I find my grounding by returning annually to the spot my grandmother indelibly stamped in my memory as the happiest; Alice has found hers by moving back home, a move that she found surprisingly easy. On the Internet she found a job at a day care center and a suitable apartment. Nearly as soon as she'd had the thought, she found herself back in Durham.

She has not chosen to become a recluse or a nun; there are still men in her life, though they have caused as much heartbreak as happiness. "You see these gray hairs?" Alice asked me at dinner. "I intend to color them, once I get rid of this extra weight and get my blood pressure down. I let myself go a little after that last man. I got so depressed I had to take off work. He just up and left me for some woman from Baltimore. I was hurt and angry, but most of all, I wanted him to tell me: What was the point?"

As my eyes scanned Alice's close-cropped, nearly masculine coiffure, I couldn't see any gray hairs. Perhaps when one looks at the people one loves, one sees only the best and the most beautiful, for she claimed not to see any white hairs on my head, and I know there are many. I was surprised and happy to find that our talk was as intimate and normal as if we had spoken every day, though it had been seven years since I'd last sat down with Alice at a Sunday afternoon supper at Aunt Jennie's house, up on the hill.

"I just want you to be careful, Alice," I told her. "You have to be so careful these days."

"There are so many diseases," she concurred. Then she shook her head and smiled an impish smile. "Honey, I don't need a man. I don't want to be bothered. When the last one hauled it out, I told him, 'Put that away, I've seen bigger and better.' In fact, it had been so large I'd thought it looked more like the sex of a horse!"

I liked listening to her stories. But I wanted to know—since she was on her own, man-wise, and since she'd left her entire old life behind—what truly made her happy nowadays.

"Oh," she answered, "the simple things. Sitting on the porch talking to Aunt Jennie and eating a pint of Häagen-Dazs. You know what I did this summer that I really enjoyed? I went down to the orchard and picked apples. I should have lived in the country my whole life. Picking those apples was wonderful. And the orchard was so pretty.

"You know, I had one big disappointment this summer," she volunteers. "I planted a whole garden, and nothing came up. Not one thing! I bought seeds, fertilizer, everything, and I planted string beans, watermelons, tomatoes. But I guess I waited too late in the season and probably didn't distribute the seeds evenly in the rows. I'll do better next year."

If I try to take an outsider's perspective on what Alice told me—about apple picking, filling gallon containers with water from an unseen, untreated source—I realize how boring it could sound, how provincial. I see how it could boggle the mind that I find such beauty in Alice's weekend junkets into a place of fresh biscuits, well water, and wood-burning stoves.

I knew, when we sat at the table, that Aunt Jennie and Alice would somehow resolve the demands of getting wood from the shed to the stove, even if Alice's statement about the subject ("I can't stop her from killing herself.") proved true.

Alice has really only one obsession—to obey the unspoken rules of preserving pride of place. She winces when she thinks of Aunt Jennie having to sell her house and the family land if she becomes truly infirm. As long as Aunt Jennie remains in that humble house with few (if any) luxuries except faith to a spouse and home, Alice has her place in the world.

"You know," she admitted, "I can't put a label on why I love this water so much. It's as clear as a bell ringing from the church belfry, and I think it's one of the things that have contributed to the longevity of the people who've lived in this country. But I couldn't say why it's so important to me."

I had been thinking, meanwhile, how wonderful it was that we were able to feel the warmth of our mutual love of place, just talking about fresh country spring water.

Alice is a handsome woman—big-boned and chesty, with fair, almond-hued skin. Like me, she has a huge gap between her upper front teeth. Ever since she was a child, she has projected an air of calm self-assurance. Yet one can see her soft core when she speaks of regretting not bearing children, and the depth of her stores of love becomes evident when she talks of her late terrier, Hennessy, who lived for thirteen years. For the last two of those years, she had to chase him around the yard every morning, trying to read a urine sample to monitor her little dog's diabetes. In the end, the disease killed him, as it killed my father. When Alice talks about Hennessy's death after all those years of faithful companionship, tears well up in her dark eyes, and the simplicity of her moral code sparkles into view.

"I am not," she told me, "a wealthy woman of affairs. I couldn't afford to have his effigy carved in onyx or agate." But she did believe it was important to commend her dog to God's care, exactly as she would commend any other good friend. She had Hennessy cremated and housed the ashes in an urn until she could get to Roxboro for a proper funeral. She chose a spot out the living room windows of the little shack she so loves, right past Aunt Jennie's beds of zinnias, roses, and sweet peas, near the apple trees that my father once transplanted as saplings from the deep woods to the front lawn, and which now bloom every spring and bear fruit in the summer.

"Aunt Jennie did the singing," Alice said. "Rothane's husband, Roger, did the talking. And I did the crying. But I know I can visit him anytime, right on the other side of the flower garden."

"Are you going to get another dog?" I asked her.

"No," she replied. "I couldn't replace him. I couldn't go through having to funeralize another dog."

To me, Alice's life seems rich in complexity of sentiment: it is as if she is a quilt sewn up of patches of love, family, faith, and the Christian ideals of charity and love for her neighbor. I think that it is through her service and devotion to others that Alice has gained her sense of self-worth, and it is as durable as the finest Meissen or Sèvres porcelain.

Well water runs through her tissues, so although her porcelain surface may just be beginning to show the lines of age and wear, she has a beauty that will remain, though time may pass and places may change.

As I gazed through the small, round bottom of the glass, savoring my second glass of Alice's luxurious gift, it was a hot, bright, delicious August day. A week before, I had escaped the galaxy of fashion and ego, and record-breaking 103-degree heat in New York City, and driven my air-conditioned car to the place of my roots, a house surrounded by flourishing magnolia trees planted in the very year my grandmother died. Their waxy green leaves glistened as dark as cognac and glowed in the headlights that first night as I turned into my driveway. The drive itself had recently been pressure washed, so it glowed nearly white, and seemed to lead me, through that dark night, to the one place where I could find a sip of serenity, a brief spell of perfect peace.

My grandmother's house is still my favorite place. It reminds me of her goodness and the way she helped shape me to become the complex person I am. Staying at her house takes me, mentally, thousands of miles from the stylized, exaggerated, and frequently absurd world of high fashion. In New York, my mind often feels like it flows in a number of powerful streams simultaneously. In Durham, my mind is like a calm, clear lake at eventide, with huge, wild geese flapping their wings in flight overhead.

Uncertainty is the one sure thing when you work in fashion. You never know if the layouts you work so hard on will see life on the printed page. You wait anxiously to find out if your editor and art director think you've done your work well enough to create an emotional impact and, as they say, "bring home the bacon."

These two powerful people choose the images for an article without the input of the photographer or sittings editor. While we work, we talk to them by cell phone or fax and try to do everything possible to meet their desires, but sometimes they decide otherwise at the end of the day. It is difficult to describe the joy one feels if a piece actually makes it into the magazine and millions of homes, and equally difficult to describe the pain and frustration of watching a piece get scrapped. No matter how many Polaroids one takes at a sitting such as Mrs. Simon Howard's, the whole layout can be, as they bluntly put it, "killed." (Sometimes an editor will, in trying to save the sittings editor's feelings, simply say that "the pictures didn't work.") Years in the industry do not always save one from being scarred by such a turn of events; it is always sad to see ideas, images, and words die before they come to the printed page. And one rarely gets an explanation. If, after years of living this life of gilded uncertainty, one still maintains a sense of self, a sense of the value of hard work and achievement, that can seem a miracle. And living with this uncertainty—the dark side of the beautiful imperiousness of fashion magazines—one simply must have a parachute on one's back, or an emergency lever to pull to catapult one from the depths of rejection.

The power of place isn't a guarantee that a person can find soul survival. Figuring out what brings you—not people in general, but you in particular—contentment, can be an arduous task. I think it is particularly difficult in the times we live in now. It must have been easier to know your place, and to appreciate belonging there, when people still whiled away evenings on their front porches; but front porch life is now a lost art. In Durham, my next-door neighbors, the Stogners, have a beautiful front porch with grand columns, their house a mini Tara. Pristine white wicker *fauteuils* with rockers complement their impeccably kept lawn. Yet, as in most homes now, no one ever sits on this porch. The elegant glasses of tea with fresh mint have disappeared. (Now if anyone has tea it comes from a metal canister, and it's probably expensive green tea.) People who have become allergy-prone, spoiled by twenty-four-hour ventilation systems, no longer even open their windows. The sounds of bullfrogs and crickets singing in the trees at night are blocked out, and we are deprived of their symphonic beauty. All my blood kin have screened-in back porches but use them infrequently. The only people I know who use their front porch as part of a quiet, yet active, social life in the hot summer months, are my Aunt Jennie and her devoted Alice.

Aunt Jennie's shack, nestled among what's left of her acreage, has two porches—a formal one in front, and a larger one in back that is sheltered along its entire length by stately old shade trees. Depending on how many visitors come, Aunt Jennie will bring chairs out from the house to one porch or the other, and any number of people might sit outside for an entire afternoon, sipping cool, ice-laden glasses of tea or lemonade under those trees. I miss this tradition of porch life. When it was in its heyday, in my childhood, the world seemed full of heat, sun, huge insects, tall, sweating glasses, and a panorama of swaying paper church fans on carved balsa wood sticks. It seemed complete.

Sometimes I feel like a migratory bird, making the return journey to my heartland every August. It is a solitary journey, a time for introspective unraveling and for detoxification from the world of fashion. The roads I travel to get there feel like they're framed on three sides—on two by verdant trees, and overhead by a ceiling of blue sky, dappled with clouds on a clear day. Though my life in fashion sometimes seems full of more duties than I can keep track of, the road home always seems to point to one determined beautiful place.

Homecoming isn't always a journey of bliss. Even when the past was blissfully happy, coming face to face with it can be painful. I feel my grandmother all around me when I am in North Carolina, yet sometimes I am overwhelmed. At other times, I realize that she lives on in myriad ways—in my values and in the lives of all those I've met who turn such values into a beautiful way of life. Cousin Alice reminds me more than almost anyone of my grandmother: She is solid, dutiful, committed to home, and full of that same unconditional love. People like Alice are rare, but I thank Heaven they are not impossible to find.

Although I miss my grandmother terribly, I never despaired that the world was full of such good people, though I confess I did sometimes wonder if I would ever find another teacher and friend as singular and formidable as Mrs. Vreeland. The truth has of course proven to be that although no other person will ever be made in Mrs. Vreeland's mold, I am fortunate to count some remarkable women among my friends and role models. Baroness Liliane Rothschild is in her mid-eighties, but this past July, we had lunch at a Chinese restaurant in Paris and laughed like school friends, though we couldn't have come from more different worlds. She taught me how to swim, at the age of fifty, in Karl Lagerfeld's pool. Imagine having the social empress of Paris, world-renowned for her collection of Marie Antoinette's personal artifacts, as your swimming instructor. I am also friends with Beatrice de Rothschild, née Caracciolo. At any moment she could choose to go into her closet and come out wearing a stupendous YSL or John Galliano couture dress. Her mind is focused on her children and on painting, which I love about her. We found beauty and majesty climbing the branches of a three-hundred-year-old live oak in Savannah. I share a passion for things French with Sao Schlumberger, whom I met with Andy Warhol in 1975, and whose background also differs wildly from my own. I met her years ago at Andy Warhol's studio, when Sao went to have her portrait painted. Everyone in the Warhol circle immediately recognized how wonderful she was, and we have been friends ever since. But the difference in our upbringings means that while I can adore and write about Versailles, when the French sought to redo the King's bedroom there in the 1960s, she and her now-deceased husband gave a million dollars to assist in the reweaving of the original hangings and reprinting of the original wallpaper. And of course, there is my wonderful friend, the renowned decorator Mica Ertegun.

Mica originally came from Romania and moved as a young woman to Paris, where she worked as a mannequin for a couture house. From there she emigrated to Canada, married a chicken farmer, and lived on the farm for seven or eight years. (When one sees Mrs. Ertegun now, one can hardly imagine her driving a tractor, but according to her, that is exactly what she did! I sometimes think we get along so well because of what I can only describe as a streak of down-home Southernness in her otherwise very European and sophisticated nature.) After a divorce, she moved to America and met Ahmet Ertegun, to whom she has been married for the past forty years. Ahmet was the son of a Turkish ambassador and, as a young executive for Atlantic Records, played as vital a role as anyone in the shaping of popular music as we know it today. He frequented the Harlem clubs back before hardly anyone from Downtown knew they were even there, and it was he who signed on such musicians as Ray Charles, Aretha Franklin, LaVern Baker, and Ruth Brown. He devoted his superhuman efforts to bringing them to prominence. Ahmet went to rent parties, fought for fair contracts, supported artists in every way he could, and managed thus to become one of the most important people in the music industry and an integral part of that wonderful chapter of our cultural history. Mica is his second wife, and a woman of great beauty and culture. She is *une femme d'une certaine age,* but she looks no older than fifty—and not because of strategic surgery or expensive creams. Mica exercises every day, but primarily, her beauty and incredible stature come from being a true lady of ritual, maintenance, and discipline. And also, of course, from her great spirit.

Mrs. Ertegun's iconoclastic design work has appeared in the pages of *Vogue* since I was a young man. I remember when she and her now-deceased best friend, Chessy Rayner, opened their decorating business, MAC II; I was reading *Vogue* voraciously then, and Mica Ertegun was an important part of the aesthetic that shaped me. In my early years in the fashion world, I worked with her on a few sittings, and when Chessy died, I sent her a condolence letter and received a lovely thank-you note in return. We rebounded as close friends recently, and under the strangest of circumstances.

In February 2001, I was admitted to Lenox Hill Hospital for surgery on a blood clot in my knee. Four or five years previously, I had injured the knee while playing squash with Alex Denis, who is a champion squash player and a trainer at the Ritz in Paris. When he and I were playing there one day, my racquet hit my knee, which smarted enough to force me to halt the match. Alex told me to go put ice on it, but it was about seven hours before I got around to doing it. From then on, the knee intermittently gave me problems. I finally went in for an MRI, and they discovered that the cartilage was torn and required arthroscopic surgery, which is, of course, routine—but six weeks later a blood clot appeared in the back of my knee. I was nervous to death. It was the first time in my life I'd been in the hospital, and a hospital is a frightening place. I don't care how great your health insurance is, how much you trust your doctor: When you go to the hospital, you realize your own mortality. Thankfully I was only there for a five-day stay. During that time, I had been scheduled to have lunch with my friend Joseph Holtzman, the editor of a beautiful interior design magazine called *Nest.* When Joseph called me on my cell phone to confirm the lunch, I regretfully said, "I'm afraid I'm going to have to cancel. I'm in the hospital."

"Which hospital?" he asked.

"Lenox Hill."

"Well, what kind of flowers do you like?" he asked.

"Parrot tulips," I answered, remembering Mrs. Vreeland's living room. I thought it was kind of him to think of sending over an arrangement.

As it turned out, he brought the flowers over himself, vases and vases of them, which was a wonderfully cheering surprise. But as soon as he walked into the room—literally before he even sat down—he presented me with something even more surprising. He said, "André, I have the greatest idea." I know I am not the only person in the world who becomes suspicious upon hearing that phrase, but Joseph *is* a fountain of great ideas, so my ears only pricked up a little. "I want to decorate your room and put it in the magazine," he went on. "I've always wanted to do a hospital room, to show how it can become something beautiful.

Would you let me decorate your room and put a photograph in the magazine?"

I would not ordinarily say yes to this sort of proposition, because it would involve hassle at a time when I needed to rest. But Joseph is both a visionary editor and a good friend, so I agreed.

"Wonderful!" he exclaimed. "Now tell me, who's your favorite interior designer?"

"Mica Ertegun, of course," I said, without missing a beat.

"Good, then. Shall we call her?"

I said, "Sure. Call her and see if she'll do it." I didn't think she would.

"I'll tell you what," Joseph said. "I think Mica would appreciate it if you called her and told her about the idea yourself. But we can take it from there."

So I called Mica Ertegun that afternoon and told her that *Nest* wanted her to pick fabric and furniture and completely do over my hospital room. Mica had never heard of *Nest,* but much to my surprise, she said, "I'd love to do it. I'll come over in the morning."

The next morning she stopped by with her assistant, who is also named Mica, on her way home from yoga class. There was Mica Ertegun in gray exercise leggings, warm boots, and a shearling coat—not the sort of attire in which one ordinarily sees her. I thought she looked fabulous. I was sitting up in the chair at the time, so Mica sat down on the bed. I said to her, "Mica, this is the room they want you to do." As she looked around we both laughed. I'm sure you can imagine how utterly it lacked in character. "And you'd have to do it in two days, because after that I'll be leaving."

Mica continued to look around, appraising the space. "Well," she said, "I'm on my way to Europe, but I'll make notes while I'm here, and Mica can take care of the details."

Her visit lasted no more than half an hour, and the next morning she left for Switzerland. Before she left, however, she picked out everything for the room—the fabric, the notepads and pencils, the kinds of flowers and where they should be placed, the lamps, the paintings, everything. And within two days, her assistant, Mica, had everything ordered and delivered; MAC II decorated the room in a whirlwind hurry, and *Nest* shot a whole photographic spread of me in a hospital room decorated by Mica Ertegun.

That room she designed for me was incredible! The fabric was a chinoiserie chintz, with black-and-white images of pagodas and Chinese men. She sent over yards upon yards of this fabric and had it shirred all along the walls, like a Turkish tent. Mica picked out sumptuous Frette celadon green sheets for the bed, beautiful lamps, and vases overflowing with flowers. The room ended up being one of the most wonderful I'd ever stayed in—not just because of Mica's impeccable taste, but because of the kindness and generosity she had showed in doing the project on such short notice. The space she created completely changed my experience of being in the hospital.

I had always admired Mica, but I now admired her doubly for being open to so spontaneous an idea and for using it as the springboard to create such original work.

Soon after, Anna Wintour mentioned that she would love to have Mica appear in a *Vogue* feature called "Women of All Ages," in which one woman would represent each decade of a fashionable life. Would I want to be the editor for the profile of Mica? I could not turn down the opportunity—and, thankfully, Mica was delighted by the prospect as well. For the next two months, therefore, we spoke on the phone almost every day in order to work on the *Vogue* article. The piece was to center on a big celebration that was about to happen in her life: Her friends the Henry Kissingers, the Julio Santo Domingos, and the Oscar de la Rentas were planning to take over the St. Regis ballroom and throw a huge fête to celebrate Mica and Ahmet's fortieth wedding anniversary. As the preparations for this party were under way, Mica came to have lunch with me one day in the *Vogue* cafeteria. Now, Mica eats nothing. She eats grape leaves, or a little Feta cheese and tomatoes with olive oil. We sat down at our table—I with a meal before me, she with hardly a snack—and she asked, "What kind of dress do you think I should wear for my big party? I'm not buying any ball gowns, but I know I have to have something. I'm going to see Oscar de la Renta this afternoon—what should I ask him to do?"

Immediately an image popped into my mind from years ago, from a big opening at the Metropolitan Museum of Art with Mrs. Vreeland. It was an evening on which everyone who was anyone had a dress from Paris or a New York designer and wore all of her jewels. There they all were in their biggest, most important dresses, dripping in diamonds and pearls, and Mica arrived in a black shirt and a big black skirt. The skirt was so large that when, late in the evening, I saw her going into Studio 54, she descended the steps and disappeared from view, but the skirt remained in my vision. I remember thinking that the dress must have been by Mme. Grès, of whom Mrs. Vreeland was so fond and whose gowns were the pinnacle of both fashion and good taste. (Having one of her dresses in one's closet was like having a Brancusi sculpture on the coffee table.) And Mica had been one of Mme. Grès's largest couture clients. I remembered going up to Mica at the bar and asking, "Mica, excuse me, is this outfit by Mme. Grès? It's so unusual—I mean, here's everyone in these enormous ball gowns, and you're in a big gypsy skirt."

"Oh," she answered brightly, "this is OMO. I found it at Norma Kamali."

At the time I thought, *At Norma Kamali?* I recalled the first time I'd gone to meet Kamali, up in her Madison Avenue studio; she was sitting at her sewing machine making vintage parachutes into clothes. She created an entire collection from old parachutes; she was sitting there breaking boxes of needles, needles by the gross, as she put together parachute jumpsuits and parachute skirts with the pull cords left intact. There had been some outrageous things in that collection, but nothing to parallel the skirt Mica was wearing. This skirt was beyond a skirt—huge, layered, and voluminous, with what must have been layers of petticoats underneath.

So more than twenty years later, when we were sitting together in the *Vogue* cafeteria and she was trying to figure out what to wear, I said, "Mica, when I remember you in that black gypsy skirt, I think that was your look, no one else's. You should get a big shirt and a big, big skirt, and wear it with your rubies from India, the ones Ahmet gave you."

Her eyes sparkled with pleasure. She said, "I think that's exactly what I'll do."

She did, in fact, go and get herself a gypsy skirt—an enormous one in silk taffeta and red, red, red. It had about a dozen ruffles, and exquisite ruching, and was so large that wearing it, she couldn't get into the elevator in her house unless someone stuffed her and the skirt in. (Granted, it's a small elevator, but still.) She had so much style that evening—she wore the skirt with a blouse of a deep petroleum blue, almost black, and with ropes and ropes of rubies from Jar of Paris around her neck. And she looked extraordinary.

The party itself, in April, was the party of the season. Everyone from every world was there: Diane Sawyer, Ed Bradley, the Rothschilds, Mick Jagger, the late, lamented Katharine Graham, and Bette Midler, who sat right next to Ahmet; all in all, about two hundred people in the St. Regis ballroom. I sat at the de la Rentas' table. This was the sort of party I remembered from my first years in New York, when Andy Warhol and Diana Vreeland were still alive and frequently blended their worlds together for spectacular evenings. In those days, people just got together. It doesn't happen like that anymore, because parties aren't like they used to be; the grandest parties tend to be fund-raisers, motivated by something other than simply gathering people together for a glorious evening of celebration. The Erteguns' anniversary party was not pictured in any newspaper or magazine, yet it was a meeting of the worlds of power, society, fashion, and the arts such as one hardly sees anymore. The singer Solomon Burke came in from California, with a big ten-gallon Texas hat on and wearing a huge mink-lined cape (he himself must weigh nearly four hundred pounds), and at some point during the night, he stood up, threw that cape off, and started singing. Ahmet got up and sang a duet with him, and everyone applauded. Though everyone looked fantastic, no one looked better than Mica in her wonderful outfit, and no one else had that kind of originality in their dress. In the days of Mrs. Vreeland, people had such originality, women like Mica and Chessy Rayner.

Something happened that evening that I hadn't imagined would happen again in my lifetime: I danced, with as much joy as I had with Anne Bibby at the close of our prom night.

I have nothing against dancing, mind you, but Karl Lagerfeld and I have always said that you should never dance after you're fifty, because you look like a fool on the dance floor. Of course, it depends on where you are dancing. It took Lagerfeld's weight loss of ninety-three pounds and my own shedding of sixty pounds of my former Rabelaisian girth to change our minds. Now we both are out there, swirling the most elegant women across dance floors, including the cushioned and padded parquet in Lagerfeld's Paris ballroom.

Before that much needed shedding of extra baggage, the last time I had danced had been in 1992, at a dinner party for Sylvester Stallone at Sao Schlumberger's fantasia apartment in Paris, when my friend Eric de Rothschild, in front of his wife, Beatrice, twisted me around in a quick tango/waltz. I've been to many weddings and other parties in the meanwhile and have felt no desire to dance at any of them. I had to shed the weight to feel comfortable enough in my own skin to give it a whirl. But there was Mica. She had been walking all around the party, greeting everyone, being the perfect hostess, and then danced with Ahmet. When she was returning from the dance floor, she walked past me, the pleated taffeta of her gypsy skirts almost whistling. Without even thinking twice, I said, "Mica, would you like to dance with me?" I meant this as a gesture of my respect for her; I didn't expect her to say yes! But greatly to my surprise, she did.

I had, of course, never danced with Mica. But we danced like we'd been dancing together for years. I was totally in awe of her—her rhythm and style were remarkable, and she was obviously having a great time. Somewhat to my surprise, I had a ball as well; and no one could believe it, because no one ever sees me dancing. We didn't dance together in any specific style—it wasn't a waltz or disco dancing—we just danced. And after we finished I left the party, although it was only 10:30 in the evening, because I knew that was the perfect moment; nothing else could happen to top that wonderful experience.

Mica's turned out to be the most extraordinary shoot in that issue of *Vogue.* When the article appeared in August, it received more favorable letters from readers than any other piece in the magazine. People were dazzled by her regal elegance, the spare beauty of her interior design, and the incontrovertible proof that one can live a stylish and vivid life well past the age when most people slide into frumpery. Mica is impressive in her every detail. When she came for a photo sitting, for example, I was astonished at the care she had taken to pack her shoes for an intracity trip. For each pair of shoes, she had a ticking-striped drawstring pouch bearing her quilted initials, ME. When she took each shoe out of its pouch, it had a little fabric shoe tree inside, which one removed by pulling on a brass ring. She is fastidious about every such detail. She has made an extraordinary life for herself and her husband, with a unique vision that blends the worlds of society, fashion, and the arts in a totally unpretentious, down-to-earth way. She is a person who can go into a room and talk to anyone there. I remember going with her to a party that Ahmet was giving for the Rock and Roll Hall of Fame. When I walked in, she was sitting beside and having an animated conversation with Kid Rock.

Behind the veneer of elegance, there is a pragmatic woman who runs a house on a grand scale but with the same sense of values my grandmother used in running hers. Everything in Mica's house seems spit-polished, and though she updates things from time to time, she has not substantially changed her house since decorating it twenty years ago. She doesn't redo things on a whim. And she has managed to create a home that feels, like Mrs. Vreeland's did, grand yet cozy: incredible Russian furniture next to a Magritte painting, or (indeed) a Brancusi head lying around on the coffee table. The rooms in her Southampton home are designed to look like those in a Russian dacha, yet have all the opulence of a Turkish palace. Sleeping in the Oriental red guest suite, with huge French doors open to the sun rising over Shinnecock Bay, is one of the most peaceful rests I've ever experienced. Her taste in design is much like her taste in clothing, which we captured in the *Vogue* piece, for which she wore her own clothes. Mica's taste has never been faddish or trendy. She's not at the forefront of fashion—she isn't wearing destroyed clothes or anything—yet she always looks incredible. On the day we were doing the group shot for the issue, a shot including all the women representing the decades of a woman's life, the younger women were completely in awe of her. They'd never seen anyone with that kind of poise. Everybody else had clothes that were beautiful and clothes of their choice, but seeing her, the eldest, with the most assuredness about who she was and how she looked was probably the most successful ingredient of the piece.

Around the same time that we were working on the article, I recommended that Ahmet be recognized by a committee I serve on at Abyssinian Baptist Church, which annually gives awards to recognize outstanding contributions (by prominent people and ordinary citizens) to the community and legacy of Harlem, and to African Americans in general. I thought the award was tailor-made for Ahmet, whose contribution to black music had been so very, very great, and the committee just about unanimously agreed. So shortly after the anniversary party, Ahmet and Mica came with me to a very touching awards breakfast, where Ahmet received his honor with consummate grace and was delighted to meet the people of my church. Mica was very impressed by the whole affair and asked if she could come to church with me one Sunday.

Thanks to our busy schedules, that Sunday did not materialize until I returned from Paris in August, but Mica was still eager to go. Before she did, I called Dr. Butts, the minister of my church, and asked if he'd be there that Sunday; I really wanted Mica to come when she could hear him preach. When I told Dr. Butts I would be bringing Mica Ertegun, he gave a hearty assent and said he'd greatly look forward to seeing her there. Ahmet had just had open-heart surgery (performed by the famous New York heart surgeon Mehmet Oz, himself a Turk)—from which he is, thankfully, well recovered—and Mica thought she would go to church on her way to visit him in the hospital that Sunday, and perhaps bring him news of an uplifting experience or sermon. Well, her expectations were more than met. Dr. Butts made the extraordinary gesture of speaking from the pulpit about Ahmet's truly great contributions to Harlem, African Americans, and American culture at large and reiterated much of what he'd said when we'd honored him earlier in the summer. Mica stood up and received a warm welcome from the church.

I felt so proud to be beside this woman in church. It reminded me so much of being in church with my grandmother—not in a morbid way, but in the soul-satisfying way of being full of admiration for the woman beside me, who sat there in a well-tailored navy blue suit. At that moment I realized how great my good fortune was in becoming friends with Mica. Everything about her reflects style at its best, everything. The simple way she wears her hair, or the way she places the table in a living room, the way she puts candles on a table to create exactly the right glow. She does all of these things effortlessly because she knows who she is. Many of us believe that that confidence will come to us with age, but Mica, I know, had her same exquisite sense of style in her earliest youth, exactly as Jacqueline Kennedy did, or Mrs. Vreeland. Mica is a woman of great elegance, but nothing about it is artificial. Her style is based on choices that relate to her, such as the skirt and blouse instead of a ball dress; and though she loves and surrounds herself with beautiful things (besides the Brancusi, she has a David Hockney and other magnificent works of art in her home), she remains unpretentious and has a sense of humor about herself and her famous husband. She has proven to me once again that beauty and style have nothing to do with youth and little to do with wealth. She is supremely articulate, both in the way she speaks and in the way she dresses and moves. I think of the way she glided through the room in that big skirt—a skirt almost Scarlett O'Hara big, with ruffles to the floor. Most people just can't do that. And she had it down, the effortless glide. There is a term to describe the way the ladies of the court used to walk at Versailles—*glissade;* they walked as smoothly as if they were roller-skating, but apparently one still had a sense that there were legs and feet beneath them as they moved. Mica has that beauty in her movement. To attain that, one has to have a passion for the world, an appreciation of beauty, and diligence in (and love of) enriching one's world with a sense of beauty. There is no other way to find one's own style so naturally and completely.

There are few women like Mica anymore. People have forgotten how to have that kind of panache, or they're too busy, too focused on other things. People don't throw huge parties like her anniversary celebration—they don't celebrate on a grand scale like that. It isn't the money the Erteguns and their friends spent that made their party so incredible; it was the beauty of their sharing, with all the people they were fond of, the joy of celebrating something special. Mica and Ahmet's life stands as an emblem for me of the highest good one can do with money. They are generous with their friends, generous to the community, and meanwhile manage to live a life of impeccable style, as if they were pre-Revolutionary Russian nobility. Everything they own is beyond compare—their dinner plates, their art collection, the candles on their table; if they serve a Portuguese goulash, it will be the most extraordinary, perfect stew imaginable, and if they serve a fancy jellied crab, their chief goal is to share a wonderful dining experience with friends, and that makes the dish all the more magnificent. They might serve you lunch on a simple, polished table, with no tablecloth—but what a table! It's the sharing that's important; the fact that they share, and the fact that their friends truly appreciate the time and thought they put into their wonderful entertaining. Mica, with her radiant, beautiful heart, has once again shown me that beauty and style bubble up from a wellspring deep within, in order to touch, with their grace, the lives of all around.

Miuccia Prada is to me the epitome of glamour, and what a fashion designer should be. We always have so much to talk about, nonfashion. She once sent her private plane to whisk me from Paris to Turin for a lunch, just for the two of us, just for fun. Dressed in a white T-shirt, a silver skirt of metal worked on the bias, her mother's '20s rock crystal necklace, forty-carat diamond earrings the size of quarters, and a white full-length ermine, she conveys original elegance. There is something of Marlene Dietrich (with a dollop of Tallulah Bankhead's dry chic) about her style that makes me think of my Aunt Louvenia, who, without the same resources as Miuccia, still knew how to dress. She and my grandmother were the best-dressed of all the Roberson siblings.

In another time, Lee Radziwill would have been part of what is known in French as *le gratin.* Lee is a kindred spirit who can bond with you over seeking the beauty and humor in life, as well as "a cozy, indulgent day," as she calls it. Lee and I really have a great deal in common, as we both had our first jobs in high fashion with Empress DV. Diana Vreeland absolutely doted on her. When Lee's sister, Jacqueline Onassis, died in 1994, I went to see Hubert de Givenchy, who was still working as a couturier in Paris. It was Lee, he told me, who had introduced her sister to Paris couture. Look at pictures of the young Lee and you see a confident, original dresser, not someone following the herd. Mrs. Vreeland always said that Lee had the sum total of refined taste.

In her role as the voice and image of *Vogue,* Anna Wintour is a walking masterpiece. Designers are inspired by her klieg-light, supernova glamour. The House of Dior will fly Raphael Ilardo, the chief of its couture tailoring workrooms, to New York for the day just to fit a dress for her. As with Diana Vreeland, the fashion drums beat to the pace she sets. I was humbled when she recently wrote in *Vogue,* "When I'm thinking about my fall wardrobe—and I'm afraid that these things take a little bit of planning—I tend to skim designer look books, flag pages of this magazine, and consult my colleague André (my most trusted advisor) for inspiration and guidance." And it was a surprise when, at her wedding, she thrust her bouquet directly into my hands. Behind a lacquered surface as brilliantly and carefully maintained as Empress Vreeland's, Anna has great depth of soul, feeling for family and children, and loyalty to friends.

I don't have time to do everything the way my grandmother and Mrs. Vreeland taught me, the way Mica Ertegun, Miuccia Prada, Lee Radziwill, and Anna Wintour do things even today. I agree with all of them that polished furniture is the only furniture, and I'd still like to shine the bottoms of my shoes with a rhinoceros horn, but the truth is that one has to make choices and has to get on with it. When I was a young man living in Paris, I wasn't ready to compromise yet, and I ended up spending a huge amount of my salary at various hand laundries where they could take care of my possessions as I wished. But that didn't turn out to be a life plan for me; it was too complicated and too expensive. For a while, I frequently spent a Saturday night washing and ironing my own sheets, but that cost too much in terms of time. This is a wash-and-wear world we live in now, and I make my peace with that. Now my Calvin Klein sheets come out of the dryer and go straight on the bed, which isn't so bad. A bed can be plenty beautiful and still not require much fuss. If I could afford to hire someone to do nothing but iron my linens, another to do nothing but tend to my clothes, a third to cook, and a fourth to clean the house, life would be easy and grand. But more important than the taste for luxury that both my grandmother and Mrs. Vreeland encouraged in me is the ability, also learned from them, to find luxury in my actual life, rather than pining after an unobtainable ideal.

When I was leaving recently for a trip to Paris, someone asked me, "Aren't you having someone come to pack your clothes?" And I thought, *A butler? Are you kidding?* It's wonderful to have a butler, but it costs money. I pack my own clothes. And because I don't have the time or the patience to polish my grandmother's silver, it's packed up in a closet for now, but it still gives me pleasure knowing it's there. One of these days, I'll find a way to make use of it.

The grittiness of the real world is always there, and it's not going to go away. If one has an inheritance, one can throw money, but for the rest of us—for the vast majority of us—the trick is to figure out ways to find pockets of pleasure and luxury that take us away from the grime of everyday reality long enough to feel nourished and rested. The things that make you feel that way may not be the same as your neighbor's: For someone, it might be a beautiful pair of candlesticks, for someone else, a fuzzy mohair blanket; this one might enjoy decorating with fabric, while that one buys fresh flowers; one person will have good wine if he has to forgo all other luxuries, while another will abstain from ordering drinks in order to save for a larger purchase—but they can make all the difference in the world. Of course, it's luxurious to ride around in a limousine, or to wear couture, but if you keep your Toyota as neat and clean as my cousin Alice does, or can wear a Norma Kamali gypsy skirt with Mica's panache, either of those things can be an oasis of luxury, too.

I try to do as Bennie Frances Davis did in being of service to others. I do what I can at church and for my friends, and I try to keep my eyes open for opportunities to serve in unexpected ways. In the year 2000, one such opportunity presented itself in the form of a letter that came to me at *Vogue* from the Savannah College of Art and Design in Georgia (a school I had never even heard of) asking me to come down there to accept an award. Although I am always flattered when people approve of my work, I might not have given the letter a second glance had

I not noticed that it had come from the school on the recommendation of Santiago Gonzalez, a young man who had been an intern at Manolo Blahnik the previous summer and who was then a senior at SCAD. Santiago came from a wealthy, cultured family in Colombia and always made a good impression with his poise. He had sat working quietly at his desk the entire summer; I had never exchanged a word with him on any of my frequent visits to Manolo but must have impressed him, because he went back to school in the autumn and recommended that I be nominated for their highest award. This touched me deeply.

I was glad to have made an impact upon Santiago, so I agreed to go down to Savannah to accept the award from his fashion department. I had some hesitation about going because I had never been to Savannah and had the notion that I might find the antebellum South alive and thriving there, but there was nothing of the sort at the school.

Indeed, SCAD was utterly modern, and booming. Though it had been founded only twenty-three years previously, it now has more than five thousand students. The school is accredited, and its campus is made up of spectacular old buildings; people come from all over the world to study there. The awards ceremony was elegant and dignified, and I enjoyed speaking to that auditorium full of students and felt deeply honored to be there.

The students and faculty were apparently impressed by my acceptance speech, because after it was over, they graciously asked if I would stay to talk to the students and look over their work. I was more than happy to accept and remained another two days, inspecting their work in the studios and talking to them in small groups. I showed them a slide show of images from the most recent couture in Paris—Chanel, Karl Lagerfeld, whatever images I wanted to show them, but they loved seeing the pictures and getting a taste of my point of view. By the time I left Savannah to return to my work in New York, they had decided to change the name of the award they'd given me to the André Leon Talley Lifetime Achievement Award, because they had been so impressed with my passion for the students' dreams and work. This was an honor beyond compare—to have an award not only named for me, but to be given the honor of choosing its recipient each year.

The first year I chose it was 2001, and I selected Oscar de la Renta. That May, he traveled to Savannah to meet with the students and accept the award, and both he and they reported that it was an incredible experience. Karl Lagerfeld accepted the award in 2002; Miuccia Prada was the recipient in 2003. I, meanwhile, went there for a week in the autumn of 2001 and spent the entire week giving lectures to and working with the students. I visited them in the workrooms of the fashion department and showed them film and photographs from the fashion shows; really just taking the time to be available to them, to answer questions, and encourage them in what they want to do. And it makes a huge, huge difference in a young person's life to have someone do that. I was lucky enough to have Mrs. Vreeland, Carrie Donovan, Andy Warhol, and Fred Hughes all rooting for my success. Sadly, I can never repay them personally, but I'd like to be able to repay that debt by doing for other people what they did for me.

Paula S. Wallace, one of the founders of the Savannah College of Art and Design, asked me to become a member of its board of trustees, and I also consider this a great honor. I feel like everything has come full circle, if I can make a difference in some young person's life the way Mrs. Vreeland did in mine. Recently, I was invited by the Yale Entrepreneurial Society to speak to a body of 120 graduate and undergraduate students from various departments. I put on my best Richard Anderson suit, a white Charvet shirt and tie, and my best shoes. I spoke about motivation, inspiration, education, humility, and aspirational values. The students' eagerness to hear the story of how I got over, or up, filled me with warmth. It was certainly the high point of my sessions of talking to students—the absolute zenith!

Most of the time, the rewards for generosity are less tangible, but I keep giving, regardless. People have been so generous with me in this lifetime that I could keep giving for the rest of my life and never feel like I've repaid all the kindnesses others have done me.

I invite all my friends to experience the natural beauty of the human spirit that flourishes at the Abyssinian Baptist Church. It makes me very happy when they can appreciate the degree of warmth and kindness that electrifies the congregants there. And there is no greater joy than watching friends discover the eloquence, dignity, and tradition of the sanctuary choir, which assistant minister Reverend Kevin Johnson has described as "the best choir this side of heaven." Soprano soloist Joan Faye Donovan's annual rendering of "Silent Night" takes me right back to the warmth of my grandmother's kitchen at Christmastime. One recent Christmas I proudly walked my friend Lee Radziwill down the aisle of my church for a performance by the sanctuary choir of Handel's Messiah, accompanied by the Harlem Festival Orchestra, a performance she pronounced "outstandingly refined." (She later took me to Christmas Eve mass at Saint Ignatius Loyola, the Catholic church where both she and her sister were baptized.) After a special Christmas concert by the choir at the Morgan Library for their annual trustees dinner, Annette de la Renta remarked that, after hearing that music, she wouldn't be afraid of dying.

Annette and Oscar de la Renta love the Abyssinian Baptist Church almost as much as I do, which they demonstrate through their continual contributions to a development fund that raises money for education, community programs, and outreach in Harlem. They give out of love, and out of respect for the André that most people do not know, the one who sits every Sunday in the sanctuary of the Abyssinian Baptist Church.

In early 2002 I was in Paris reporting on the spring couture for *Vogue* and visited John Galliano in his studio at Dior. With a gleam in his dark brown eyes, and a kind of wicked grin, John handed me a blue leather box with the gold monogram C.B.E. At first I thought it was a small Christmas present. In the box, however, was an enamel cross on a pale pink and silver ribbon, his Commander of the British Empire bestowed by Queen Elizabeth II at Buckingham Palace in November 2001. John had added one special touch: He had laced onto the ribbon a crucifix with an image of a black Jesus—because, he said, of my faith in God.

John could have handed this medal to his mother, whom he loves, or to M. Bernard Arnault, who had given him the privilege to reinvent Dior into a modern luxury image. But he wanted me to have it, as a more than gracious gesture of friendship and remembrance for having helped jump-start his career in Paris in 1993. I told him I would consider this a beautiful loan, and that anytime he wanted it back, he could have it. I wear the ribbon and cross only on special evenings or sometimes to church.

I think about Mrs. Vreeland's generosity, that time she saw me in her office before she left for Santo Domingo; I think of my father and grandmother working hard all their lives to provide me with advantages they never had; I think of Cousin Alice, helping me with the simplest of gifts to reconnect to the home and history I cherish; and I realize how solemn a duty that old-time spiritual refers to. I get more letters than I can answer, but I do read them all, combing them for that special spark, that whatever-it-is that makes someone's words move me. And if there is a spark, I always respond. I think it's especially important to respond to letters from young people, because something as simple as a letter of encouragement from a stranger can change the course of someone's life.

I try to be a voice that can make the difference in someone's life. Diana Vreeland and my grandmother stood for that. With the highest standards, in lives so diverse and so remote from each other, these two great mentors embodied courage, generosity, grace, and great style.

Even when I myself am not happy, I try to do what I can to make others feel happy. Even when people are not acting exactly as I think they ought to, I try to reach out and make them feel good about themselves and their situation. Now that I am in the habit of it, it hardly costs any time or effort to pay a compliment, write a note, or place a quick telephone call. I don't know how much it means to Alice when I tell her I admire what she's doing for Aunt Jennie; I don't know if, when I bestow an award upon Oscar de la Renta or Karl Lagerfeld, it lights up their days the way receiving that honor lit up mine; and I don't know if Bennie Frances Davis and Diana Vreeland ever fathomed the depths of love and gratitude I tried so hard to express to them in word and deed. But I do know this: that making even the tiniest positive impact upon the life of someone I care for is the most beautiful feeling in the world. It seems like the least I can do to repay my wonderful, blessed mentors for having given me the precious gift of a sense of meaning and purpose in my life. Payback is golden.

If I strive for one thing, it is to make a difference. To live every day is a prayer not to give in, but to be tough and hang in there. Valleys and peaks, the highs and lows are all miracles. My life is one long continous prayer.

Bennie Frances Davis. *(Collection of the author)*

ACKNOWLEDGMENTS

From the Introduction of this book to its final chapter, I thank so very much four people who made the difference: Anna Wintour, Karl Lagerfeld, Manolo Blahnik, and George Malkemus III.

I thank Dr. Janis A. Mayes of Syracuse University, for reading the first pages of the journey from home to the world of *Vogue* and home again.

I thank Emily Barton, award-winning author of *The Testament of Yves Gundron,* for many pleasurable hours of honing the narrative.

I thank John Fairchild, for being an inspiration with his book *The Fashionable Savages,* and for his guiding light at *W* and *WWD.*

I thank Patrick McCarthy, editor of *W.*

I thank Michael Coady, for being my Maxell Perkins at *W* and *WWD.*

I thank my wonderful agent, Luke Janklow, and my patient and sensitive editor at Villard, Bruce Tracy.

I thank Natasha Fraser and Miuccia Prada, for their calls, faxes, and enthusiasm.

I thank my extended family, Oscar and Annette de la Renta, Ahmet and Mica Ertegun, Diane von Furstenberg, Beatrice and Eric de Rothschild, Liliane de Rothschild, and my friend and minister of the Abyssinian Baptist Church in New York, Dr. Calvin O. Butts III, for his continued spiritual guidance.

ABOUT THE AUTHOR

ANDRÉ LEON TALLEY received his M.A. in French studies from Brown University. He joined *Vogue* in 1983 as fashion news director and served as creative director from 1988 to 1995. After living in Paris for a number of years, he returned to *Vogue* in 1998 as editor at large. He was nominated for an Emmy Award for his weekly segment on Metro TV's *Full Frontal Fashion* called "Vogue's Talley." He is a member of the board of trustees of the Savannah College of Art and Design in Savannah, Georgia, where a Lifetime Achievement Award has been named for him. He lives in Hastings-on-Hudson, New York.